Latin Alive and Well

LATIN
Alive and Well

An Introductory Text

P. L. CHAMBERS

UNIVERSITY OF OKLAHOMA PRESS : NORMAN

Library of Congress Cataloging-in-Publication Data

Chambers, P. L. (Peggy L.)
    Latin alive and well : an introductory text / P. L. Chambers.
      p. cm.
    ISBN 13: 978-0-8061-3816-5 (pbk. : alk. paper)
    1. Latin language—Grammar—Problems, exercises, etc. I. Title.

  PA2087.5.C43 2006
  478.2'421—dc22

2006050948

The paper in this book meets the guidelines for permanence and durability of the Committee on Production Guidelines for Book Longevity of the Council on Library Resources, Inc. ∞

Copyright © 2007 by the University of Oklahoma Press, Norman, Publishing Division of the University. All rights reserved. Manufactured in the U.S.A.

1 2 3 4 5 6 7 8 9 10

Also by P. L. Chambers

Latin Alive and Well: An Introductory Text (Norman, 1987, 1989, 1990, 1992, 1994, 1997, 2000, 2002, 2004)

Latin Alive and Well Teacher Key (Norman, 1987, 1989, 1990, 1992, 1994, 1997, 2000, 2002, 2004)

The Attic Nights of Aulus Gellius: An Intermediate Reader/Grammar Review (Norman, 1992, 1993, 1995, 1996, 2000)

The Attic Nights of Aulus Gellius Teacher Key (Norman, 1992, 1993, 1995, 1996, 2000)

Pliny the Younger's Character as Revealed Through His Letters: An Intermediate Reader/Grammar Review (Norman, 1995, 1997, 1998, 2000)

Pliny the Younger's Character as Revealed Through His Letters Teacher Key (Norman, 1995, 1997, 1998, 2000)

The Natural Histories of Pliny the Elder (Norman, 2000)

The Natural Histories of Pliny the Elder Teacher Key (Norman, 2000)

Contents

CONTENTS

Authors and Subjects of Passage Readings

A Note to the Student

Latin Alive and Well is the result of many years of teaching, and I am much indebted to my students, whose comments and suggestions are the basis of the current text. My goal has been to develop a text that is addressed to you, the student, in a way that is understandable and that presents the essential elements of Latin grammar in an order and format that enables you to read classical authors immediately. I have endeavored to select exercise material that is worthy of translation effort and that includes the most famous quotations and excerpts of the best Roman writers and thinkers.

Grammar presentation is the primary task of any introductory language text, but it also is my goal to acquaint you with Roman thought, mythology, history, and philosophy by letting the Romans speak for themselves. To this end I demonstrate Latin grammar in context through the writers of the period, but my presentation is basic, direct, and comprehensible to contemporary students. My approach to Latin as a subject is the same as that of the French philosopher René Boylesve: "Let us remember that we do not learn Latin in order to conjugate verbs and decline nouns and shine on examinations, but that by means of this language we are able to penetrate a magnificent realm which remains unknown to the greater part of mankind—the realm of human thought."

Through an informal conversational style, I have sought to offer encouragement and learning tips as well as empathy for particularly tedious grammatical points. Regarding the use of technical terminology, I have adhered to the Latin proverb *Nihil praeter necessitatem*! (Nothing beyond necessity!) Essential technical terminology is briefly explained, and when necessary for clarity, I recap it under the heading "Summary of New Terminology" at the end of the same chapter in which it is introduced. The continuous passage readings begin in Chapter V. These readings are mostly prose, though some poetry has been included in order to present a valid spectrum of Roman writers.

Learning a new language is always a wonderful experience, and it is even more meaningful when you realize you are reading authors whose works date back two thousand years. *Bona fortuna* (good fortune) in this new adventure! I am delighted to have the opportunity of introducing you to the Roman world.

A Note to the Teacher

My goal in writing *Latin Alive and Well* is to teach students to read Latin. Over many years in the classroom I have discovered that the following methods are effective in helping students reach that goal:

- Because macrons occur neither in modern texts (e.g., Loeb Library) nor in most intermediate and advanced readers, I employ them only for new vocabulary.
- I ask students not to write in this book. This way, they can go back later and see that they can translate with no aids.
- I emphasize parsing (identifying grammatical constructions) when translating. This begins with individual words and proceeds to clauses. I maintain the term *parsing* and indicate what I am after by underlining and boldface type.
- The text is periodic and progressive in its presentation of grammar and in readings.
- Continuous-passage readings are labeled "Text Translations." The first Text Translation is an adaptation of Virgil; the last is unedited Virgil. The readings follow Roman mythology and history and conclude with the closing lines of the *Aeneid.*
- Exercises at the end of each chapter are comprehensive and pertinent to the content of the chapter.
- In early Exercises and Text Translations, words that are not a part of the assigned chapter vocabulary are numbered and are indexed by number. This helps students, telling them that if they must look up any word not indexed, they need to review the previously assigned vocabulary. By the end of the book new vocabulary is listed alphabetically.
- To ease the student into new vocabulary and new grammar, I employ foreshadowing. Thus, in sentences assigned for translation I introduce words not in the chapter vocabulary and provide, beneath the sentences, definitions of the new words. Then, when some of these words appear as part of the assigned vocabulary in succeeding chapters, the student will be somewhat familiar with them. Very occasionally I do the same thing for new grammar. For example, I introduce **-ne** in a Text Translation in the chapter before it is formally presented as an enclitic introducing interrogative sentences. I insert, as a vocabulary item, one or two 1st Conjugation deponent verbs several chapters before the chapter in which they are formally introduced. I simply point out that these verbs have only passive forms but are to be translated actively. My students *like* foreshadowing. It prepares them for upcoming forms.
- Exercises and translations are the basis of teaching. None are skipped. In my classes, completion of daily assignments constitutes 20 percent of the final grade. All assigned material is reviewed in class. In these reviews we identify the inevitable mistakes and correct them. In class, as a group, we parse a portion or all of each Text Translation before I assign it as homework. As the course progresses, we parse beforehand only the more difficult passages. The more difficult poetry Text Translations are not assigned as homework but are worked out in class as a team effort. A couple of chapters before the chapter in which they are formally identified, I orally introduce declined pronouns (calling

them instead "the class yell") as three word jingles (e.g., "*hic, haec, hoc,*" "*huius, huius, huius*" "*huic, huic, huic,*" "*hunc, hanc, hoc,*" and "*hoc, hac, hoc*"). The next day each student answers the roll with the assigned recitation. This turns drudgery into entertainment and gets the memorization done before we deal with declined meanings.

- You will discover some made-for-fun translations that I spring on the class as an oral group effort. These contain new grammar and are presented in a format generally familiar to the student.
- Some readings contain subject matter introduced in an earlier chapter. Familiarity with the stories will enable the student to translate such readings quite easily.
- I limit technical terminology to the minimum required. For example, instead of using *substantive adjective* I simply point out that a Latin author need not write out *bonus vir* when the masculine singular ending in *bonus* accomplishes the same purpose.
- I introduce nine broad ablative categories as a basis for general translating, and students *can translate* with these nine. Likewise, I introduce nine broad and inclusive categories of the subjunctive. (In my accompanying readers, specific and particular ablative usages are identified and formally discussed, as are more specific and particular subjunctive usages.)
- The only way to confirm that students are mastering grammar and vocabulary is with weekly testing. For a *two-semester* course, I begin with a twenty-minute quiz at the end of the first week and follow with a one-hour exam at the end of the second week, and then I continue this pattern throughout both semesters. For an intensive, *one-semester* course the pattern is a weekly quiz for three weeks, and then, at the end of the fourth week, an exam.

In grammar presentation *Latin Alive and Well* is *different* from other introductory texts in the following ways.

- By chapter V, the student has been introduced to:
  Present Indicative of all conjugations;
  Present, Imperfect, and Future Indicative of *sum*;
  1st–2nd Declension Nouns and Adjectives.
- Verb tenses are explained and identified by systems.
- Future Indicative for all conjugations is presented in a single chapter.
- Imperfect Indicative for all conjugations is presented in a single chapter.
- Perfect Active System for all conjugations is presented in a single chapter.
- Present Passive System for all conjugations is presented in a single chapter.
- Perfect Passive System for all conjugations is presented in a single chapter.
- Demonstrative Pronouns and irregular 1st–2nd Declension Adjectives are presented in chapter VI and before the introduction of 3rd Declension Nouns.

I teach all levels of Latin but the introductory course is by far my favorite. It is a wonderful experience to observe and be a part of the joy of a student's mastering a new concept, and then gaining assurance and competence in translating and simultaneously becoming enamored of Roman mythology and history. My hope is that this text helps and perhaps even enables you and your students to have the same experience.

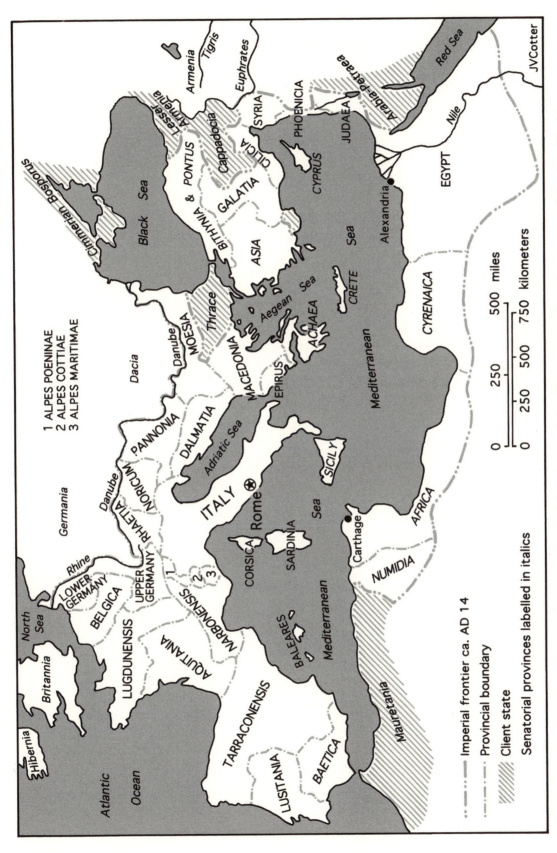

The Roman Empire at the death of Augustus, A.D. 14. (Map by John Cotter, reproduced courtesy of Paul A. Zoch)

xv

Latin Alive and Well

Introduction

Latin is a member of the large group of related languages that in ancient times were spread across India and Europe and for this reason are called Indo-European or I.E. languages. Below you will find a listing of some of the original I.E. languages followed by the modern languages that come from them.

Indo-European Languages

Slavic:	Russian
Celtic:	Irish, Gaelic
Germanic:	Scandinavian, Dutch, German, English
Greek:	Modern Greek
Iranian:	Persian
Sanskrit:	Modern I.E. Languages of India
Latin:	Italian, Spanish, French, Portuguese, Romanian

Notice that Latin is the parent language of Italian, Spanish, French, Portuguese, and Romanian. The reason for this is that Latin was the official language of the Roman Empire, and the modern nations of Italy, Spain, France, Portugal, and Romania were once all part of the Roman Empire.

All languages that come from Latin are called Romance languages because of their Roman origin. Some of you may be familiar with a few Italian, Spanish, or French words. The chart below will show you how each of these languages is simply a variant of Latin. The Romance-language words are listed as *derivatives* because they are *derived* (taken directly) from Latin.

Latin Word	Romance Language	Derivative	English Meaning
amicus	Italian:	*amico*	friend
	Spanish:	*amigo*	
	French:	*ami*	
manus	Italian:	*mano*	hand
	Spanish:	*mano*	
	French:	*main*	
tempus	Italian:	*tempo*	time
	Spanish:	*tiempo*	
	French:	*temps*	

The Relation of Latin to English

Although English is not a Romance language, it is filled with Latin words because England was once a part of the Roman Empire and also because England was later occupied by the French. In addition Latin was the official language of the Christian church as well as the common language of the literary and scientific world until the early nineteenth century.

It has been said that 60 percent of the English language comes from Latin. In my letter below, all the pure Latin or Latin-derivative words have been underlined.

Curriculum Coordinator
Education Systems of the United States

Thank you for permitting me the opportunity of addressing your faculty and students on the benefits of providing and maintaining a Latin program in the public schools. It is interesting that while the current trend has been to delete Latin per se, terms such as curriculum, electives, mandatory courses, minimum requirements, grade point averages, *etc.*, have managed to remain in our vocabulary like the immortal spirits of the Homeric heroes in the Elysian Fields. I am confident that a careful and objective examination of the pros and cons will at least elicit some serious consideration regarding this subject as a subject.

As with all disciplines and skills, Latin represents a cumulative knowledge that is extremely demanding and even at times difficult, tedious, and frustrating—much like my golf game. Also like my golf game, it is not always an ego elevator. In fact it very often has the opposite effect, i.e., of producing unmitigated humility. Unlike the fleeting joy of an occasional perfect golf shot, however, even moderate comprehension of Latin affords benefits in English vocabulary, written skills, literature, the arts, sciences, and technology that are enduring, infinite, timeless, and exhilarating.

Certainly the Romans had no televisions or electronic computers, much less aerospace technology and communication satellites, but all these terms are Latin! Latin as a spoken language may be moribund, but the fact is that we encounter the corpus dilecti on a daily basis.

All of us in education have certificates which represent our intellectual credentials and abilities. We might not have all graduated magna cum laude, but we did satisfy at least the minimal degree requirements.

Almost everyone receives per diem salaries, writes memoranda, and pays ad valorem taxes in addition to a certain percentage of his or her per capita income to support our local and national governments. Our law courts are overrun with phrases such as habeas corpus, nolo contendere, and non compos mentis as well as the testimonies of witnesses and decisions of judges. The medical profession is filled with Latin eponyms such as N.P.O., I.V., and I.M., not to mention surgical procedures, postmortem, and the cryptic P.R.N., Q.I.D., and H.S. of prescription codes issued by our doctors.

Obviously I could continue ad nauseam to illustrate the point that 60 percent of our English language is derived directly or indirectly from Latin in addition to innumerable verbatim adoptions. The Romance languages (Spanish, French, Italian, Portuguese, and Romanian) represent regionally corrupted Latin that evolved out of Roman military conquests and the subsequent loss of those conquests after the fall of the Roman Empire. A basic Latin background provides not only a firm foundation in English (which, although a Germanic language, is couched in a Latin format), but also the base vocabulary and grammatical forms for all the Romance languages.

This takes me to another major point. The side benefit of learning Latin is that in addition to attaining a skill, the student is made aware of the origins of Western civilization. The rationalism, art, and ideas of our cultural forefathers, the Greeks, were expanded and transmitted by the Romans by means of the Latin language to all western Europe and Britain. These concepts were maintained by the Christian church through the Dark Ages of Europe and were brought to life again in the Renaissance. As we all know, they were then transported to the New World, where they have been thoroughly incorporated.

It has been noted that a citizen is one who, if necessary, can refound his or her civilization. It may be that one reason why so many of our youth have no direction for the future is that they have no idea where they are in time. We Americans need to learn our cultural identity. As Cicero said, and he was paraphrasing Aristotle, those who do not know the past will always remain children. We as a nation (and humankind in general) cannot know where we are going if we do not know where we are or where we have been.

We are all by definition *Homo sapiens*—sensible persons, but in no sense have we lately been nurturing informed or prepared citizens. Americans sorely lack the ability to refound the cultural progression that links us with the rest of the world. In addition our youth are desperately deficient in verbal and written skills. In order to compete and even survive in the modern world, we must have mastery of our own language and culture and must develop this same skill and knowledge in other cultures. We simply must learn to think and communicate in the linguistic framework of others as well as our own. Sensibly, this is only going to be accomplished when citizens see to it that their offspring: (1) know not only where they are in space, but also in time; and, (2) develop the communication skills to nurture as well as transmit a national and international civilization.

It is a fact that knowledge of Latin provides a firm foundation for English written and verbal skills as well as a grammatical and historical point of reference for additional linguistic studies and cultural advances. *Quod erat demonstrandum*, I hope. *Ipso facto,* we can compute the benefits of Latin simply by observing the present status quo.

Sincerely,

P. L. Chambers

The Alphabet and Pronunciation

The Latin alphabet is exactly like ours except that it lacks the letters *j* and *w*. However, the Romans had their own particular way of pronouncing certain letters or combinations of letters.

Consonants

Consonants are those letters of the alphabet that are sounded by stopping or hindering the flow of air from the mouth. Latin consonants are pronounced the same as in English with the following exceptions.

1. *bs* is pronounced as *ps* (*urbs*)
2. *bt* is pronounced as *pt* (*obtinere*)
3. *c* and *ch* are always like *k*, as in *coat* (*cura, chorus*)
4. *g* is always hard, as in *goat* (*gens*)
5. *i*-**consonant**: *i* before a vowel is like *y,* as in *yes* (*iacio*)
6. *ph* is like the hard *p* and aspirated *h* in *up hill* (*philosophia*)
7. *r* is **trilled** (*errare*)
8. *s* is always like the *s* in *silly* (*sententia*)
9. *t* is always hard, as in *toy* (*tacere*)
10. *th* is like the hard *t* and aspirated *h* in *pothole* (*theatrum*)
11. *qu* is like the *kw* sound in *queen* (*qui*)
12. *v* is always like *w*, as in *will* (*verbum*)
13. *x* is like *x* in *example* (*exemplar*)

Vowels

Vowels are those letters of the alphabet that are sounded without the flow of air from the mouth being stopped by the lips or the tongue; *a,e,i,o,* and *u* are vowels. In pronouncing a word we sound some vowels for a longer length of time than others, and we call these "long vowels." Vowels that are not sounded for a long time are called "short vowels." Most of the long-vowel sounds in Latin are different from the long-vowel sounds in English, as you will see in the examples below.

Long Vowels		**Short Vowels**	
1. $\bar{a}$ as in *father*	(*pāter*)	1. *a* as in *attention*	(*musa*)
2. $\bar{e}$ as in *they*	(*rēs*)	2. *e* as in *let*	(*et*)
3. $\bar{\imath}$ as in *marine*	(*fīdes*)	3. *i* as in *fin*	(*hic*)
4. $\bar{o}$ as in *most*	(*mōres*)	4. *o* as in *hot*	(*opus*)
5. $\bar{u}$ as in *rule*	(*tū*)	5. *u* as in *hut*	(*locus*)

Diphthongs

Diphthongs are two vowels pronounced as one. Some diphthongs in Latin are the same as those in English, some have the same sound but with different spellings, and others are not a part of the English language.

1. *ae* as the *ai* in *ai*sle (*puellae*)
2. *au* as the *ou* in *pou*ch (*laudare*)
3. *ei* as the *ei* in *rei*gn (*deinde*)
4. *oe* as the *oi* in f*oi*l (*foedus*)
5. *ui* as our word *we* (*huic*)

NOTE: *ei* and *ui* are sometimes not pronounced as diphthongs but as separate letters, as in *di-e-i* and *ma-nu-i*.

Syllables

A syllable is a word or a part of a word, usually a combination of a consonant and a vowel that is pronounced with a single sounding of the voice. A Latin word contains as many syllables as there are vowels and diphthongs and is pronounced according to the rules below.

1. A single consonant goes with the following vowel: *mā-ter, a-mī-cus*.
2. Double consonants are separated: *mit-to, se-dūc-tor*.
3. Double vowels or a vowel and a diphthong are separated: *sē-u, de-ae*.
4. A syllable is long by nature if it contains a long vowel or a diphthong; a syllable is long by position if it has a short vowel followed by two or more consonants (*x* is treated as a double consonant.): *a-mī-cus, lau-dān-tem*.

Accent

In pronouncing a word we sound some syllables more loudly than others; this is called *accenting*. An accent is the emphasis of a particular syllable. Like all languages, Latin follows particular rules regarding accent. The easiest and most helpful rule is to never accent the last syllable.

1. The accent is on the first syllable of a word of two syllables: *frá-ter, nós-ter*.
   For words of more than two syllables:
   (1) the accent is on the next to the last syllable if it is long: *lau-dá-re, for-tú-na*;
   (2) otherwise, the accent is on the third syllable from the end: *pá-tri-a, cor-ró-bo- ro*.

Inflection of Verbs
Four Principal Parts of Verbs
Indicative Mood
1st Conjugation Verbs
Imperative Mood

I

Objectives

To enable you to:

1. recognize and conjugate 1st Conjugation Verbs in the Present Tense of the Indicative Mood;
2. form the Imperatives of 1st Conjugation Verbs;
3. understand that every Regular Verb has Four Principal Parts;
4. understand a Conjugated Verb indicates Tense, Voice, Mood, Person, Number.

Inflection of Verbs

Latin is a highly inflected language, that is, the ends of words are changed (inflected) in order to make a word indicate different things. Changing a verb ending is called conjugating. A **conjugated verb** indicates five things:

1. **tense** or time (Present, Past, or Future);
2. **voice**, which is Active (there is a Direct Object of the verb) or Passive (the Subject of the verb receives the action);
3. **mood**, which can be Indicative (relays facts), Imperative (commands), or Subjunctive (informs other than facts or commands);
4. **person,** 1st (the speaker—I or we), 2nd (the one[s] spoken to—you), 3rd (the one[s] spoken about—he, she, it, they);
5. **number**, singular or plural.

Four Principal Parts of Verbs

In English we identify a verb by a single Infinitive meaning, such as "to call" or "to praise" or "to love"; in Latin all regular verbs have four parts. For example, the four principal parts of the Latin verb meaning "to call" are:

voco, vocāre, vocāvi, vocātum

The 1st Principal Part of any Latin verb is the 1st Person Singular of the Present Tense: *vocō* = "I call." The 2nd Principal Part of a Latin verb is the Infinitive. The Infinitive provides the general meaning for the verb (*vocare* = "to call") and is the verb part we use to obtain the verbal stem for Personal Endings (explained below). We will only be concerned with the first two principal parts of verbs for quite some time, but **all four parts will have to be committed to memory**. (And, trust me, better to do it **now** than later, when you will be concerned with other "details.")

Personal Endings

In English we need to use **personal pronouns** such as **I, you** (singular), **he, she, it, we, you** (plural), and **they** to indicate who the Subject of the verb is. In Latin there are special verb endings that indicate a particular pronoun:

Singular		Plural	
1st Person *-ō* or *-m*	**I**	*-mus*	**we**
2nd Person *-s*	**you** (sing.)	*-tis*	**you** (pl.)
3rd Person *-t*	**he, she, it**	*-nt*	**they**

To conjugate a verb in the **Present Tense Indicative Mood**, you simply attach these personal endings to the **Verbal Stem**. The **Verbal Stem** (underlined below) is attained by dropping the **-re** from the 2nd Principal Part of the verb, which, as you discovered above, is the Infinitive.

vocō, vocāre, vocāvi, vocātum

vocō	I call, am calling, do call
vocās	you call, are calling, do call
vocat	he, she, it calls, is calling, does call
vocāmus	we call, are calling, do call
vocātis	you (plural) call, are calling, do call
vocant	they call, are calling, do call

10

Indicative Mood

The Indicative Mood simply tells or indicates a fact, e.g. *(exempli gratia* = for example), "The sky is blue." "I love Latin." The paradigm (model) above represents a conjugation of ***voco, vocare, vocavi, vocatum*** in the Present Indicative Mood followed by the possible English translations.

1st Conjugation Verbs

In Latin verbs are divided into four major categories based on the spelling of the Infinitive, which, if you will remember, is the 2nd Principal Part of the verb. Infinitives of 1st Conjugation verbs always end in *-āre*.

> *vocō, vocāre, vocāvi, vocātum* = to call
> *laudō, laudāre, laudāvi, laudātum* = to praise
> *amō, amāre, amāvi, amātum* = to love

With only a few exceptions 1st Conjugation verbs follow the regular pattern illustrated by the examples above, with the 3rd Principal Part ending in *-āvi* and the 4th ending in *-ātum*. A very few, however (such as *do, dare, dēdi, datum*), do not follow the norm, and these will have to be committed to memory as exceptions. This is easier than it sounds, and we will not be learning the whole language in one day, just one short step at a time.

Imperative Mood

The Imperative Mood is used for **commands**, e.g., "Do your homework!" "Come to class every day!" "Don't be late!" In English it is not always clear whether a command is addressed to a single person or to a group, as the verb form is the same for both. In Latin there is never any confusion about to whom a command is addressed, as there are specific verb forms for singular and plural commmands. The Singular Imperative is the verbal stem; i.e. *(id est* = that is), the Infinitive minus *-re*. To form the Plural Imperative of a 1st Conjugation Verb, add *-te* to the the verbal stem.

voco, <u>voca</u>re, vocavi, vocatum

Singular Imperative: ***Vocā***   (You) Call!
Plural Imperative: ***Vocāte***   (All of you) Call!

I have included the **understood Subjects** of the above commands **in parentheses** only to emphasize that the Subject of a Singular Imperative is singular while the Subject of a Plural Imperative is plural. **Understood subjects of commands are not included in translations**. Also, commands do not have to have exclamation points after them.

Summary of New Terminology

1. Indicative: a verb mood indicating a fact
2. Imperative: a verb mood indicating a command
3. Infinitive: the 2nd Principal Part of a Verb; gives general meaning of verb; provides the stem for Present Tense verb endings
4. Inflect: to change the ending of a Latin word to make it have a different and particular meaning
5. Conjugate: to inflect a verb
6. Paradigm: a model format illustrating a uniform changing of endings
7. Stem: the part of an inflected word to which endings are added

Vocabulary

Now, let's begin with a few words that we can play with in translating and composing Latin sentences. A working vocabulary is the key to learning any language, so be sure you commit to memory the vocabulary at the end of each chapter as soon as possible. If you keep a vocab list taped to the edge of your dressing mirror, on the outside of your notebook, or wherever you see it often, you will be surprised at how quickly you can master a few words at a time. Repeating vocabulary words aloud to yourself will speed up this process, and flash cards are very beneficial. There is a vocabulary flash-card set available for this text in which the vocabulary is collated according to each of the thirty-six chapters of *Latin Alive and Well*. Alternatively, it is very simple to make your own flash cards, entering the Latin on one side and the English meaning on the reverse side.

NB (**Nota Bene** = note well/take note): Regular 1st Conjugation Verbs have only the 1st Principal Part listed, followed by a (1). This indicates the standard pattern of: *vocō, -āre, -āvi, -ātum* for the four Principal Parts.

amō (1) to love

cōgitō (1) to think/understand/consider

culpō (1) to blame

dō, dare, dedī, datum to give

errō (1) to err/go astray

festīnō (1) to hasten

laudō (1) to praise

servō (1) to save/protect/preserve

vocō (1) to call

et and

lentē adv., slowly

mē me

nihil nothing

nōn adv., not

quid what?

saepe adv., often

sī if

Exercises

A. Fill in the paradigm below with the Latin Personal Endings for the persons indicated, followed by the English pronoun equivalents.

	Singular	Plural
1st Person	_____	_____
2nd Person	_____	_____
3rd Person	_____	_____

B. Using the paradigm above, **conjugate** (i.e., add the personal endings to the verbal stem) *dō, dare, dedī, datum* in the Present Tense, followed by the English translation of each conjugated form.

	Singular	Plural
1st Person	_____	_____
2nd Person	_____	_____
3rd Person	_____	_____

C. Form the Singular and Plural Imperatives of the following verbs, followed by the English translation of each form.

1. laudō, laudāre, laudāvī, laudātum
2. amō, amāre, amāvī, amātum
3. cōgitō, cōgitāre, cōgitāvī, cōgitātum

D. Translate the following verb forms.

1. errant
2. cōgitā
3. laudāmus
4. dātis
5. festīnāte
6. vocat
7. amō
8. vocā
9. errās
10. dō

E. Render the following sentences into Latin.

1. They praise nothing.
2. What do we praise?
3. Often he calls me.
4. You are not thinking.
5. You blame me.

F.   Sentence Translations.

Best Method:
• Do not write in the book.
• Copy down each sentence, then write your translation below each line of Latin.

1. Lingua Latīna mē vocat. (*Lingua Latīna* = Latin)
2. Cicerō et Caesar mē vocant.
3. Festīnā lentē! (Proverb of the emperor Augustus)
4. Sī festinās, saepe errās.
5. Lente cogitō.
6. Sī nōn errō, laudā mē.
7. Venus mē servat. (The goddess Venus was the protector goddess of Rome.)
8. Saepe non cōgitāmus.
9. Mē laudant; non mē culpant.
10. Quid cōgitātis? Nihil cōgitāmus.
11. Servāte mē!

Cases
1st Declension Nouns
2nd Conjugation Verbs
Word Order

Objectives

To enable you to:

1. decline 1st Declension Nouns into Six Cases, Singular and Plural;
2. recognize and conjugate 2nd Conjugation Verbs in the Present Tense of the Indicative Mood;
3. form the Imperatives of 2nd Conjugation Verbs;
4. recognize SMIDAV word order;
5. recognize nouns as listed by the Nominative and Genitive Singular Forms.

Cases

As I mentioned in chapter I, Latin is an inflected language, which means the endings of words are altered, in a standard way, to make a word mean different things. In chapter I we added the personal endings *-o, -s, -t, -mus, -tis, -nt* to a verb stem to form a Conjugated Verb indicating a particular tense, voice, mood, person, and number. Because Latin word order is so varied, the endings of nouns must also be altered to indicate their use as the Subject of the verb, the Direct Object, the Indirect Object, or whatever. I will show you what I mean.

In English we employ "linear syntax," a fancy way of saying a standard word order. So when I write "The poet loves the girl," you know that the Subject of the sentence is "the poet" and the Direct Object is "the girl," because we use left-to-right linear syntax (**Subject→Verb→Direct Object** word order). If I change the order of the nouns, the sentence means something different, i.e., "The girl loves the poet." Since Latin lacks such word order, I have to add a specific ending to a noun stem in order to indicate the particular function of the noun in the sentence. The possible grammatical usages of nouns are called **cases** and include the following:

- **Nominative**:
  Subject of the verb; tells "who" or "what" is doing something.
  *The **poet** loves the girl.*
- **Genitive**:
  Shows possession and is always translated "of" whom or what.
  *The girl loves the fame **of the poet**.*
- **Dative**:
  Indirect Object of the verb; tells "to or for whom or what" something is being done.
  *The poet gives roses **to the girls**.*
- **Accusative:**
  Direct Object of the verb; tells "whom" or "what" received the Action or the verb affected.
  *The girls love the **roses**.*
- **Ablative:**
  Prepositional Phrases; translated with prepositions such as "by, in, from, about, with."
  *The poet loves life **with the girl**.*
- **Vocative**:
  Direct Address.
  ***Girls,** avoid poets.*

1st Declension Nouns

While Latin verbs have four Principal Parts, Latin nouns are identified by two parts: the Nominative and Genitive Singular forms, e.g., ***puella, puellae*** = girl. The Nominative Singular is the first word; the Genitive Singular is the second word. **Inflecting (changing) noun endings** to make a noun serve different functions is called *declining*. To *decline* a noun into cases, you must first find the noun stem, which is what remains after dropping the case ending from the Genitive Singular form. The Genitive Singular ending of all 1st Declension nouns is *-ae*; the stem of *puella, puellae* is therefore *puell-*. To decline *puella, puellae*, you must add 1st Declension Noun case endings to this stem. The complete 1st Declension case endings (in paradigm format) are:

	Sing.			Pl.		
Nom.	*-a*	*puella*	the girl	*-ae*	*puellae*	the girls
Gen.	*-ae*	*puellae*	of the girl	*-ārum*	*puellārum*	of the girls
Dat.	*-ae*	*puellae*	to/for the girl	*-īs*	*puellīs*	to/for the girls
Acc.	*-am*	*puellam*	the girl	*-ās*	*puellās*	the girls
Abl.	*-ā*	*puellā*	by/with/from the girl	*-īs*	*puellīs*	by/with/from the girls
Voc.	*-a*	*puella*	"Girl,"	*-ae*	*puellae*	"Girls,"

The long mark over the *-ā* in the Ablative Singular form is used to distinguish it from the Nominative Singular. After this chapter I will not mark the other long vowels in the Exercises and Text Translations, but I will always mark the long *-ā* in the Ablative Singular. You will notice from the paradigm above that a noun has plural endings in addition to singular ones. Thus, a **declined noun indicates three things: case, number, and gender (sex)**. Most 1st Declension Nouns are feminine.

Look at the example sentences at the top of page 16. Try to render these in Latin employing the required case endings for the nouns, given that: *amica,-ae* = girlfriend; *poeta,-ae* = poet; *rosa,-ae* = rose; *de* = from. (To check whether you got them right; see the correct forms on page 19.)

2nd Conjugation Verbs

2nd Conjugation Verbs are characterized by an *e* in the 1st Principal Part of the verb and an *-ēre* (long *ē*) in the 2nd Principal Part.

> *videō, vidēre, vīdī, vīsum* = to see
> *moneō, monēre, monuī, monitum* = to warn or advise

Unfortunately, the four Principal Parts of 2nd Conjugation Verbs do not have the same consistent endings as do the four Principal Parts of 1st Conjugation Verbs. This means that the four Principal Parts of 2nd Conjugation verbs have to be committed to memory on an individual basis. But there are relatively few 2nd Conjugation verbs, and the majority of these will follow the *-eō, -ēre, -uī, -itum* pattern of **moneō**.

2nd Conjugation Verbs are conjugated exactly the same way as 1st Conjugation Verbs. As always, the **1st Person Singular Indicative is given**; to conjugate the verb into the other Persons of the Present Tense, go to the second Principal Part (the Infinitive), **drop the *-re***, and **add the Personal Endings**.

2nd Conjugation

videō, vidēre, vīdī, vīsum

Sing.		Pl.	
videō	I see, do see, am seeing	*vidēmus*	we see, do see, are seeing
vidēs	you see, do see, are seeing	*vidētis*	you see, do see, are seeing
videt	he/she/it sees, does see, is seeing	*vident*	they see, do see, are seeing

Imperatives

The Imperatives of 2nd Conjugation Verbs are formed in the same way as the Imperatives of 1st Conjugation Verbs. To form the Singular Imperative, drop the *-re* from the Infinitive; to form the Plural Imperative, add *-te*. I have included Direct Objects in the examples below so the commands make sense.

| Singular Imperative: | *Vidē me!* | See me! |
| Plural Imperative: | *Vidēte me!* | See me! |

Latin Salutations

Two 2nd Conjugation Verbs are noteworthy because their Imperative forms were used as salutations. *Salvē!* and *Salvēte!* (Imperatives of *salveō, salvēre*) literally mean "Be in good health!" but were used as we use the greeting **"Hello!"** *Valē!* and *Valēte!* (from *valeō, valēre, valuī, valitūrus*) literally mean "Be strong!" and were used as we use "Good-bye!"

Word Order of a Simple Latin Sentence

While there is no left-to-right linear syntax (word order) in Latin, a relative order is often employed, best remembered by the acronym **SMIDAV.** This stands for:

<u>S</u>ubject-<u>M</u>odifier-<u>I</u>ndirect Object-<u>D</u>irect Object-<u>A</u>dverb-<u>V</u>erb

In translating Latin always find the Verb first, then identify the agreeing Subject, then find the Direct Object, and the rest will be fairly obvious.

Summary of New Terminology

1. Case: a specific form of a noun indicating its function in a sentence.
2. Declining: the changing of a noun ending to make it indicate a specific case.
3. Linear Syntax: left-to-right word order.
4. Salutation: a greeting.
5. Noun Stem: what is left after dropping the ending from the Genitive Singular form; the base to which to add case endings.

Vocabulary

fāma,-ae f., fame/rumor
fortūna,-ae f., fortune/luck
ira,-ae f., anger
patria,-ae f., country/native land
pecūnia,-ae f., money
philosophia,-ae f., philosophy/wisdom
poena,-ae f., penalty/punishment
porta,-ae f., gate
puella,-ae f., girl
vīta,-ae f., life

doceō, docēre, docuī, doctum to teach
moneō, monēre, monuī, monitum to advise/warn
salveō, salvēre (only two Principal Parts) to be in good health
valeō, valēre, valuī, valiturus to be strong
videō, vidēre, vīdī, vīsum to see/understand
vītō (1) to avoid/shun

quis who?
-que and (-*que* may be used in place of *et* when connecting two nouns or two adjectives;
   when -*que* is used, it is always attached to the end of the 2nd noun or adjective, i.e.,
   fama fortunaque.)
dē + abl. about/from

Correct Latin forms for example sentences on page 17.
Poeta puellam amat.
Puella famam poetae amat.
Poeta puellis rosas dat.
Puella rosas amat.
Poeta vitam cum puellā amat. (*cum* + abl. = with)
Puellae, vitate poetas.

Exercises

A. Using the paradigm format indicating case and number, decline ***porta, -ae***. Give the English meaning of each declined form.

B. Give the declined English meaning of each of the following forms.

1. puellārum
2. philosophiam
3. irae
4. poenās
5. portīs

6. vitae
7. pecuniīs
8. fāma
9. fortūna
10. patriae

C. Conjugate the following verbs in the Present Tense. Write the English translation after each conjugated form.

1. vītō, vītāre, vītāvī, vītātum
2. doceō, docēre, docuī, doctum

D. Form the Singular and Plural Imperatives of the following verbs, followed by the English translation of each.

	Sing.	Pl.
1. videō, vidēre	_____	_____
2. festīnō, festīnāre	_____	_____
3. moneō, monēre	_____	_____
4. salveō, salvēre	_____	_____
5. laudō, laudāre	_____	_____

E. Translate the following conjugated verb forms.

1. vident
2. salveō
3. docet
4. valent
5. dāmus

6. salvē
7. monēmus
8. valēs
9. errātis
10. cōgitō

F. Render the following sentences into Latin.

1. The gates are strong.
2. Who does not err?
3. She advises me.
4. He avoids anger.
5. They are calling.
6. Save me from punishment!

G. Sentence translations.

1. Fāmam fortūnamque patriae laudāmus.
2. Saepe pecuniam laudātis.
3. Quid vidētis? Portās vidēmus.
4. Portae valent.
5. Philosophia iram non videt.
6. Mē philosophiae dō.
7. Fāma volat. (Virgil) *volo* (1) = to fly
8. Poenam irae saepe vidēmus.
9. Philosophia dē vītā docet.

2nd Declension Nouns
1st–2nd Declension Adjectives
Noun and Adjective Agreement
Present Indicative of *sum, esse, fui, futurus*

III

Objectives

To enable you to:
1. recognize and decline 2nd Declension Masculine and Neuter Nouns;
2. decline 1st–2nd Declension Adjectives;
3. make Adjectives agree in Case, Number, and Gender with the Nouns they modify;
4. form the Present Tense of the Irregular Verb *sum, esse, fui, futurus*.

2nd Declension Nouns

There are five categories or divisions of nouns in the Latin language, based on the spelling of the Genitive Singular ending. Those with a Genitive Singular ending in *-ae* are 1st Declension Nouns and follow the declension outlined in the previous chapter. The Genitive Singular ending of 2nd Declension Nouns is *-ī*.

amīcus, amicī	= m., friend	*puer, pueri*	= m., boy
filius, filiī	= m., son	*ager, agrī*	= m., field
vir, virī	= m., man	*dōnum, dōnī*	= n., gift

Masculine 2nd Declension Nouns

Most 2nd Declension nouns are masculine, with a Nominative Singular ending in *-us*, and follow the declension of *amīcus,-ī*; but there are also 2nd Declension Masculine nouns that have Nominative forms ending in *-ius, -ir*, and *-er*. As for all nouns, the stem to which the case endings are added is found by dropping the Genitive Singular ending.

22

amicus,-i = m., friend

	sing.				pl.		
Nom.	**-us**	*amīcus*	friend	**-ī**	*amīcī*	friends
Gen.	**-ī**	*amīcī*	of a friend	**-ōrum**	*amīcōrum*	of friends
Dat.	**-ō**	*amīcō*	to/for a friend	**-īs**	*amīcīs*	to/for friends
Acc.	**-um**	*amīcum*	friend	**-ōs**	*amīcōs*	friends
Abl.	**-ō**	*amīcō*	by a friend	**-īs**	*amīcīs*	with friends
Voc.	**-e**	*amīc**e****	"friend,"	**-ī**	*amīcī*	"friends,"

	filius,-i = m., son		*vir,-i* = m., man		*ager, agri* = m., field	
	sing.	pl.	sing.	pl.	sing.	pl.
Nom.	*filius*	*filiī*	*vir*	*virī*	*ager*	*agrī*
Gen.	*filiī*	*filiōrum*	*virī*	*virōrum*	*agrī**	*agrōrum*
Dat.	*filiō*	*filiīs*	*virō*	*virīs*	*agrō*	*agrīs*
Acc.	*filium*	*filiōs*	*virum*	*virōs*	*agrum*	*agrōs*
Abl.	*filiō*	*filiīs*	*virō*	*virīs*	*agrō*	*agrīs*
Voc.	*filī**	*filiī*	*vir*	*virī*	*ager*	*agrī*

***NB:** 1. the **-e** ending for the Vocative Singular of 2nd Declensions with a Nominative Singular ending in **-us**;
2. the single **-ī** ending in the Vocative Singular of 2nd Declensions with a Nominative Singular ending in **-ius** (later on the Genitive Singular was also reduced to a single **-i**);
3. the possibility of a stem change in the Genitive Singular as in *ager, a**grī***.

Neuter 2nd Declension Nouns

Neuter 2nd Declension Nouns differ from other 2nd Declension Nouns in that the Nominative, Accusative, and Vocative forms are identical, ending in **-um** in the singular and **-a** in the plural.

donum,-ī = n., gift

	sing.	pl.
Nom.	*donum*	*dona*
Gen.	*donī*	*donōrum*
Dat.	*donō*	*donīs*
Acc.	*donum*	*dona*
Abl.	*donō*	*donīs*
Voc.	*donum*	*dona*

1st–2nd Declension Adjectives

Like nouns, adjectives have three possible genders: masculine, feminine, and neuter. Listing their possible nominative forms indicates the fact that they are adjectives and have three possible gender declensions. 1st–2nd Declension Adjectives have a Genitive Singular ending in *-ī* or *-ae*.

bonus,-a,-um (good)

	Singular			Plural		
	M.	F.	Neut.	M.	F.	Neut.
Nom.	*bonus*	*bona*	*bonum*	*bonī*	*bonae*	*bona*
Gen.	*bonī*	*bonae*	*boni*	*bonōrum*	*bonārum*	*bonōrum*
Dat.	*bonō*	*bonae*	*bono*	*bonīs*	*bonīs*	*bonīs*
Acc.	*bonum*	*bonam*	*bonum*	*bonōs*	*bonās*	*bona*
Abl.	*bonō*	*bonā*	*bono*	*bonīs*	*bonīs*	*bonīs*
Voc.	*bone*	*bona*	*bonum*	*bonī*	*bonae*	*bona*

Noun and Adjective Agreement

Adjectives must be declined to agree with the nouns they modify (describe) in case, number, and gender, e.g., **bonus amicus, bona puella, bonum donum.** This does not mean, however, that the adjective and noun will always have the same ending as in, for example, **puer bonus** and **vir bonus**. In addition there are three common 1st Declension Nouns that are masculine: **nauta,-ae** (sailor), **poeta,-ae** (poet), **agricola,-ae** (farmer). This means that these nouns have 1st Declension endings but that the agreeing adjectives have 2nd Declension endings.

nauta bonus   **poeta magnus**   **agricola bonus**

There is one irregular vocative form that needs to be noted. **Mi** is the irregular singular masculine vocative form of **meus**. Since **bone** and **fili** are the vocative singular forms of **bonus** and **filius** and follow the rules for 2nd Declensions with nominative forms ending in **-us** or **-ius**, if you simply memorize the Latin phrase **mi bone fili** (my good son), you will have mastered any variation that could otherwise cause a problem.

Present Indicative of sum, esse, fui, futurus

Sum, esse, fuī, futūrus are the four Principal Parts of the Latin verb meaning "to be." In languages the more often a verb is used, the more irregular it becomes. Very frequently this is a result of mispronunciation and then a passing on and acceptance of the "new" pronunciation and new spelling. The Present Tense of *sum, esse, fuī, futūrus* certainly illustrates this phenomenon, but note that even though there is no regular stem, the pronoun endings (*-o/m, -s, -t, -mus, -tis, -nt*) are still consistent.

1st Person	*sum*	I am	*sumus*	we are
2nd Person	*es*	you are	*estis*	you (pl.) are
3rd Person	*est*	he, she, it is, there is	*sunt*	they are, there are

<u>Important</u>: The verb "to be" cannot have a Direct Object, i.e., it is intransitive. In noun-adjective relationships, conjugated forms of *sum, esse* act like "equals" signs, in which the adjective on one side of the verb must "equal" (agree in case, number, and gender with) the noun or pronoun on the other side of the verb.

1. *Vita est bona*. Life is good.
   Vita (Nom. Sing. F.) = *bona* (Nom. Sing. F.)
2. *Bella sunt mala*. Wars are evil.
   Bella (Nom. Pl. Neut.) = *mala* (Nom. Pl. Neut.)
3. *Sumus amicae*. We are friends.
   What is the gender of "friends"? How do you know?
4. *Sumus amici*. We are friends.
   What are the possibilities for the gender of "friends"?

Vocabulary

ager, agrī m., field/farm
agricola,-ae m., farmer
amīca,-ae f., friend
amīcus,-ī m., friend
bellum,-ī n., war
donum,-ī n., gift
filia,-ae f., daughter
filius,-ī m., son
nauta,-ae m., sailor
periculum,-ī n., danger
poeta,-ae m., poet
puer,-ī m., boy
sapientia,-ae f., wisdom
vir,-ī m., man

bellus,-a,-um pretty
bonus,-a,-um good
magnus,-a,-um great
malus,-a,-um bad/evil
meus,-a,-um my
multus,-a,-um much/many
stultus,-a,-um foolish
tuus,-a,-um your (sing.)

sum, esse, fuī, fūturus to be/exist

etiam adv., even/also

Exercises

A. Using a paradigm format indicating case and number, decline the following nouns, giving the English translation of each declined form:

    1. puer, pueri   2. Vergilius, Vergilii (Virgil was a famous Roman poet. The plural forms indicate the Vergilian family.)

B. Using a paradigm format, decline ***multus,-a,-um*** into each of its three possible genders.

C. Using a paradigm format, decline:

    1. magnus vir
    2. bona amica
    3. magnum periculum

D. Render the following into the Latin declined forms indicated.

    1. bad sailor (nom. sing.)   4. foolish poets (acc. pl.)
    2. many evils (acc. pl.)   5. for your farmer (dat. sing.)
    3. my good son (voc. sing.)   6. of pretty girls

E. Translate the following into Latin verb forms.

    1. I am   6. you (pl.) are
    2. they are   7. we are
    3. we praise   8. you (sing.) are
    4. he is   9. there are
    5. there is   10. she gives

F. Conjugate the following verbs in the Present Indicative. Give the English translations of each conjugated form.

    1. laudo (1)   2. moneo, monere, monui, monitum

G. Render the following sentences into Latin.

    1. You are a good friend.
    2. My friends are not your friends.
    3. The gifts of wisdom are many and great.
    4. We avoid foolish dangers.
    5. Many poets are not good poets.

H. Sentence translations.

    1. Experientia est magister stultorum.
        experientia,-ae = f., experience
        magister,-tri = m., teacher

    2. Fortuna patriae est magna.

    3. Vir in agro est agricola.
        in + abl. = in/on

    4. Sunt multae puellae bellae.

    5. Pericula belli sunt magna.

    6. Nautae boni estis.

    7. Multi viri pecuniam laudant.

    8. De nihilo, nihil!
        nihilum,-i = n., nothing

    9. Terra Italiae est in Europa.
        terra,-ae = f., land
        Italia,-ae = f., Italy
        Europa,-ae = f., Europe

    10. Puella poetam non amat. Vale, puella! (Catullus)

3rd, 3rd-*io*, and 4th Conjugation Verbs
Formation of the Present Indicative

Objectives

To enable you to:
1. recognize 3rd, 3rd-*io*, and 4th Conjugation Verbs;
2. conjugate 3rd, 3rd-*io*, and 4th Conjugation Verbs in the Present Tense.

3rd, 3rd-io, and 4th Conjugation Verbs

Just as Latin has five Declensions of nouns, it has five divisions of verbs (four Conjugations and a variant). The various divisions of verbs are called Conjugations. Verb Conjugations in Latin are determined by the spelling of the Infinitive; Conjugations are distinguished from each other by the spelling of the first two Principal Parts.

voco, vocare, vocavi, vocatum   1st Conjugation, because the Active Infinitive ends in **-are**.

video, vidēre, vidi, visum   2nd Conjugation, because the Active Infinitive ends in **-ēre** (long **ē**) and the First Principal Part ends in **-eo**.

Identifying 3rd, 3rd *-io*, and 4th Conjugation Verbs

There are two types of 3rd Conjugation Verbs:

Regular 3rd Conjugation: *mittō, mittere, mīsī, missum* (to send)
3rd *-io* Conjugation: *capiō, capere, cēpī, captum* (to capture)

Like 2nd Conjugation Verbs, 3rd Conjugation Verbs have Infinitives ending in **-ere**, but the **-e-** is short. 3rd Conjugation verbs are easily distinguished from 2nd Conjugation verbs in that the First Principal Part does not end in **-eo**. 3rd *-io* verbs differ from Regular 3rd Conjugation Verbs in that the First Principal Part ends in **-io**.

4th Conjugation: *sciō, scīre, scīvī, scītum* (to know)

4th Conjugation Verbs have a distinctive *-ire* ending in the Infinitive and the First Principal Part ends in *-io*.

Present Indicative Tense of 3rd, 3rd-io, and 4th Conjugation Verbs

To form the Present Tense of 3rd, 3rd-*io,* and 4th Conjugation Verbs, follow these steps.

1. Find the verbal stem by **dropping the last three letters of the Infinitive**:

    mittere → **mitt**   *capere* → **cap**   *scīre* → **sc**

2. For Regular 3rd Conjugation Verbs, add these endings to the verbal stem:

Endings		*mitto, mittere*		
-ō	*-imus*	*mittō*	I send	*mittimus*
-is	*-itis*	*mittis*		*mittitis*
-it	*-unt*	*mittit*		*mittunt*

3. For 3rd-*io* and 4th Conjugation Verbs, add the endings below to the verbal stem. Note that an *-i-* precedes every ending.

Endings		*capio, capere*			*scio, scire*		
-iō	*-imus*	*capiō*	I capture	*capimus*	*scio*	I know	*scimus*
-is	*-itis*	*capis*		*capitis*	*scis*		*scitis*
-it	*-iunt*	*capit*		*capiunt*	*scit*		*sciunt*

Nota Bene

In conjugating 3rd, 3rd-*io*, and 4th Conjugation Verbs, the important things to remember are that:

1. 1st Person Singular for all conjugations is always given;
2. *-i-* is the general Present Tense Sign for 3rd, 3rd-*io*, and 4th Conjugation Verbs;
3. *-unt* is always the 3rd Person Plural Ending for 3rd, 3rd-*io,* and 4th Conjugation Verbs;
4. if the 1st Principal Part ends in *-io*, there will be an *-i-* in 3rd Person Plural (*-iunt*).

The persistent *-unt* in the 3rd Person Plural will be difficult to remember. It might help to recall that this is the same ending that occurs in the 3rd Person Plural of *sum, esse, fuī, futūrus*:

sum	I am	*sumus*	we are
es	you are	*estis*	you (pl.) are
est	he, she, it is	*sunt*	they are

Vocabulary

audiō, audīre, audīvī, audītum to hear/listen to
capiō, capere, cēpī, captum to capture/seize
dīcō, dīcere, dīxī, dictum to say/tell/speak
discō, discere, didicī to learn
dūco, dūcere, dūxi, ductum to lead/consider
faciō, facere, fēcī, factum to do/make
habeō, habēre, habuī, habitum to have/hold/possess
inveniō, invenīre, invēnī, inventum to discover/come upon/find
mittō, mittere, mīsī, missum to send
nesciō, nescire, nescīvī, nescitum to not know
sciō, scīre, scīvī, scitum to know
veniō, venīre, vēnī, ventum to come

cūra,-ae f., care/anxiety
magister, magistrī m., teacher/master
mora,-ae f., delay
ōtium,-ī n., leisure
verbum,-ī n., word

beātus,-a,-um blessed/happy/fortunate
parvus,-a,-um small/little
paucī,-ae,-a few

nunc adv., now

Exercises

A. Identify the Conjugation and then form the Present Tense of each of the verbs below, giving the English translation of each conjugated verb form.

1. duco, ducere, duxi, ductum
2. facio, facere, feci, factum
3. habeo, habere, habui, habitum
4. nescio, nescire, nescivi, nescitum

B. Using a paradigm format listing cases and number, decline:

1. a small farmer
2. few words
3. blessed leisure

C. Translate the following verb forms into English or Latin as required.

1. est
2. dicunt
3. dant
4. scimus
5. habes
6. venio
7. we are
8. you (pl.) are sending
9. I do not know
10. they are calling
11. he hears
12. he is speaking

D. Render the following sentences into Latin.

1. What are you sending?
2. I am slowly learning.
3. Who listens to/hears the words of the poet?
4. Now we understand the dangers of leisure.
5. They do not know about the delay.

E. Sentence translations.

1. Quis patriam nunc ducit?
2. Remedium irae est mora. (Seneca) *remedium,-i* = n., remedy/cure
3. Quid facimus? Discimus multa.
4. Magistri, dum docent, discunt. *dum* = while
5. Verba poetae saepe non sunt beata.
6. Nautae multas fabulas dicunt. *fabula,-ae* = f., fable/tale/story
7. Otium sine curis est beatum. *sine* + abl. = without
8. Vita multa pericula habet.
9. Portae oppidi sunt parvae. *oppidum,-i* = n., village
10. Vir paucorum verborum et multorum factorum est. *factum,-i* = n., deed

Vocabulary Chapters I–IV

ager, agrī m., field/farm
agricola,-ae m., farmer
amīca,-ae f., friend
amīcus,- ī m., friend
amō (1) to love
audiō, audīre, audīvī, audītum to hear/to listen to

beātus,-a,-um blessed/happy/content
bellum,- ī n., war
bellus,-a,-um pretty
bonus,-a,-um good

capiō, capere, cēpī, captum to capture/seize
cōgitō (1) to think/understand/consider
culpō (1) to blame
cūra,-ae f., care/anxiety

dē + abl. about/from
dīcō, dīcere, dīxī, dictum to say/tell/speak
discō, discere, didicī to learn
dō, dare, dēdī, datum to give
doceō, docēre, docuī, doctum to teach
donum,- ī n., gift
dūcō, dūcere, dūxī, ductum to lead/consider

errō (1) to err/go astray
et and
etiam adv., so/too/even/also

faciō, facere, fēcī, factum to make/do
fāma,-ae f., fame/rumor
festīnō (1) to hasten
filia,-ae f., daughter
fīlius,- ī m., son
fortūna,-ae f., fortune/luck

habeō, habēre, habuī, habitum to have/hold/possess
inveniō, invenīre, invenī, inventum to discover/come upon/find
ira,-ae f., anger
laudō, laudāre, laudāvī, laudātum to praise
lentē adv., slowly

magister, magistrī m., teacher/master
magnus,-a,-um great
malus,-a,-um bad/evil
mē me
meus,-a,-um my

mittō, mittere, mīsī, missum to send
moneō, monēre, monuī, monitum to advise/warn
mora,-ae f., delay
multus,-a,-um much/many

nauta,-ae m., sailor
nesciō, nescīre, nescīvī, nescitum to not know
nihil nothing
nōn adv., not
nunc adv., now

ōtium,- ī n., leisure

parvus,-a,-um small/little
patria,-ae f., country/native land
paucī,-ae,-a few
pecunia,-ae, f., money
periculum,- ī n., danger
philosophia,-ae f., philosophy/wisdom
poena,-ae f., penalty/punishment
poeta,-ae m., poet
porta,-ae f., gate
puella,-ae f., girl
puer,- ī m., boy

-que and
quid what?
quis who?

saepe adv., often
salveō, salvēre (only two Principal Parts) to be in good health
sapientia,-ae f., wisdom
sciō, scīre, scīvī, scitum to know
servō (1) to save/protect/preserve
sī if
stultus,-a,-um foolish
sum, esse, fuī, futūrus to be

tuus,-a,-um your (sing.)

valeō, valēre, valuī, valitūrus to be strong
verbum,- ī n., word
veniō, venīre, vēnī, ventum to come
videō, vidēre, vīdī, vīsum to see/understand
vir,- ī m., man
vīta,-ae f., life
vītō (1) to avoid/shun
vocō (1) to call

Imperatives, All Conjugations
Imperfect and Future Indicative Tenses of
sum, esse, fui, futurus

V

Objectives

To enable you to:

1. form the Imperatives of 3rd, 3rd-*io*, and 4th Conjugation Verbs;
2. form the Imperfect and Future Tenses of the Irregular Verb ***sum, esse, fui, futurus***.

Imperatives, All Conjugations

We have already discussed the **Imperative Mood** (used for commands) and learned how to form the **Imperatives** (commands) for 1st and 2nd Conjugation verbs. If you will recall, to form the Singular Imperative, simply drop the *-re* from the Active Infinitive. You will be delighted to find out that this is the way to form the Singular Imperative for all conjugations of verbs.

		Singular Imperative	
1st Conjugation	*voco, vocare*	*Vocā mē!*	Call me!
2nd Conjugation	*video, videre*	*Vidē mē!*	See me!
3rd Conjugation	*mitto, mittere*	*Mitte me!*	Send me!
3rd *-io* Conjugation	*capio, capere*	*Cape virum!*	Capture the man!
4th Conjugation	*scio, scire*	*Scī tuōs amicōs!*	Know your friends!

To form the **Plural Imperative**:

1. for 1st, 2nd, and 4th Conjugation verbs, add *-te* to the Singular Imperative.

Voca	*+ te*	→	*Vocāte*
Vide	*+ te*	→	*Vidēte*
Sci	*+ te*	→	*Scīte*

33

2. for 3rd and 3rd-*io* Conjugation verbs, drop the final *-e* from the Singular Imperative and add *-ite*.

$$Mitt(e) + \textbf{\textit{ite}} \quad \rightarrow \quad \textbf{\textit{Mittite}}$$
$$Cap(e) + \textbf{\textit{ite}} \quad \rightarrow \quad \textbf{\textit{Capite}}$$

Now, let's put it all together in a paradigm format listing the first two principal parts of the verb.

	Verb	**Imperatives**			
		Sing.		Pl.	
1st	*voco, vocare*	**Vocā**	Call!	**Vocāte**	Call!
2nd	*video, videre*	**Vidē**	See!	**Vidēte**	See!
3rd	*mitto, mittere*	**Mitte**	Send!	**Mittite**	Send!
3rd-*io*	*capio, capere*	**Cape**	Capture!	**Capite**	Capture!
4th	*scio, scire*	**Scī**	Know!	**Scīte**	Know!

There is an important jingle that will come in handy for remembering <u>the four</u> **Irregular Imperatives** in the entire Latin language:

"**Dūc, Dīc, Fac,** and **Fer** have an *-e* that isn't there!"

Only the Singular Imperatives of these verbs are irregular; they are irregular in that over the years, the final *-e* was eventually omitted. (All these verbs, except for **fer**, were in the vocabulary for chapter IV.)

Imperfect and Future Indicative Tenses of sum, esse, fui, futurus

Because it is used so often, the verb **"to be"** is irregular in every language, and Latin is no exception. This means you simply have to memorize the individual forms for the Present, Imperfect, and Future of *sum, esse*. The good news is that you already know the Present Tense, which I am listing again only as a review. The Imperfect is a general past tense.

Present	Imperfect	Future
sum I am	*eram* I was	*erō* I will be
es you are	*erās* you were	*eris* you will be
est he, she, it, there is	*erat* he, she, it, there was	*erit* he, she, it, there will be
sumus we are	*erāmus* we were	*erimus* we will be
estis you (pl.) are	*erātis* you were	*eritis* you will be
sunt they, there are	*erant* they, there were	*erunt* they, there will be

Be sure to notice the possibility of translating Third Person Singular and Plural impersonally with "there." When you translate using "there," the form of the verb is dependent on whether the subject is Singular or Plural.

1. There was much danger.   *Erat periculum multum.*
2. There were many gifts.   *Erant dona multa.*

Vocabulary

fūgiō, fūgere, fūgī, fūgitūrus to flee
incipiō, incipere, incēpī, inceptum to begin
superō (1) to overcome

antīquus,-a,-um old/ancient
Graecus,-a,-um Greek

arma, armōrum n., weapons/arms
auxilium,- ī n., help/aid
cūlpa,-ae f., fault
fōrma,-ae f., shape/form/beauty
historia,-ae f., story/history
Italia,-ae f., Italy
liber, librī m., book
Rōma,-ae f., Rome

dēnique adv., finally
ergō adv., therefore
quondam adv., once
semper adv., always

cum + abl. with
ex (ē) + abl. out of/away from (ē is used before consonants)
in + abl. in/on
in + acc. into/against
sine + abl. without
ubi when/where

Exercises

A. Identify the conjugation of each of the following verbs then form the Singular and Plural Imperatives followed by the English translations of each.

1. venio, venire
2. supero, superare
3. incipio, incipere
4. duco, ducere

5. facio, facere
6. habeo, habere
7. dico, dicere
8. fugio, fugere

B. Translate the following verb forms into English or Latin as required.

1. eramus
2. erunt
3. estis
4. erit
5. es

6. I will be
7. you (sing.) were
8. we are
9. she was
10. they were

C. Decline *auxilium,-i* using a paradigm format indicating cases and number.

D. Give the Latin declined or conjugated forms for the following.

1. we are beginning
2. Send me!
3. small boys (acc.)
4. few cares (nom.)
5. of little leisure

6. for blessed friends
7. without delay
8. of great anxieties
9. they see
10. he is coming

E. Render the following sentences into Latin.

1. There is nothing without fault.
2. The history of Rome is old and great.
3. I am beginning to understand!

F. Sentence translations.

1. Vitate Graecos cum dono in formā equi! *equus,-i* = m., horse
2. Ab antiquā philosophiā multam sapientiam discimus. *ab* + abl. = from
3. Antiquus liber non semper est magnus liber.
4. Sumus et semper erimus amici.
5. Saepe vir famae de famā fugit.
6. Semper multa forma est in parvis pueris puellisque.
7. Ubi sine periculis erimus?
8. Cogito ergo sum. (Descartes)
9. Graeci Romanique semper non erant amici. *Romanus,-a,-um* = Roman
10. Italia erat patria Romanorum.

Text Translation

Now that you have acquired a workable vocabulary, there will be readings like the one below at the end of each chapter to help you become familiar with text format translation. Vocabulary that you have not had will be given.

Historia Romae in Troiā[1] incipit ubi quondam

magnum bellum inter[2] Graecos Troianosque[3] erat.

Denique Graeci cum auxilio equi[4] lignei[5] Troianos

superant. Quis historiam equi lignei nescit?

Venus filium de Graecis servat. Aeneas[6] cum paucis

amicis ē Troiā fugit. Navigat[7] multos annos.[8]

Denique ad[9] Italiam venit. Publius Vergilius Maro[10]

historiam Aeneae dicit: "Arma virumque cano."[11]

(*Aeneid* Bk. I)

1. **Troia,-ae** f., Proper Noun, Troy, an ancient city
2. **inter + acc.** between
3. **Troianus,-a,-um** Trojan
4. **equus,-i** m., horse
5. **ligneus,-a,-um** wooden
6. **Aeneas,-ae** m., Proper Noun, mythological founder of the Roman people
7. **navigo (1)** to sail
8. **annus,-i** m., year
9. **ad + acc.** into
10. **Publius Vergilius Maro** Proper Noun, Virgil, a famous Roman poet; author of the *Aeneid*.
11. **cano, canere, cecini, cantum** to sing/to tell about

Demonstrative Pronouns *hic, haec, hoc*
Demonstrative Pronouns *ille, illa, illud*
Personal Pronoun *is, ea, id*
Irregular 1st–2nd Declension Adjectives

VI

Objectives

To enable you to:

1. recognize and recall the Masculine, Feminine, and Neuter Singular and Plural forms of the Pronouns: ***hic, haec, hoc***
ille, illa, illud
is, ea, id;

2. determine the declension stem of 1st–2nd Declension Adjectives with a Masculine Nominative Singular ending in *-er*.

Demonstrative Pronouns hic, haec, hoc
ille, illa, illud

Demonstrative Pronouns point out a specific person, place, or thing. The singular forms are irregular, but their declined forms are similar to each other and can easily be committed to memory by group and individual recitations in class. The plural forms of Demonstrative Pronouns have regular 1st–2nd Declension endings for the most part (in bold print on the next page).

	hic, haec, hoc this/the latter				*ille, illa, illud* that/the former			
	Singular				Singular			
	M.	F.	N.		M.	F.	N.	
Nom.	hic	haec	hoc	*this*	ille	illa	illud	*that*
Gen.	huius	huius	huius	*of this*	illius	illius	illius	*of that*
Dat.	huic	huic	huic	*to/for this*	illī	illī	illī	*for that*
Acc.	hunc	hanc	hoc	*this*	illum	illam	illud	*that*
Abl.	hōc	hāc	hōc	*with this*	illō	illā	illō	*with that*
Voc.	The Vocative is not listed here and will no longer be listed because, with the exception of 2nd Declension Masculine Nouns with a Nominative Singular ending in *-us* or *-ius,* the Vocative is always the same as the Nominative.							

Plural Forms of the Above Pronouns

	hic, haec, hoc this/the latter				*ille, illa, illud* that/the former			
	Plural				Plural			
	M.	F.	N.		M.	F.	N.	
Nom.	hī	hae	haec	*these*	illī	illae	illa	*those*
Gen.	hōrum	hārum	hōrum	*of these*	illōrum	illārum	illōrum	*of those*
Dat.	hīs	hīs	hīs	*to/for these*	illīs	illīs	illīs	*for those*
Acc.	hōs	hās	haec	*these*	illōs	illās	illa	*those*
Abl.	hīs	hīs	hīs	*with these*	illīs	illīs	illīs	*in those*
Voc.	No longer listed.							

NB: When **demonstratives** are used **alone**, they are **pronouns**; when demonstratives **modify nouns**, they act as **adjectives**.

Pronoun Usage	Adjective Usage
hic = this (man)	*hic poeta* = this poet
haec = this (woman)	*haec mora* = this delay
hoc = this (thing)	*hoc bellum* = this war

Personal Pronoun is, ea, id

Is, ea, id are Personal Pronouns and mean respectively **"he, she, it."**

	M.		Singular F.		N.	
Nom.	is	*he*	ea	*she*	id	*it*
Gen.	eius	*of him/his*	eius	*of hers/her*	eius	*of it*
Dat.	eī	*to/for him*	eī	*to/for her*	eī	*to/for it*
Acc.	eum	*him*	eam	*her*	id	*it*
Abl.	eō	*with him*	eā	*with her*	eō	*with it*

			Plural			
Nom.	eī	*they*	eae	*they*	ea	*they*
Gen.	eōrum	*of them/their*	eārum	*of them/their*	eōrum	*of them/their*
Dat.	eīs	*to/for them*	eīs	*to/for them*	eīs	*to/for them*
Acc.	eōs	*them*	eās	*them*	ea	*them*
Abl.	eīs	*with them*	eīs	*with them*	eīs	*with them*

Is, ea, id may also serve as Demonstrative Adjectives meaning **"this"** or **"that,"** as you will notice in the examples below.

1. *Eos viros saepe videmus.*   We often see these men.
2. *Eae patriae valent.*   Those countries are strong.

Irregular 1st–2nd Declension Adjectives

Several 1st–2nd Declension Adjectives follow the **-ius** and **-ī** endings in the Genitive and Dative Singular cases but are completely regular in all other cases. The most common include:

nūllus,-a,-um = none   *solus,-a,-um* = alone/only
ūllus,-a,-um = any   *ūnus,-a,-um* = one
totus,-a,-um = whole/entire

An easy way to remember the above adjectives as a group is to recall the little phrase "**nuts**" to "**u**."

ūllus,-a,-um = any

	Sing. M.	F.	N.	Pl. M.	F.	N.
Nom.	ūllus	ūlla	ūllum	ūllī	ūllae	ūlla
Gen.	ūllius	ūllius	ūllius	ūllōrum	ūllārum	ūllōrum
Dat.	ūllī	ūllī	ullī	ūllīs	ūllīs	ūllīs
Acc.	ūllum	ūllam	ūllum	ūllōs	ūllās	ulla
Abl.	ūllō	ūllā	ūllō	ūllīs	ūllīs	ūllīs

1st–2nd Declension Adjectives with a Masculine Ending in -er

For 1st–2nd Declension Adjectives with a Masculine ending in **-er** such as **noster, nostra, nostrum** (our), the <u>feminine stem</u> is the stem used for declining all genders.

noster, nostra, nostrum = our

	Sing. M.	F.	N.	Pl. M.	F.	N.
Nom.	noster	nostra	nostrum	nostrī	nostrae	nostra
Gen.	nostrī	nostrae	nostrī	nostrōrum	nostrārum	nostrōrum
Dat.	nostrō	nostrae	nostrō	nostrīs	nostrīs	nostrīs
Acc.	nostrum	nostram	nostrum	nostrōs	nostrās	nostra
Abl.	nostrō	nostrā	nostrō	nostrīs	nostrīs	nostrīs

Vocabulary

hic, haec, hoc this/the latter
ille, illa, illud that/the former
is, ea, id he, she, it, this, that
iste, ista, istud* such that of yours/that
scrībo, scribere, scripsī, scriptum to write
animus,-ī m., soul/spirit; **pl.,** pride/courage
numerus,-ī m., number
officium,-ī n., duty/office
populus,-ī m., people/nation

nimium or nimis indecl. adj./adv., too much/excessively
satis enough (indeclinable noun/adv.)
ad + acc. toward/to (with verbs of motion)
nōn sōlum—sed etiam correlative,** not only—but also

līber, lībera, līberum free
noster, nostra, nostrum our
nūllus,-a,-um none/no
Rōmānus,-a,-um Roman
sōlus,-a,-um alone/only
tōtus,-a,-um whole/entire
ūllus,-a,-um any
ūnus,-a,-um one
verus,-a,-um true/real/proper
vester, vestra, vestrum your (pl.)

*Iste, ista, istud is an Irregular 1st–2nd Declension Pronoun and Adjective following the same declension pattern as *ille, illa, illud*.

	Sing.			Pl.		
	M.	F.	N.	M.	F.	N.
Nom.	*iste*	*ista*	*istud*	*isti*	*istae*	*ista*
Gen.	*istius*	*istius*	*istius*	*istorum*	*istarum*	*istorum*
Dat.	*isti*	*isti*	*isti*	*istis*	*istis*	*istis*
Acc.	*istum*	*istam*	*istud*	*istos*	*istas*	*ista*
Abl.	*isto*	*ista*	*isto*	*istis*	*istis*	*istis*

** Correlatives are words that regularly appear together but are not adjacent. See page 321 for a Compiled Chart of Common Correlatives.

Exercises

A. Using *is, ea, id* as a Pronoun or Adjective as required, render the following phrases into Latin.

1. her
2. of these things
3. to him
4. it
5. these things (acc. pl.)
6. with them
7. he
8. these (nom. m.)
9. for her
10. them (acc. m.)

B. Give the case, number, and gender of each of the following as well as the declined English meaning.

1. illis
2. solius
3. illae
4. eius
5. illa
6. horum
7. uni
8. illos
9. has
10. his
11. ea
12. ulli

C. Translate the following according to the declined meaning.

1. hos numeros
2. illorum populorum
3. illud officium
4. huius totius libri
5. Graecis solis
6. hanc puellam
7. illa poena
8. in hāc vitā
9. illis moris
10. Satis huius!

D. Conjugate *scribo, scribere, scripsi, scriptum* in the Present Indicative, followed by the English translation of each conjugated form.

E. Render the following sentences into Latin.

1. That man is not a true Roman.
2. Your (pl.) friends are not our friends.
3. When duty and courage are strong, the country is strong.

F.   Sentence translations.

    1. Hic de culpis illorum scribit.
    2. Nostrae culpae non sunt bellae.
    3. Supera animos et iram tuam. (Ovid)
    4. Officium liberos viros semper vocat.
    5. Totus populus hanc puellam laudat.
    6. Fortuna multis dat nimis, satis nulli. (Martial)
    7. Nondum satis pecuniae habeo. *nondum* = not yet
    8. Non solum arma sed etiam animi populum magnum faciunt.
    9. Infinitus est numerus stultorum. *infinitus,-a,-um* = infinite

Text Translation

At the request of the emperor Augustus, Virgil composed the *Aeneid*, an epic poem glorifying and affirming the Roman Nation. Virgil incorporated the myth that the gods planned the founding of Rome. In the Dido episode Aeneas, the main character of the *Aeneid*, abandons the young queen, who has saved his life, because the gods have called him to get on with his purpose in life: founding the Roman Nation. Most scholars agree that the Dido myth was included to explain and excuse the future conflict between Rome and Carthage.

Karthago[1] erat oppidum[2] in Africā.[3] Dido[4] erat regina[5] oppidi huius. Dea[6] Juno[7] hunc populum amat. Juno Aeneam[8] odit[9] quod[10] ea scit de factis[11] futuris[12] eius. Juno Aeolo,[13] deo[14] ventorum,[15] dicit. Aeolus magnos ventos mittit. Hi venti naviculas[16] Aeneae delent.[17] Quod Venus[18] Troianos[19] amat, Juppiter[20] ventos prohibet.[21] Aeneas cum amicis ad terram[22] natat.[23] Dido miseros[24] viros invenit et hos iuvat.[25] Dido Aeneam statim[26] amat. (Venus est causa[27] huius!) Aeneas in Africā multos annos remanet.[28] Denique Juppiter Mercurium,[29] nuntium[30] deum, ad Aeneam mittit. Mercurius vocat Aeneam ad officium eius: Quid agis?[31] Cur[32] muros[33] in Africā struis?[34] Dediscis**ne**[35] tuum[36] regnum?[37]

(*Aeneid* Bks. I–IV)

1. **Karthago** f., Proper Noun, Carthage	17. **deleo, delere, delevi, deletum** to destroy
2. **oppidum,-i** n., town/village	18. **Venus** f., Venus, goddess of love
3. **Africa,-ae** f., Proper Noun, Africa	19. **Troianus,-a,-um** Trojan
4. **Dido** f., Proper Noun, Dido	20. **Juppiter** m., Proper Noun, Jupiter, king of the gods
5. **regina,-ae** f., queen	
6. **dea,-ae** f., goddess	21. **prohibeo, prohibere, prohibui, prohibitum** to stop
7. **Juno** f., Proper Noun, Juno, queen of the gods	
8. **Aeneas,-ae** m., Proper Noun, Aeneas	22. **terra,-ae** f., land
9. **odit** he/she/it hates	23. **nato (1)** to swim
10. **quod** because	24. **miser, misera, miserum** wretched/miserable
11. **factum,-i** n., deed	25. **iuvo, iuvare, iuvi, iutum** to help
12. **futurus,-a,-um** future	26. **statim** adv., immediately
13. **Aeolus,-i** m., Proper Noun, Aeolus	27. **causa,-ae** f., cause
14. **deus,-i** m., god	28. **remaneo,-manere,-mansi,-mansum** to remain
15. **ventus,-i** m., wind	
16. **navicula,-ae** f., little ship	29. **Mercurius,-i** m., Proper Noun, Mercury

30. **nuntius,-i** m., messenger
31. **ago, agere, egi, actum** to do
32. **cur** why?
33. **murus,-i** m., wall
34. **struo, struere, struxi, structum** to build/pile up
35. **dedisco, dediscere, dedidici** to forget
36. **-ne** added to the end of the 1st word of a sentence to indicate a question
37. **regnum,-i** n., rule/realm

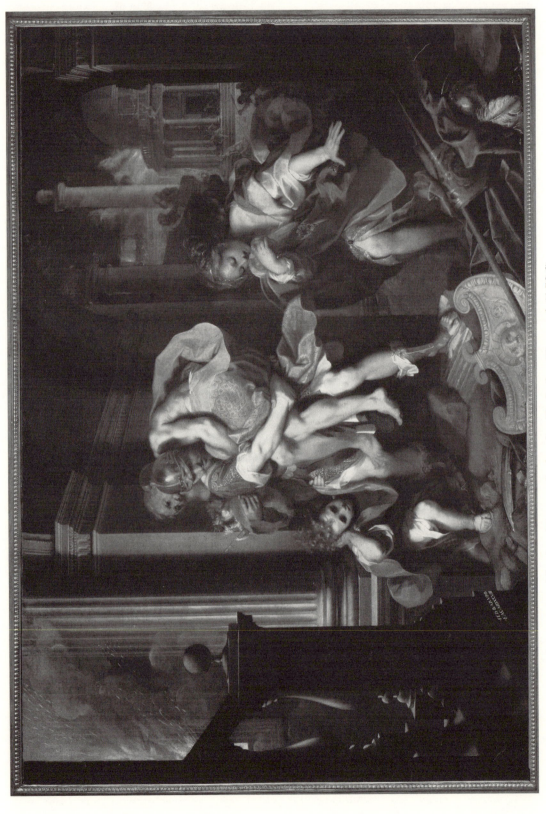

Aeneas, Anchises, and Ascanius Fleeing Troy, painting by Federico Barocci (1596)

Irregular Verb *possum, posse, potui*
Complementary Infinitives
-ne to Indicate a Question
Intensive Pronoun *ipse, ipsa, ipsum*

Objectives

To enable you to:

1. conjugate the Irregular Verb **possum, posse, potui** into the Present, Imperfect, and Future Tenses;
2. recognize Complementary Infinitives;
3. recognize and form Interrogative Latin Statements Employing **-ne**;
4. decline the Intensive Pronoun **ipse, ipsa, ipsum.**

Irregular Verb possum, posse, potui

The conjugation of the verb **possum, posse, potui** (to be able) represents a combination of the first three letters of the adjective **potis** (able) and conjugated forms of the verb **sum, esse, fui, futurus** (to be). Because it is difficult to pronounce "**t**" plus "**s**" as would occur in *pot + sum (potsum)*, this combination became "**ss**," as you will see in the underlined forms below.

Present Indicative		Imperfect Indicative		Future	
*po**ss**um*	I am able	*poteram*	I was able	*potero*	I will be able
potes	you are able	*poteras*	you were able	*poteris*	you will be able
potest	he, she, it is able	*poterat*	he, she, it was able	*poterit*	he, she, it will be able
*po**ss**umus*	we are able	*poterāmus*	we were able	*poterimus*	we will be able
potestis	you (pl.) are able	*poterātis*	you (pl.) were able	*poteritis*	you (pl.) will be able
*po**ss**unt*	they are able	*poterant*	they were able	*poterunt*	they will be able

Complementary Infinitives

Some verbs require an Infinitive to <u>complete</u> their meaning, thus the origin of the term <u>Complementary</u> Infinitive. *Debeō, debēre, debuī, debitum* (to ought) and *possum, posse, potuī* (to be able) always require Complementary Infinitives to complete their meanings.

1. *Debeo facere hoc.*	I ought to do this.
2. *Poterunt venire.*	They will be able to come.

While "can" and "could" are perfectly acceptable English translations for the Present and Imperfect Tenses of *possum*, the more literal translation "to be able" will always point out the obvious necessity of a Complementary Infinitive.

-ne *to Indicate a Question*

As the Romans had no punctuation marks, they had to indicate questions through vocabulary. You have already had the interrogative pronouns *quis* (who?) and *quid* (what?); in this chapter you will be introduced to the interrogative adverb *cur* (why?). The <u>grammatical way</u> of indicating a simple question is to attach *-ne* to the first word of a sentence.

1. *Sumusne amici?*	Are we friends?
2. *Puellane est bella?*	Is the girl pretty?

Intensive Pronoun ipse, ipsa, ipsum

The Intensive Pronoun *ipse, ipsa, ipsum*, meaning respectively "himself, herself, itself," follows the same declension pattern of *ille, illa, illud*, with *-ius* in the Genitive Singular and *-i* in the Dative Singular.

	Singular			Plural		
	M.	F.	N.	M.	F.	N.
Nom.	ipse	ipsa	ipsum	ipsī	ipsae	ipsa
Gen.	**ipsius**	**ipsius**	**ipsius**	ipsōrum	ipsārum	ipsōrum
Dat.	**ipsī**	**ipsī**	**ipsī**	ipsīs	ipsīs	ipsīs
Acc.	ipsum	ipsam	ipsum	ipsōs	ipsās	ipsa
Abl.	ipsō	ipsā	ipsō	ipsīs	ipsīs	ipsīs

The Intensive Pronoun is used to rename a noun or pronoun for emphasis.

1. The poet himself says this.   *Poeta ipse hoc dicit.*
2. She herself says this.   *Ipsa hoc dicit.*
3. The plan itself is bad.   *Consilium ipsum est malum.*
4. These are gifts from the farmers   *Ea dona sunt de agricolis ipsis.*
   themselves.
5. They blame the wars themselves   *Bella ipsa eis famis culpant.*
   for these rumors.

Vocabulary

agō, agere, ēgī, āctum to do/lead/act/drive
  Idioms:
  vitam agere to live life
  gratias agere to thank
dēbeō, dēbēre, dēbuī, dēbitum to ought/owe
dēleō, dēlēre, dēlēvī, dēlētum to destroy/delete/wipe out
possum, posse, potuī to be able
tolerō (1) to tolerate/endure

cūr why?
-ne enclitic added to end of word to indicate a question
quod because
propter + acc. on account of/because of
sed but

ibi adv., there
tum adv., then
insidiae,-ārum f., plots/treachery
oculus,- ī m., eye
terra,-ae f., land
tyrannus,- ī m., tyrant/absolute ruler
vitium,- ī n., vice/fault

miser, misera, miserum wretched/miserable
perpetuus,-a,-um perpetual/continuous

ipse, ipsa, ipsum intensive pron., himself/herself/itself

Exercises

A. Using a paradigm format, decline and translate:

    1. vitium malum   2. tyrannus miser

B. Conjugate the following verbs into the Present Indicative; translate each form.

    1. ago, agere, egi, actum   2. debeo, debere, debui, debitum

C. Form the Imperatives of the following verbs.

    1. scribo, scribere, scripsi, scriptum   4. tolero, tolerare, toleravi, toleratum
    2. deleo, delere, delevi, deletum   5. ago, agere, egi, actum
    3. facio, facere, feci, factum   6. incipio, incipere, incepi, inceptum

D. Translate the following verb forms into English or Latin as required.

    1. poterit   6. poteram
    2. possumus   7. poteris
    3. poterant   8. possum
    4. potero   9. we were able
    5. potes   10. are you (pl.) able?

E. Give the English for the declined meanings of the following pronouns.

    1. ipsi (sing.)   6. iste
    2. istis   7. ipse
    3. ipsam   8. ipsius
    4. ipsa (pl.)   9. istos
    5. istorum   10. ipsum

F. Supply the correct declined form of *is, ea, id*.

    1. them (m.)   6. with these (women)
    2. her   7. he
    3. to them   8. they (m.)
    4. of it   9. for him
    5. of those (men)   10. these (things)

G. Render the following sentences into Latin.

    1. Our nation will not be able to endure such treacheries.
    2. Virgil himself tells this story.
    3. Will the courage of one such man be able to save our country?

H. Sentence translations.

1. Si animus infirmus est, non poterit bonam fortunam tolerare. (Pubilius Syrius)
    infirmus,-a,- um infirm/not strong
2. Poterisne otium pecuniae vitaeque sine curis superare?
3. Quid facere debemus?
4. Vita non est vivere sed valere. (Martial)
    vivo, vivere, vixi, victum to live
5. Sine deo, animus non potest bonus esse. (Seneca)
    deus,-i m., god
6. In liberā terrā vitam agimus.
7. Nec nostra vitia nec remedia tolerare possumus. (Livy)
    nec . . . nec neither . . . nor
    remedium,-i n., remedy
8. Cur hoc agitis?
9. Potestne fortuna bona esse perpetua?
10. Nihil mali potest venire ulli viro bono. (Socrates)
11. Aurora musis amica est.
    aurora,-ae f., dawn
    musa,-ae f., muse (goddess of music and arts/learning)

Text Translation

Livy begins his history of Rome with the arrival of Aeneas in Italy.

Denique, post[1] multos annos et post magnas miserias[2] in terrā altoque,[3] fugitivi[4] Troiani[5] in Italiam veniunt. Quomodo[6] potest ira unius deae[7] esse causa[8] tantorum[9] malorum, Musa?[10] Troiani cibum[11] in proximis[12] agris avide[13] petunt.[14] Agri sunt Latini.[15] Latinus est rex[16] Latii.[17] Cum[18] Latinus facta[19] Troianorum invenit, bellum gerit[20] cum Aeneā amicisque. Troiani Latinum populumque eius vincunt.[21] Etiam Latinus Aeneam Troianosque vivere[22] in Latio invitat.[23] Latinus nullos filios et solam unam filiam, Laviniam,[24] habet. Post longum[25] bellum cum Turnō,[26] Aeneas in matrimonium[27] ducit Laviniam. Aeneas Laviniaque novum[28] oppidum[29] condunt.[30] Appellant[31] oppidum Lavinium de Laviniā. In Lavinio et toto Latio linguam[32] Latinam[33] dicunt. Aeneas Laviniaque filium habent. Appellant puerum Ascanium.[34] (Iulus[35] est altera[36] forma Ascanii.)

(*Ab Urbe Condita* Bk. I, i–iii)

1. **post + acc.** after
2. **miseria,-ae** f., affliction/misery
3. **altum,-i** n., depth/deep sea
4. **fugitivus,-a,-um** fugitive
5. **Troianus,-a,-um** Trojan
6. **quomodo** how?
7. **dea,-ae** f., goddess
8. **causa,-ae** f., cause
9. **tantus,-a,-um** such/so great
10. **Musa,-ae** f., muse (goddess of literature and other arts)
11. **cibus,-i** m., food
12. **proximus,-a,-um** nearest
13. **avide** adv., hungrily
14. **peto, petere, petivi, petitum** to seek
15. **Latinus,-i** m., Proper Noun
16. **rex** m., king
17. **Latium,-i** n., Proper Noun, an area in Italy in which Rome is later situated
18. **Cum + Indic. Verb** when
19. **factum,-i** n., deed
20. **gero, gerere, gessi, gessum** to carry on/conduct/wage
21. **vinco, vincere, vici, victum** to conquer
22. **vivo, vivere, vixi, victum** to live
23. **invito, invitare** to invite
24. **Lavinia,-ae** f., Proper Noun
25. **longus,-a,-um** long
26. **Turnus,-i** m., Proper Noun, the prince from a neighboring village to whom Lavinia had been betrothed
27. **matrimonium,-i** n., marriage
28. **novus,-a,-um** new
29. **oppidum,-i** n., town/village

52

30. **condo, condere, condidi, conditum** to found
31. **appello (1)** to name/call
32. **lingua,-ae** f., language
33. **Latinus,-a,-um** Latin
34. **Ascanius,-i** m., Proper Noun
35. **Iulus,-i** m., Julius
36. **alter, altera, alterum** another

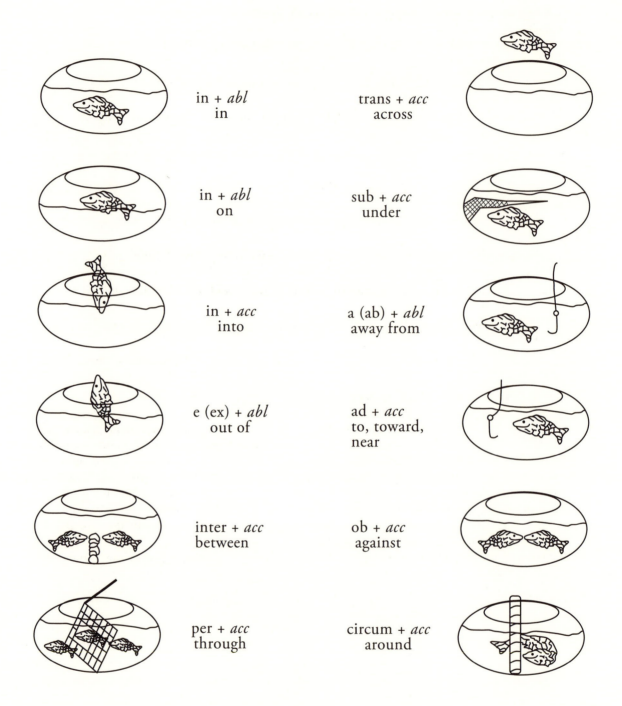

in + *abl*
in

trans + *acc*
across

in + *abl*
on

sub + *acc*
under

in + *acc*
into

a (ab) + *abl*
away from

e (ex) + *abl*
out of

ad + *acc*
to, toward,
near

inter + *acc*
between

ob + *acc*
against

per + *acc*
through

circum + *acc*
around

3rd Declension Nouns
Six Specific Ablative Uses
Accusative of Duration of Time

Objectives

To enable you to:
1. recognize and decline 3rd Declension Masculine, Feminine, and Neuter Nouns;
2. recognize and translate Specific Ablative Usages;
3. recognize and translate the Accusative of Duration of Time.

3rd Declension Nouns

3rd Declension Nouns are characterized by an *-is* in the Genitive Singular as well as distinctive endings in the other cases.

	M./F. Sing.	Pl.	N. Sing.	Pl.
Nom.	(variable)	**-ēs**	(variable)	**-a**
Gen.	**-is**	**-um**	-is	**-um**
Dat.	**-ī**	-ibus	-i	-ibus
Acc.	**-em**	**-ēs**	(same as Nom.)	-a
Abl.	**-e**	-ibus	-e	**-ibus**
Voc.	(same as Nom.)	**-ēs**	(same as Nom.)	**-a**

While most 1st Declension Nouns (Genitive Singular ending = *-ae*) are feminine and 2nd Declension Nouns (Genitive Singular ending = *-i*) are either masculine or neuter, 3rd Declension Nouns (Genitive Singular ending = *-is*) may be masculine, feminine, or neuter. As always, to find the stem of the noun, drop the Genitive Singular ending.

55

	rex, regis = m., king		*pax, pacis* = f., peace		*tempus, temporis* = n., time	
	sing.	pl.	sing.	pl.	sing.	pl.
Nom.	rēx	rēgēs	pāx	pācēs	tempus	tempora
Gen.	rēgis	rēgum	pācis	pācum	temporis	temporum
Dat.	rēgī	rēgibus	pācī	pācibus	temporī	temporibus
Acc.	rēgem	rēgēs	pācem	pācēs	tempus	tempora
Abl.	rēge	rēgibus	pāce	pācibus	tempore	temporibus

This means, of course, that you will have to memorize the gender along with the meaning. There are, however, some general guidelines regarding genders of 3rd Declension Nouns that have few exceptions.

1. 3rd Declension Nouns with a Nominative Singular ending in *-or* and a Genitive ending in *-oris* are **masculine** (*labor, laboris* = m., labor).

2. 3rd Declension Nouns with the following Nominative and Genitive Singular ending combinations are **feminine**:

   -tas,-tatis   (*civitas, civitatis* = f., state)
   -tus,-tutis   (*virtus, virtutis* = f., virtue/courage/character)
   -tio,-tionis (*natio, nationis* = f., nation)

Six Specific Ablative Uses

Since there is no left-to-right linear syntax in Latin, the Romans incorporated the Ablative Case in several standard formations, with and without prepositions, to relay the following particulars.

1. An Ablative of **Time When** or **Time Within Which** always contains a noun referring to time, is translated "in" or "at," and is never introduced with a preposition.

   *Venit **unā horā**.*   He is coming in one hour.
   ***Eo tempore** poterimus venire.*   We will be able to come at that time.

2. An Ablative of **Place Where** answers the question "where" and is always preceded by the preposition *in*.

   *Non erit **in foro**.*   He will not be in the forum.
     forum,-i = n., forum
   *Erasne **in periculo**?*   Were you in danger?

56

3. An Ablative of **Place from Which** indicates <u>motion away from</u> a person, place, or thing and is introduced and translated by the prepositions *ab, de,* or *ex.*

Nunc eramus ē periculo.	Now we were out of danger.
Ducit populum ā bello.	He is leading the people away from the war.
Fugit de foro.	He is fleeing (from) the forum.

4. An **Ablative of Accompaniment** answers the question "with whom" and is always preceded by the preposition *cum.*

Venimus cum amicis nostris.	We are coming with our friends.
Venit cum puellā.	He is coming with a girl.

5. An **Ablative of Manner** answers the questions "how" or "in what manner." An Ablative of Manner is preceded by *cum* unless it is used with an adjective, in which case the use of *cum* is optional. If *cum* is used with an adjective, *cum* falls between the noun and adjective. (This ablative is the easiest of all to remember, because everyone wants to graduate *cum laude* or, even better, *magnā cum laude* or, the best of all possible worlds, *summā cum laude*!)

Poteris vivere cum honore.	You will be able to live with honor.
Hic poeta scribit magnā (cum) formā.	This poet writes with great beauty.

6. An **Ablative of Means** answers the question "with what" or "by (means of) what" and usually appears without a preposition.

Possumus videre oculis nostris.	By means of our eyes we are able to see.
Tyrannus superat bello.	A tyrant overcomes by means of war.

Accusative of Duration of Time

To indicate <u>how</u> <u>long</u> the Romans used the accusative case.

1.	*Viri nostri unam horam in periculo erant.*	Our men were in danger (for) one hour.
2.	*Eramus amici multos annos.*	We were friends (for) many years.

Vocabulary

annus,- ī m., year
cīvitās, cīvitātis f., state
corpus, corporis n., body
homō, hominis m., human being/man
honor, honōris m., honor/office/esteem
labor, labōris m., labor/task/effort
laus, laudis f., praise
mōs, mōris m., custom/habit;
      pl., character/morals
nātiō, nātiōnis f., nation
pāx, pācis f., peace
rēx, rēgis m., king
tempestās, tempestātis f., storm/wind
tempus, temporis n., time
virtus, virtutis f., virtue/courage/character
modus, -ī m., model/mode/measure
hōra,-ae f., hour

dūrus,-a,-um hard/harsh
longus,-a,-um long
novus,-a,-um new

ab (ā) + abl. from/away from/by (*ā* is used before a consonant)
sub + abl. under (*sub rege*)
sub + acc. under (*sub terram*)

audeō, audēre, ausus sum to dare
obtineo, obtinēre, obtinuī, obtentum to hold/possess/obtain
vincō, vincere, vīcī, victum to conquer
vīvō, vīvere, vīxī, vīctum to live

Exercises

A. Using a paradigm format, decline the following:

    1. magnum corpus   2. perpetuus labor

B. Using a paradigm format, form the Present Indicative of:

    1. audeo, audere, ausus sum   2. vivo, vivere, vixi, victum

C. Form the Imperatives of the following verbs.

    1. obtineo, obtinere   2. vinco, vincere

D. Render the following phrases into Latin.

    1. evil character   3. to men of peace
    2. with such honors   4. away from the storm

E. Translate the following.

    1. unius parvi regis   5. longam pacem
    2. bona tempora   6. in multis tempestatibus
    3. magnarum civitatum   7. bonus homo
    4. magnā laude   8. multas horas longas

F. Render the following passage into Latin.

By means of food we are able to be; by means of money we are able to obtain many things; with great effort we are able to obtain knowledge; by means of knowledge we learn to live.

        cibus,-i = m., food   *scientia,-ae* = f., knowledge

G. Sentence translations.

    1. Sub principe duro temporibusque malis audes esse bonus. (Martial)
       princeps, principis = m., leader
    2. Populus stultus viris indignis honores saepe dat. (Horace)
       indignus,-a,-um = unworthy
    3. O tempora, O mores! Ubi vivimus!? (Cicero)
    4. Illā horā eram solus.
    5. Possumusne scire mentem dei?
       mens, mentis = f., mind   *deus,-i* = m., god
    6. Eo tempore, nostra civitas erit libera.
    7. Sumus liberi homines; in pace vivimus; sapientiam laudamus; adversa mentibus nostris superamus.
       adversus,-a,-um = adverse

8. Multi de duris tyrannis fugiunt et novam vitam in novā terrā incipiunt.

9. Malum est in necessitate vivere, sed in necessitate vivere necessitas nulla est. Si homo non desiderat, non caret. (Seneca)

   necessitas, necessitatis = f., need/necessity

   desidero (1) = desire

   careo, carere, carui, cariturus = to lack

10. Est bonum esse rex! (Mel Brooks)

Text Translation

Titus Livius or Livy (circa 59 BC–AD 17) was the author of the authorized version of the history of the Roman Republic. Although of Republican sentiments, he spent forty years in the employment of the emperor Augustus writing the <u>Ab Urbe Condita</u>, a 142-book history of the Roman Nation beginning with the founding of the city in 753 BC. The justification of his source material and his reasons for undertaking such a monumental task are included in his introduction. This reading is an adaptation of a portion of his introduction.

Rome has just gone through one hundred years of civil war. The Republic, because of the greed and corruption of the aristocracy, has been replaced with a new order—no one knows what the future will bring.

Meus labor est magnus sed multum gaudium[1] in studio[2] antiquorum

invenio, quod possum meos oculos de presentiā[3] vertere.[4] Fabulas[5] ante[6]

tempus urbis[7] Romae nec[8] adfirmare[9] nec refellere[10] in meo animo est.

Nulla ratio[11] est cum[12] historia inter[13] humana[14] et inhumana[15] non semper

distinguit.[16] Haec sunt parva; magna sunt: vitae moresque maiorum[17]

nostrorum; quomodo[18] imperium[19] Romanum obtinent et extendunt.[20] Tum

investigare[21] deteriorem[22] disciplinae[23] morumque ad haec tempora cum

nec nostra vitia nec remedia possumus tolerare. Studium historiae est

optima[24] medicina[25] aegrae[26] menti.[27] In historiā tabulam[28] infinitorum[29]

modorum experientiae[30] humanae habes. In hāc tabulā potes invenire tibi[31]

et tuae patriae bona exemplaria[32] habere et mala vitare.

(*Ab Urbe Condita* Bk. I, Praefatio)

1. **gaudium,-i** n., joy
2. **studium,-i** n., study
3. **presentia,-ae** f., present
4. **verto, vertere, verti, versum** to turn
5. **fabula,-ae** f., fable
6. **ante + acc.** before
7. **urbs, urbis** f., city
8. **nec . . . nec** neither . . . nor
9. **adfirmo (1)** to affirm
10. **refello,-fellere,-felli** to refute
11. **ratio, rationis** f., reason
12. **cum + indic. verb** when
13. **inter + acc.** between
14. **humanus,-a,-um** human
15. **inhumanus,-a,-um** not human/inhuman
16. **distinguo,-tinguere,-tinxi,-tinctum** to distinguish
17. **maiores, maiorum** m., ancestors
18. **quomodo** adv., how
19. **imperium,-i** n., absolute power/command
20. **extendo,-tendere,tendi,-tensum** to extend
21. **investigo (1)** to investigate/trace

22. **deterior, deterioris** m., deterioration
23. **disciplina,-ae** f., discipline/education/instruction
24. **optimus,-a,-um** best
25. **medicina,-ae** f., medicine
26. **aeger, aegra, aegrum** sick
27. **mens, mentis** f., mind
28. **tabula,-ae** f., record
29. **infinitus,-a,-um** infinite
30. **experientia,-ae** f., experience
31. **tibi** for yourself
32. **exemplar, exemplaris** n., example

Vocabulary: Chapters V–VIII

ab (ā) + abl. from/away from/by
ad + acc. toward/to (with verbs of motion)
agō, agere, ēgī, āctum to do/lead/act/drive
animus,-ī m., soul/spirit; pl., courage
annus,-ī m., year
antīquus,-a,-um old/ancient
arma, armōrum n., weapons/arms
audeō, audēre, ausus sum to dare
auxilium,-ī n., help/aid

cīvitās, cīvitātis f., state
corpus, corporis n., body
culpa,-ae f., fault/blame
cūr why?

dēbeō, dēbēre, dēbuī, debitum to ought/owe
dēleō, dēlēre, dēlēvī, dēlētum to
    destroy/delete/wipe out
dēnique adv., finally
dūrus,-a,-um hard/harsh

ergō adv., therefore
ex/ē + abl. out of/from

fōrma,-ae f., shape/form/beauty
fugiō, fugere, fūgī, fugitūrus to flee

Graecus,-a,-um Greek

hic, haec, hoc this/the latter
historia,-ae f., story/history
homō, hominis m., human being/man
honor, honōris m., honor/office
hōra,-ae f., hour

ibi adv., there
ille, illa, illud that/the former
in + abl. in/on
in + acc. into/against
incipiō,-cipere,-cēpī,-ceptum to begin
īnsidiae,-ārum f., plots/treachery
ipse, ipsa, ipsum himself/herself/itself
is, ea, id, he/she/it/this/that
iste, ista, istud such
Italia,-ae f., Italy

labor, labōris m., labor/task/effort
laus, laudis f., praise
līber, lībera, līberum free

liber, librī m., book
longus,-a,-um long

miser, misera, miserum miserable/ wretched
modus,-ī m., model/mode
mōs, mōris m., custom/habit; **pl.,** character/morals

natio, nationis f., nation
-ne enclitic added to end of word to indicate a
    question
nimis/nimium adv., too much/very much
nōn sōlum . . . sed etiam not only . . . but also
noster,-tra,-trum our
novus,-a,-um new
nūllus,-a,-um none/no
numerus,-ī m., number

obtineō,-tinēre,-tinuī,-tentum to
    hold/possess/obtain
oculus,-ī m., eye
officium,-ī n., duty/office

pāx, pācis f., peace
perpetuus,-a,-um perpetual
populus,-ī m., people/nation
possum, posse, potuī to be able
propter + acc. on account of/because of

quod because
quondam adv., once

rēx, rēgis m., king
Rōma,-ae f., Rome
Rōmānus,-a,-um Roman

satis enough (indecl. noun, adj., adv.)
scrībo, scrībere, scripsī, scriptum to write
sed but
semper adv., always
sine + abl. without
sōlus,-a,-um alone/only
sub + abl. under (e.g., *sub rege*)
sub + acc. under (e.g., *sub terram*)
superō (1) to overcome

tempestās, tempestātis f.,storm/wind
tempus, temporis n., time
terra,-ae f., land
tolerō (1) to tolerate/endure

tōtus,-a,-um whole/entire
tum adv., then
tyrannus,-ī m., tyrant/absolute ruler

ubi adv., when/where
ūllus,-a,-um any
ūnus,-a,-um one

verus,-a,-um true
vester, vestra, vestrum your (pl.)
vincō, vincere, vīcī, victum to conquer
virtus, virtutis f., virtue/courage/character
vitium,-ī n., vice/fault
vīvo, vīvere, vīxī, victum to live

Imperfect Indicative Formation, All Conjugations
3rd Declension *i*-stem Nouns
Irregular Noun *vis, vis*

Objectives
To enable you to:
1. recognize, translate, and form the Imperfect Indicative Tense;
2. recognize and decline 3rd Declension *i*-stem Nouns;
3. recognize and decline the irregular 3rd Declension *i*-stem noun **vis, vis.**

Imperfect Tense Use

The Romans employed the Imperfect Tense for general description of past events and to indicate repetitive or ongoing action in the past. The Imperfect Tense may be translated several ways, as you will see below.

Imperfect Indicative Formation, All Conjugations

The Imperfect Indicative tense sign for all conjugations of verbs is *-ba*. The general rule for forming the Imperfect Tense is: drop the *-re* from the Active Infinitive (Second Principal Part of the verb) then add *-ba* plus the personal ending.

1st Conjugation	2nd Conjugation	3rd Conjugation
vocō, vocāre	*videō, vidēre*	*mitto, mittere*
vocābam	*vidēbam*	*mittēbam*
I called/was calling	I used to see	I kept on sending
vocābās	*vidēbās*	*mittēbās*
vocābat	*vidēbat*	*mittēbat*
vocābāmus	*vidēbāmus*	*mittēbāmus*
vocābātis	*vidēbātis*	*mittēbātis*
vocābant	*vidēbant*	*mittēbant*

3rd-*io* and 4th Conjugation verbs do not follow the above general formation rule, and you will simply have to remember the standard variations below.

1. In **3rd-*io* Conjugations**, the *-i-* in the first Principal Part appears in every conjugated form.

3rd-*io* Conjugation

capi**o**, cap**e**re

capiēbam	capiēbāmus
capiēbās	capiēbātis
capiēbat	capiēbant

2. The Romans confused 3rd-*io* and **4th Conjugations** in forming the Imperfect Indicative, apparently assuming the Infinitive ended in *-ere* rather than *-ire*. Whatever the reason, you will have to remember to insert an *-e-* in the Imperfect Indicative of **4th Conjugation verbs**.

4th Conjugation

sci**o**, sc**ī**re

sciēbam	sciēbāmus
sciēbās	sciēbātis
sciēbat	sciēbant

3rd Declension i-Stem Nouns

Masculine and Feminine *i*-stem 3rd Declension Nouns have a characteristic *-i-* in the **Genitive Plural**. Neuter *i*-stem 3rd Declension Nouns have a characteristic *-i* in the **Ablative Singular** as well as in the **Genitive, Nominative, and Accusative Plural** forms. A 3rd Declension noun is *i*-stem if:

1. the Nominative and Genitive Singular forms end in *-is,-is* or *-ēs,-is* and are parisyllabic (have an equal number of syllables);

cīvis, civis = m., citizen   *nūbēs, nūbis* = f., cloud

	sing.	pl.		sing.	pl.
Nom.	cīvis	cīvēs	Nom.	nūbēs	nūbēs
Gen.	cīvis	cīvium	Gen.	nūbis	nūbium
Dat.	cīvī	cīvibus	Dat.	nūbī	nūbibus
Acc.	cīvem	cīvēs	Acc.	nūbem	nūbēs
Abl.	cīve	cīvibus	Abl.	nūbe	nūbibus

2. the Nominative Singular ends in *-s* or *-x* and the Genitive Singular Stem ends in adjacent consonants;

ars, artis = f., art/skill   nox, noctis = f., night

	sing.	pl.		sing.	pl.
Nom.	ars	artēs	Nom.	nox	noctēs
Gen.	artis	artium	Gen.	noctis	noctium
Dat.	artī	artibus	Dat.	noctī	noctibus
Acc.	artem	artēs	Acc.	noctem	noctēs
Abl.	arte	artibus	Abl.	nocte	noctibus

3. it is neuter with a Nominative Singular ending of *-e, -al,* or *-ar*.

	Mare, maris = n., sea		*animal, animalis =* n., animal		exemplar, exemplaris = n., example/model	
	sing.	pl.	sing.	pl.	sing.	pl.
Nom.	mare	maria	animal	animalia	exemplar	exemplaria
Gen.	maris	marium	animalis	animalium	exemplaris	exemplarium
Dat.	marī	maribus	animalī	animalibus	exemplarī	exemplaribus
Acc.	mare	maria	animal	animalia	exemplar	exemplaria
Abl.	marī	maribus	animalī	animalibus	exemplarī	exemplaribus

Irregular Noun vis, vis

Vīs, vīs is an irregular *i*-stem 3rd Declension Noun that must be memorized. Note that in the singular *vis* means "force," but in the plural it means "strength."

vīs, vīs = f.

	sing.	pl.
Nom.	*vīs* (force)	*vīrēs* (strength)
Gen.	*vīs*	*vīrium*
Dat.	*vī*	*vīribus*
Acc.	*vim*	*vīrēs*
Abl.	*vī*	*vīribus*

Vocabulary

animal, animalis n., animal
ars, artis f., art/skill
cīvis, cīvis m., citizen
exemplar, exemplaris n., example/model
ius, iuris n., right/law
mare, maris n., sea
mens, mentis f., mind
mors, mortis f, death
nox, noctis f., night
nūbēs, nūbis f., cloud
pars, partis f., part/share
sententia,-ae f., feeling/thought/opinion
urbs, urbis f., city
vīs, vīs f., force; pl. strength

pulcher, pulchra, pulchrum beautiful/handsome

(cog)nōscō,-nōscere,-nōvī,-nitum to recognize/know
gerō, gerere, gessī, gestum to carry on/conduct/accomplish
(re)maneō,-manēre,-mānsī,-mānsum to remain/stay behind

cum + indic. verb = when

CHAPTER IX

Exercises

A. Form the Imperfect Indicative of the following verbs.

1. maneo, manere, mansi, mansum
2. cognosco, cognoscere, cognovi, cognitum
3. tolero, tolerare, toleravi, toleratum
4. incipio, incipere, incepi, inceptum
5. venio, venire, veni, ventum

B. Translate the following verb forms.

1. manent
2. inveniebat
3. incipe
4. tolerabatis
5. faciunt
6. cognoscite
7. delebas
8. sciebamus
9. vivebat
10. incipis

C. Using paradigm formats labeling cases and number, decline the following noun/adjective combinations.

1. pulchrum exemplar
2. magna vis
3. pulcher civis

D. Provide the Latin declined forms for the following phrases.

1. with many citizens
2. to part of the animals
3. by means of great strength
4. the laws of the sea
5. beautiful clouds (acc.)
6. the thoughts of the citizens
7. on that night
8. the force of the arts
9. many examples (nom.)
10. the death of this citizen

E. Sentence translations.

1. Nosce te ipsum. (Motto on the Temple of Apollo at Delphi)
   te = acc, you
2. Et Deus aquas maria appellabat. (Genesis)
   aqua,-ae = f., water
   appello (1) = to call/name
3. Italia illis temporibus erat plena Graecarum artium et multi Romani ipsi has artes colebant. (Cicero)
   plenus,-a,-um = full
   colo, colere, colui, cultum = to cultivate/pursue
4. Hunc nemo vi neque pecuniā superare potest. (Ennius)
   neque = nor
   nemo = no one, nom. case

5. Ille Alexander magno labore animum ad virtutem de pueritiā confirmabat. (Cicero)

> *pueritia,-ae* = f., boyhood
>
> *confirmo* (1) = to train/mold

6. Saepe in hāc civitate malos cives morte multabant. (Cicero)

> *multo* (1) = to punish

7. Non semper magna viribus gerimus sed saepe sapientiā et arte.

8. Cognoscisne iura huius terrae?

9. Post mortem animus a corpore volat.

> *volo* (1) = to fly

10. Cognosce tuos amicos tuosque inimicos.

> *inimicus,-i* = m., enemy

11. Asinus asino et sus sui pulcher.

> *asinus,-i* = m., an ass/blockhead/dolt
>
> *sus, suis* = m., pig

Text Translation

Livy traces the story of Aeneas in Italy.

NB: You will notice Present and Imperfect Tenses in this reading. The Present Tense is often used in narration to describe a past act vividly, both in English and in Latin. This is called the *historical present*. It is so common in both languages that its presence in a sentence is usually unnoticed.

Cum Aeneas in Italiam veniebat, Latinus[1] erat rex illius terrae. Latini[2] cum

Troianis[3] bellum gerebant. Troiani Latinos vincunt et Latinus filiam

Laviniam[4] Aeneae in matrimonium[5] dat. Tum Aeneas novam urbem

condit;[6] a nomine[7] uxoris[8] urbem Lavinium[9] appellat.[10] Aeneas Laviniaque

filium habent; puerum Ascanium[11] appellant. Post mortem Aeneae Ascanius

regnabat.[12] Sed mox[13] aliam[14] urbem condit. Novam urbem Albam[15]

Longam appellabat.

(*Ab Urbe Condita* Bk. I, i–iii)

1. **Latinus,-i** m., Proper Noun
2. **Latinus,-a,-um** Latin
3. **Troianus,-a,-um** Trojan
4. **Lavinia,-ae** f., Proper Noun, daughter of Latinus
5. **matrimonium,-i** n., marriage
6. **condo, condere, condidi, conditum** to found/put together
7. **nomen, nominis** n., name
8. **uxor, uxoris** f., wife
9. **Lavinium,-i** n., Proper Noun, name of city in Latium
10. **appello (1)** to call/name
11. **Ascanius,-i** m., Proper Noun
12. **regno (1)** to rule/reign
13. **mox** adv., soon
14. **alius,-a,-um** another
15. **Alba Longa, Albae Longae** f., Proper Noun, name of city in Latium

3rd Declension Adjectives
Possessive Adjectives
Reflexive Possessive Adjective *suus, -a, -um*

Objectives

To enable you to:

1. recognize and decline 3rd Declension Adjectives;
2. recognize and understand the usage of the 3rd Person Reflexive Possessive Adjective *suus,- a,-um*;
3. understand the reflexive use possibility of 1st and 2nd Person Possessive Adjectives.

3rd Declension Adjectives

With the exception of Comparatives and a few particular words, 3rd Declension Adjectives are all *-i-*stem; i.e., they differ in declension from 3rd Declension Nouns in that they have a characteristic *-i-* in:

1. the Ablative Singular of all genders;
2. the Genitive Plural of all genders;
3. the Nominative and Accusative Plural of neuters as well as in the cases mentioned above.

Remember that adjectives are listed by their Nominative Singular forms, so when you see *bonus,-a,-um*, you know that it is a 1st–2nd Declension Adjective that can be declined into masculine, feminine, and neuter singular and plural forms. 3rd Declension Adjectives are also listed by their Nominative Singular forms, except that they may have three Nominative forms (just like 1st–2nd Declension Adjectives) or they may have just two Nominative forms or they may have only one Nominative form.

3rd Declension Adjective of Three Endings

celer, celeris,* celere = swift/fast

Singular

	m.	f.	n.
Nom.	celer	celeris	celere
Gen.	celeris	celeris	celeris
Dat.	celerī	celerī	celerī
Acc.	celerem	celerem	celere
Abl.	celerī	celerī	celerī

Plural

	m.	f.	n.
Nom.	celerēs	celerēs	celer**ia**
Gen.	celer**ium**	celer**ium**	celer**ium**
Dat.	celeribus	celeribus	celeribus
Acc.	celerēs	celerēs	celer**ia**
Abl.	celeribus	celeribus	celeribus

3rd Declension Adjective of Two Endings

omnis,-e = every (sing.); all (pl.)

Singular

	m./f.	n.
Nom.	omnis	omne
Gen.	omnis	omnis
Dat.	omnī	omnī
Acc.	omnem	omne
Abl.	omnī	omnī

Plural

	m./f.	n.
Nom.	omnēs	omn**ia**
Gen.	omn**ium**	omn**ium**
Dat.	omnibus	omnibus
Acc.	omnēs	omn**ia**
Abl.	omnibus	omnibus

*The stem for all genders of a 3rd Declension Adjective of three endings is the Nominative Singular **Feminine** form minus the "*-is*."

3rd Declension Adjective of One Ending
fēlix, fēlicis = happy

Singular				Plural		
	m./f.	n.			m./f.	n.
Nom.	fēlix	fēlix		Nom.	fēlīcēs	fēlīc**ia**
Gen.	fēlīcis	fēlīcis		Gen.	fēlīc**ium**	fēlīc**ium**
Dat.	fēlīcī	fēlīcī		Dat.	fēlīcibus	fēlīcibus
Acc.	fēlīcem	fēlix		Acc.	fēlīcēs	fēlīc**ia**
Abl.	fēlīcī	fēlīcī		Abl.	flīcibus	fēlīcibus

Possessive Adjectives

Possessive Adjectives are all 1st–2nd Declension and like all adjectives must agree in case, number, and gender with the nouns they modify.

	Sing.	Pl.
1st Person	*meus,-a,-um* = my	*noster, nostra, nostrum* = our
2nd Person	*tuus,-a,-um* = your	*vester, vestra, vestrum* = your
3rd Person	*suus,-a,-um* = his, hers, its (own)	*suus,-a,-um* = their (own)

Use the genitive forms of the pronoun *is, ea, id* if the possessor is not the subject of the sentence, i.e., if the possessor <u>does not reflect</u> the subject.

(1) The girl is his friend.   *Puella est amica **<u>eius</u>**.*
(2) The girl is their friend.   *Puella est amica **<u>eorum</u>**.*
(3) Caesar saved his (not Caesar's) friend.   *Caesar amicum **<u>eius</u>** servabat.*

Reflexive Possessive Adjective suus,-a,-um

Use the Reflexive Possessive Adjective *suus,-a,-um* if the possessor is the subject of the sentence, i.e., if the possessor reflects the subject. Be sure to notice in the examples that *suus,-a,-um* reflects the subject but agrees with the noun it modifies in case, number, and gender.

(1) The girl loves her friend.   *Puella **<u>suum</u>** amicum amat.*
(2) The girl loves her friends.   *Puella **<u>suas</u>** amicas amat.*
(3) Caesar used to give gifts to his friends.   *Caesar amicis **<u>suis</u>** dona dabat.*
(4) The boy was living with his friend.   *Puer cum amico **<u>suo</u>** vivebat.*

1st and 2nd person Possessive Adjectives may also be used to reflect the subject, a fact that will give you no trouble if you note the **subject ending** (personal ending) of the verb.

1. *Amo meos amicos.*	I love my friends.
2. *Ama**mus** nostros amicos.*	We love our friends.
3. *Ama**s** tuos amicos.*	You love your friends.
4. *Ama**tis** vestros amicos.*	You (pl.) love your friends.

Vocabulary

aetās, aetātis f., age/period of life
memoria,-ae f., memory

ācer, ācris, ācre sharp/fierce/keen
celer, celeris, celere swift/quick/rapid
dulcis,-e sweet/pleasant/agreeable
felix, fēlīcis happy/lucky
fortis,-e strong/brave
omnis,-e every; pl. all
suus,-a,-um 3rd pers. refl. poss. adj., his, her, its own

iuvō, iuvāre, iūvī, iūtum to help/aid
quam adv., how
mox adv., soon

Exercises

A. Using a paradigm format identifying cases, genders, and number, completely decline *acer, acris, acre*.

B. Provide the correctly declined form of the adjective indicated, being sure to make it agree in case, number, and gender with the noun, then translate the phrase.

1. _____ memoriā
    by a rapid

6. _____ aetate
    in every

2. _____ puellae
    of the sweet

7. _____ memoriis
    for the sharp

3. _____ exemplaribus
    to the strong

8. _____ aetas
    Happy

4. _____ vires
    All

9. _____ tempestas
    Fast

5. _____ urbis
    of the happy

10. _____ dona
     Pleasant

C. Provide the correctly declined form of the Possessive Adjective or Personal Pronoun then translate the sentence.

1. Is amat _____ amicos.
        his (own)

6. Romani amabant _____ amicos.
            their (own)

2. Amas _____ amicum.
        your

7. Caesar amabat _____ amicos.
            their

3. Amo _____ amicas
        my

8. Caesar amabat _____ amicum.
            his (not Caesar's)

4. Amamus _____ amicam.
            our

9. Caesar amabat _____ amicas.
            their (fem)

5. Amatis _____ amicum.
        your

10. Auxilium _____ amicis do.
            to my

D. Form the Present and Imperfect Indicative of *iuvo, iuvare, iuvi, iutum.* Give the English translation of each conjugated form.

CHAPTER X

E. Sentence translations.

    1. Mea puella passerem suum amabat et passer ad eam solam semper pipiabat. (Catullus)

       passer, passeris = m., sparrow

       pipio (1) = to chirp

    2. Labor omnia vincit. (Motto of the State of Oklahoma)

    3. Quam dulcis est libertas! (Phaedrus)

       libertas, libertatis = f., liberty

    4. Ars poetica est non dicere omnia. (Horace)

       poeticus,-a,-um = poetic

    5. Ipse signum suum et litteras suas recognoscebat. (Cicero)

       signum,-i = n., sign/seal

       litterae,-arum = f., letter/handwriting

       recognosco,-noscere,-novi,-nitum = to recognize

    6. Quam celeris est mens! (Cicero)

    7. Fortuna fortes iuvat. (Terence)

    8. Clementia regem salvum facit; nam amor omnium civium est inexpugnabile munimentum. (Seneca)

       clementia,-ae = f., clemency

       salvus,-a,-um = safe

       nam = for

       amor, amoris = m., love

       inexpugnabilis,-e = impregnable

       munimentum,-i = n., defense

    9. Mater omnium bonarum artium sapientia est. (Cicero)

       mater, matris = f., mother

  10. Diogenes suis discipulis dicebat: "Sum civis mundi."

       Diogenes,-is = m., Proper Noun, a famous Greek philosopher

       discipulus,-i = m., student/disciple

       mundus,-i = m., world

Text Translation

The following story about the birth of Romulus and Remus is taken from the <u>Ab Urbe Condita</u> by Livy.

Post multas aetates, tandem[1] Amulius[2] Albae Longae erat rex. Regnum[3] vi ā suo fratre[4] Numitore[5] capit. Tum addit[6] scelus[7] sceleri: liberos[8] fratris occidit;[9] fratris filiam, Ream[10] Silviam, Vestalem[11] facit. Mox autem[12] Reae Silviae Martique[13] deo[14] gemini[15] filii erant. Amulius iratus[16] iubet[17] servum[18] iacere[19] geminos in Tiberim.[20] Sed aquae[21] Tiberis super[22] ripas[23] erant; sic[24] servus alveum[25] cum parvis in stagnis[26] proximis[27] ponebat.[28] Mox lupa[29] sitiens[30] e montibus[31] ad Tiberim veniebat et vagitum[32] geminorum audiebat. Lupa geminos invenit et pueros linguā[33] lambens[34] suo lacte[35] alebat.[36] Lupam cum pueris Faustulus,[37] magister regii[38] pecoris,[39] inveniebat et geminos domum[40] portabat.[41]

(*Ab Urbe Condita* Bk. I, iii, iv)

1. **tandem** adv., at last
2. **Amulius,-i** m., Proper Noun, king of Alba Longa
3. **regnum,-i** n., rule/reign
4. **frater, fratris** m., brother
5. **Numitor, Numitoris** m., Proper Noun, older brother of Amulius
6. **addo, addere, addidi, additum** to add
7. **scelus, sceleris** n., crime
8. **liberi,-orum** m., children
9. **occido, occidere, occidi, occisum** to kill
10. **Rea Silvia, Reae Silviae** f., Proper Noun, mother of Romulus and Remus
11. **Vestalis,-is** f., Vestal, a priestess of Vesta, the goddess of the hearth and domestic life
12. **autem** however
13. **Mars, Martis** m., Proper Noun, god of war
14. **deus,-i** m., god
15. **geminus,-a,-um** twin
16. **iratus,-a,-um** angered/full of wrath
17. **iubeo, iubere, iussi, iussum** to order
18. **servus,-i** m., slave/servant
19. **iacio, iacere, ieci, iactum** to throw
20. **Tiberis, Tiberis** Tiber River, the river that runs through Rome *Tiberim* = irreg. acc. sing.
21. **aqua,-ae** f., water
22. **super + acc.** above
23. **ripa,-ae** f., bank
24. **sic** adv., so
25. **alveus,-i** m., basket
26. **stagnum,-i** n., standing water
27. **proximus,-a,-um** nearest
28. **pono, ponere, posui, positum** to put
29. **lupa,-ae** f., she-wolf
30. **sitiens, sitientis** adj., thirsting
31. **mons, montis** m., mountain
32. **vagitus,-a,-um** crying
33. **lingua,-ae** f., tongue
34. **lambens, lambentis** adj., licking
35. **lac, lactis** n., milk
36. **alo, alere, alui, altum** to nourish
37. **Faustulus,-i** m., Proper Noun
38. **regius,-a,-um** royal/regal
39. **pecus, pecoris** n., cattle
40. **domum** acc. case, home
41. **porto (1)** to carry

Capitoline Wolf

Present System
Future Indicative Formation, All Conjugations

Objectives

To enable you to:

1. recognize, translate, and form the Future Indicative Tense of 1st and 2nd Conjugation Verbs;
2. recognize, translate, and form the Future Indicative Tense of 3rd, 3rd-*io*, and 4th Conjugation Verbs.

Present System

The Present System is composed of the Present, Imperfect, and Future Tenses, which are formed from variations of the first two Principal Parts of the verb. You have already learned how to form and translate the Present and Imperfect Tenses; the Future Tense has equally distinctive features.

Future Indicative Formation, All Conjugations

The only difficult part of the Future Indicative is remembering that the **Future Tense Sign** for 1st and 2nd Conjugation Verbs is *different* from that for 3rd, 3rd-*io*, and 4th Conjugation verbs. Although the tense signs vary, the steps employed to form the Future Indicative are very similar.

1st–2nd Conjugation Verbs

The <u>general</u> Future Indicative Tense sign for 1st and 2nd Conjugation Verbs is *-bi-*, with deviation in the First Person Singular and the Third Person Plural. To form the Future Indicative:

1. drop the *-re* from the Second Principal Part of the Verb (the Infinitive);
2. add the Future Tense Endings (*-bo,-bis,-bit,-bimus,-bitis,-bunt*).

1st Conjugation	2nd Conjugation
vocō, vocāre	*videō, vidēre*
vocābō I will call	*vidēbō* I will see
vocābis	*vidēbis*
vocābit	*vidēbit*
vocābimus	*vidēbimus*
vocābitis	*vidēbitis*
vocābunt	*vidēbunt*

3rd, 3rd-io, and 4th Conjugation Verbs

For 3rd, 3rd-*io*, and 4th Conjugation Verbs, the <u>general</u> Future Indicative Tense sign is **-e-**, with deviation only in the First Person Singular. To form the Future Indicative:

1. For 3rd Conjugations, drop the *-ere* from the Second Principal Part of the Verb (the Infinitive) and add these endings: **-am,-es,-et-emus,-etis,-ent**.
2. For 3rd-*io* and 4th Conjugations, drop the *–ere* or *–ire* from the Second Principal Part of the Verb (the Infinitive) and add these endings: **-iam,-ies,-iet, -iemus,-ietis,-ient**.

3rd Conjugation	3rd-*io* Conjugation	4th Conjugation
mitto, mittere	capio, capere	scio, scīre
mittam I will send*	*capiam* I will capture*	*sciam* I will know*
mittēs	*capiēs*	*sciēs*
mittet	*capiet*	*sciet*
mittēmus	*capiēmus*	*sciēmus*
mittētis	*capiētis*	*sciētis*
mittent	*capient*	*scient*

* It is also correct to translate First Person Singular and Plural of the Future Indicative as "shall," but only "will" is correct for the other persons.

Vocabulary

alius, alia, aliud* another/other
gravis,-e heavy/serious/severe
cōpia,-ae f., abundance/supply; pl. troops/forces/supplies
locus,-i m., place/passage in literature
loca, locōrum n., region
natura,-ae f., nature
ratiō, ratiōnis f., reason/judgment
senectūs, senectūtis f., old age
via,-ae f., way/road/street

teneō, tenēre, tenuī, tentum to hold/keep/possess

dum while
numquam adv., never

**alius, alia, aliud* is an irregular 1st–2nd Declension Adjective following the form of *ille, illa, illud,* with a Genitive Singular ending in *-ius* and a Dative Singular ending in *-i.* Note that the Genitive Singular form for all genders is *alterius*.

Singular

	m.	f.	n.
Nom.	alius	alia	aliud
Gen.	*alterius*	*alterius*	*alterius*
Dat.	aliī	aliī	aliī
Acc.	alium	aliam	aliud
Abl.	aliō	aliā	aliō

Plural

	m.	f.	n.
Nom.	aliī	aliae	alia
Gen.	aliōrum	aliārum	aliōrum
Dat.	aliīs	aliīs	aliīs
Acc.	aliōs	aliās	alia
Abl.	aliīs	aliīs	aliīs

Exercises

A. Form the Future Indicative of the following verbs:

    1. do, dare, dedi, datum
    2. deleo, delere, delevi, deletum
    3. dico, dicere, dixi, dictum
    4. fugio, fugere, fugi, fugiturus
    5. audio, audire, audivi, auditum

B. Form the Present, Imperfect, and Future Indicative of the following verbs.

    1. teneo, tenere, tenui, tentum—Give the English for 3rd Person Plural.
    2. gero, gerere, gessi, gestum—Give the English for 2nd Person Singular.

C. Form the Singular and Plural Imperatives of:

    1. do, dare, dedi, datum
    2. deleo, delere, delevi, deletum
    3. dico, dicere, dixi, dictum
    4. fugio, fugere, fugi, fugiturus
    5. audio, audire, audivi, auditum
    6. teneo, tenere, tenui, tentum

D. Using **paradigm formats** indicating cases and number, decline:

    1. gravis natura
    2. alius honor
    3. istud corpus

E. Sentence translations.

    1. Serva me; servabo te. (Petronius)
        te = you, direct object
    2. Mens sana in corpore sano. (Juvenal)
        sanus,-a,-um = sound/healthy
    3. Ex vitio alterius sapiens emendat suum. (Publilius Syrus)
        sapiens, sapientis = wise man
        emendo (1) = to correct
    4. Si quando satis pecuniae habebo, tum me philosophiae dabo. (Seneca)
        quando = adv., when/ever
    5. Semper gloria et fama tua manebunt. (Virgil)
        gloria,-ae = f., glory
    6. Numquam periculum sine periculo vincemus. (Publilius Syrus)
    7. Non solum eventus hoc docet (iste est magister stultorum) sed etiam ratio. (Livy)
        eventus = m., outcome, nom case
    8. Fata viam invenient. (Virgil)
        fatum,-i = n., fate
    9. Officium meum faciam. (Terence)

Text Translation

The Roman pantheon was essentially the same as that of the Greeks, with specific gods and goddesses having particular realms of authority, care, and functions.

Romani deos[1] multos habent et fabulas[2] multas de deis suis narrant.[3] In numero deorum sunt Juppiter, Neptunus, Mars et Mercurius. Juppiter in caelo vivebat; summus[4] deorum erat et caelum[5] et terras regnabat.[6] Nautae Neptunum amabant quod deus oceani[7] erat. In mari vivebat et amicus nautarum erat. Mars, deus belli, arma et proelia[8] amat. Mars viros in proeliis et in bellis servabat. Mars Romuli Remique pater[9] erat. Mercurius, nuntius[10] deorum, alas[11] habet et trans terras aquasque viris mandata[12] e deis portat.

In numero dearum sunt Juno, Diana, Minerva, Vesta et Ceres. Juno erat summa dearum et alias deas regnabat. Venus est dea amoris.[13] Ea erat mater[14] Aeneae. Diana est dea lunae[15] et silvarum.[16] Parvas puellas servat et nautae non timent[17] quod nautis in oceano fortunam bonam et auxilium dat. Minerva dea sapientiae et litterarum.[18] Vesta curam domus[19] habet. Nautae Dianam, poetae Minervam amant; feminae[20] Vestam amant. Ceres, dea agrorum, agricolas servat et iuvat.

1. **deus,-i** m., god
2. **fabula,-ae** f., fable
3. **narro (1)** to tell/narrate
4. **summus,-a,-um** highest
5. **caelum,-i** n., heaven/sky
6. **regno (1)** to rule
7. **oceanus,-i** m., ocean
8. **proelium,-i** n., battle
9. **pater,-tris** m., father
10. **nuntius,-ii** m., messenger
11. **ala,-ae** f., wing
12. **mandatum,-i** n., command
13. **amor, amoris** m., love
14. **mater,-tris** f., mother
15. **luna,-ae** f., moon
16. **silva,-ae** f., forest
17. **timeo, timere, timui** to fear
18. **litterae,-arum** f., literature
19. **domus** gen. sing., of the home
20. **femina,-ae** f., woman

Text Translation

Procurator[1] Nihil Nihil Septem[2]

Nomen[3] meum Ligamentum[4] est . . . Iacobus[5] Ligamentum. Hodie[6]

malum ingenium[7] Aureum[8] digitum[9] delebo. Sed primum,[10] latibulum[11]

secretum illius invenire debeo. Aureusdigitus captivam[12] meam pulchram

amicam, "Nulla Mens," tenet. "Nulla" autem[13] consilium[14] meum

cognoscit et me iuvabit Aureumdigitum superare. Subito[15] vox[16] mala dicit:

"Salve, Nihil Nihil Septem! Non move! Denique te[17] occidam."[18] Quid faciet

Iacobus nunc?!! "Nullane" eum servabit? Ea magnum corpus habet sed——.

Remanete "tunatum"![19] Semper noster heros[20] extremissima[21] impedimenta[22]

superare potest!

1. **procurator,-oris** m., agent
2. **septem** seven
3. **nomen, nominis** n., name
4. **ligamentum,-i** bond (<u>loose</u> translation)
5. **Iacobus,-i** m., James
6. **hodie** adv., today
7. **ingenium,-i** n., genius
8. **aureus,-a,-um** golden
9. **digitus,-i** m., finger
10. **primum** first
11. **labitulum,-i** n., hiding place
12. **captivus,-a,-um** captive
13. **autem** however
14. **consilium,-i** n., plan
15. **subito** adv., suddenly
16. **vox, vocis** f., voice
17. **te** you (sing., acc.)
18. **occido, occidere, occidi, occisum** to kill
19. **"tunatum"** tuned (Latin via Chambers)
20. **heros, herois** m., hero
21. **extremissimus,-a,-um** most extreme
22. **impedimentum,-i** n., obstacle/impediment

Relative Clauses
Relative Pronouns
Interrogative Adjectives

Objectives

To enable you to:
1. recognize and translate Relative Clauses;
2. recognize, translate, and decline Relative Pronouns;
3. recognize, translate, and decline Interrogative Adjectives.

Relative Clauses

The following underlined words are Relative Clauses; the **bold type words** are **relative pronouns**. A Relative Clause always begins with a Relative Pronoun, which is declined according to its use in the clause.

1. The girl **who** lives here is pretty.
2. The man **whose** virtues you praise lives here.
3. The boys to **whom** you gave the book are my friends.
4. The men **whom** you helped are not here.
5. The book about **which** we were speaking is large.

Notice that the Relative Clause is a Dependent Clause (does not make sense by itself) that can be completely deleted, the remaining Independent Clause still being complete and making sense by itself.

Relative Pronouns

Latin Relative Pronouns have specific declined forms for each gender. The English translations of the Plural forms are the same as the translations for the Singular forms.

	M.		F.		N.	
Nom.	*quī*	who	*quae*	who	*quod*	which/that
Gen.	*cuius*	whose/of whom	*cuius*	whose/of whom	*cuius*	of which/that
Dat.	*cui*	to/for whom	*cui*	to/for whom	*cui*	to/for which/that
Acc.	*quem*	whom	*quam*	whom	*quod*	which/that
Abl.	*quō*	by/with/from whom	*quā*	by/with/from whom	*quō*	by/with/from which/that

	M.	F.	N.
Nom.	*quī*	*quae*	*quae*
Gen.	*quōrum*	*quārum*	*quōrum*
Dat.	*quibus*	*quibus*	*quibus*
Acc.	*quōs*	*quās*	*quae*
Abl.	*quibus*	*quibus*	*quibus*

A Relative Pronoun agrees with its **Antecedent** in gender and number, but its case is determined by its use in the Relative Clause.

1. The girl who lives here is pretty.
   *Puella **quae vivit hīc** est bella.* (*hīc* = adv., here)
   quae = Nominative (subject of the Relative Clause)
   = singular, feminine (agrees with Antecedent ***puella***)
2. The man whose virtues you praise lives here.
   *Vir **cuius virtutes laudas** vivit hīc.*
   cuius = Genitive (used possessively in Relative Clause)
   = singular, masculine (agrees with ***vir***)

Now see if you can give the reason for the case, number, and gender of the Latin Relative Pronouns in the sentences below.

3. The boys to whom you used to give books are my friends.
   *Pueri **quibus libros dabas** sunt mei amici.*
4. The men whom you helped are not here.
   *Viri **quos iuvabatis** non sunt hīc.*

NB: There is one tricky thing to remember about Relative Pronouns. In English only humans are referred to by the following declined translations:

Nominative	who
Genitive	whose/of whom
Dative	to/for whom
Accusative	whom
Ablative	by/with/from whom

This means that a Latin Relative Pronoun may have a masculine antecedent (***labor***) or feminine antecedent (***pax***), but because the antecedent is not human, in English it must be translated "which" or "that." This is what I mean:

5. *Labor __quem__ facis est magnus.* The work <u>that</u> you do is great.
6. *Pax __quam__ petitis mox veniet.* The peace <u>which</u> you seek will come soon.

      peto, petere, petivi, petitum = to seek

Also, as you all know (or will know now) humans are never referred to as "which" except when "which" is used to ask a question, i.e., as an Interrogative Adjective (explained below).

Interrogative Adjectives

The Latin Interrogative Adjectives *quī? quae? quod?* (which? what?) are identical in form to Relative Pronouns but differ in use. Interrogative Adjectives modify nouns and must agree with the noun they modify in case, number, and gender; Interrogative Adjectives ask a question.

1. Which man is praising Caesar?
   __Qui__ vir laudat Caesarem?
   __Qui__   = nominative, singular, masculine because it modifies *vir*;
               = interrogative (indicated by question mark).

2. Which cities will you see?
   __Quas__ urbes videbis?
   quas   = accusative, plural, feminine because it modifies *urbes*;
               = interrogative (indicated by question mark).

3. For which reasons were they waging war?
   __Quibus__ rationibus bellum gerebant?
   __Quibus__= dative, plural, feminine because it modifies *rationibus*;
               = interrogative (indicated by question mark).

NB: When *cum* is used with an Ablative form of *qui, quae, quod*, it is attached to the end: *quōcum, quācum, quibuscum*.

Summary of New Terminology

1. Antecedent: The word to which a relative pronoun refers.
2. Clause: A group of words containing a subject and a verb.
3. Dependent Clause: A clause depending on an independent verb to complete its meaning.
4. Independent Clause: A clause expressing a complete thought and thus capable of standing independently or alone.
5. Relative Clause: A dependent clause introduced by a relative pronoun.
6. Interrogative Adjective: An adjective that asks a question.

Vocabulary

amor, amōris m., love
glōria,-ae f., glory
littera,-ae f., letter of alphabet; pl., epistle/literature
virgō, virginis f., virgin/maiden

currō, currere, cucurrī, cursum to run
trahō, trahere, trāxī, tractum to derive/draw/drag/get

quī, quae, quod Relative Pronouns, who/which/what/that
quī? quae? quod? Interrogative Adjectives, which?/what?

ante + acc. before
igitur therefore
nam for
post + acc. after
tam adv., so/to such a degree
trāns + acc. across

Exercises

A. Using a paradigm format listing cases and number, decline the following Interrogative Adjective and Noun combinations, giving the English translation of each declined form.

    1. qui amor?
    2. quae gloria?
    3. quod tempus?

B. Identify the underlined words as Relative Pronouns (RP) or Interrogative Adjectives (IA) then translate the sentences or partial sentences into English.

    1. <u>Qui</u> viri venient?
    2. Sunt viri <u>quos</u> cognoscis.
    3. De <u>quibus</u> viris currebas?
    4. Viri <u>quibuscum</u> dicebas . . .
    5. Puella <u>cuius</u> virtutem laudabas . . .
    6. Viri <u>quorum</u> filios saepe laudamus . . .
    7. <u>Quibus</u> temporibus vivimus?
    8. Litteras <u>quas</u> mittebas . . .
    9. <u>Cui</u> viro litteras scribebas?
    10. Amor verus <u>quem</u> laudamus . . .

C. Form the Present, Imperfect, and Future Indicative with the English translations of each conjugated form of:

    1. curro, currere, cucurri, cursum;
    2. supero, superare, superavi, superatum.

D. Fill in the blank with the correct form of the Relative Pronoun or Interrogative Adjective then translate the sentence.

    1. _____ viri currebant?
       which

    2. Viri _____ scribetis non sunt stulti.
        to whom

    3. In _____ urbibus invenies virtutem de _____ dicis?
        which   which

    4. Tempora _____ tolerabamus non erant felicia.
        which

    5. Copia _____ virtutum iuvabit nostram civitatem?
        of which

    6. Litterae _____ habes non sunt meae.
        which

7. Virgo de _____ dicebas in _____ viā vivit?
   whom   which

8. Gloria regum _____ urbes valebant saepe est perpetua.
   whose

9. Si poteras trahere has sententias, sunt pauca _____ non poteris discere.
   which

   sententia,-ae = f., sentence

E.   Render the following sentences into Latin.

   1. The citizens whose virtue you praise derive great strength from which books?
   2. We will overcome by means of which virtues in which places?

F.   Sentence translations.

   1. Egens aeque est is qui non satis habet, et is cui satis nihil potest esse. (Cicero)
      egens,-ntis = needy/destitute   *aeque* = adv., equally
   2. Qui pro innocente dicit satis est eloquens. (Publilius Syrus)
      pro + abl = for/on behalf of
      innocens, innocentis = innocent
      eloquens,-entis = eloquent
   3. Omnia vincit amor.(Virgil)
   4. Qui viri sunt boni cives nisi ei qui beneficia patriae memoriā tenent? (Cicero)
      nisi = unless/except
      beneficium,-i = n., benefit
      memoriā teneo = to remember
   5. Bis dat qui cito dat. (Publilius Syrus)
      bis = adv., twice
      cito = adv., quickly
   6. Liber quem recitas meus est; sed cum male eum recitas, incipit esse tuus.
      (Martial)
      recito (1) = to recite
      male = adv., badly
   7. Bis vincit qui se vincit in victoriā. (Publilius Syrus)
      victoria,-ae = f., victory
      se = himself
   8. Experentia est carus magister sed stulti habebunt nullum alium.
      experentia,-ae = f., experience
      carus,-a,-um = dear (expensive)
      alius,-a,-um = other
   9. Fortuna eum stultum facit quem nimis amat. (Publilius Syrus)

10. Non solum fortuna ipsa est caeca sed etiam eos caecos facit quos semper iuvat. (Cicero)

    caecus,-a,-um = blind

11. Punctum est id cuius nullae partes sunt. (Euclid)

    punctum,-i = n., point

Text Translation

Gaius Valerius Catullus (*floruit* 60–55 BC) came from Verona to Rome as a young man, where his talent as a lyric poet quickly brought him into contact with "Lesbia" (a cover name for Clodia, the wife of Quintus Metellus Celer), and, through her, the leading artists in Rome. The tempestuous love affair between Catullus and Lesbia is the subject of many of his poems as well as the inspiration for many invectives against her rivals, as in the poem that follows; and his rivals for Lesbia's favor, among whom was Julius Caesar.

"Id Quod Vides Id Obtines"

Quintia[1] formosa[2] est multis. mihi[3] candida[4] longa,[5]

recta[6] est: haec esse singula[7] confiteor.[8]

totum illud formosa nego:[9] nam nulla venustas,[10]

nulla in tam magno est corpore mica[11] salis.[12]

(Catullus 86)

1. **Quintia,-ae** f., proper noun
2. **formosus,-a,-um** beautifully formed/beautiful
3. **mihi** in my opinion/to me
4. **candidus,-a,-um** shining white
5. **longus,-a,-um** tall
6. **rectus,-a,-um** correct/proper
7. **singulus,-a,-um** one alone; singular
8. **confiteor** translate: "I confess"
9. **nego (1)** I deny
10. **venustas, venustatis** f., attractiveness
11. **mica,-ae** f., grain
12. **sal, salis** m., salt/wit

Vocabulary: Chapters IX–XII

ācer, ācris, ācre sharp/fierce/keen
aetās, aetātis f., age
alius, alia, aliud another/other
amor, amōris m., love
animal, animalis neut., animal
ante + acc. before
ars, artis f., art/skill

celer, celeris, celere swift/quick/rapid
cīvis, cīvis m., citizen
cognōscō,-nōscere,-nōvī,-nitum to know/be
    acquainted with
cōpia,-ae f., abundance/supply; pl.,
    troops/forces/supplies
cum + indic. verb when
currō, currere, cucurrī, cursum to run

dulcis,-e sweet/pleasant/agreeable
dum while

exemplar, exemplaris neut., example/model

fēlix, fēlīcis adj., happy/lucky
fortis,-e strong/brave

gerō, gerere, gessī, gestum carry
    on/conduct/accomplish
glōria,-ae f., glory
gravis,-e heavy/serious/severe

igitur therefore
iūs, iūris neut., right/law
iuvō, iuvāre, iūvī, iūtum to help/aid

littera,-ae f., letter of alphabet; pl. epistle/literature
loca, locōrum neut., region
locus,- ī m., place/passage in literature

mare, maris neut., sea
memoria,-ae f., memory

mens, mentis f., mind
mors, mortis f., death
mox adv., soon

nam for
natura,-ae f., nature
nox, noctis f., night
nūbēs, nūbis f., cloud
numquam adv., never
omnis,-e every; pl. all

pars, partis f., part/share
post + acc. after
pulcher, pulchra, pulchrum beautiful/handsome

quam adv., how
quī, quae, quod Rel Pro., who/which/what/that
quī? quae? quod? Interr. Adj., which?/what?

ratiō, ratiōnis f., reason/judgement
(re)maneō,-manēre,-mānsī,-mānsum to remain

senectūs, senectūtis f., old age
sententia,-ae f., feeling/thought
suus,-a,-um 3rd Pers. Refl. Poss. Adj., his own/her
    own/its own

tam adv., so
teneō, tenēre, tenuī, tentum to hold/keep/possess
trahō, trahere, trāxī, tractum to
    derive/draw/drag/get
trāns + acc. across
tuus,-a,-um your (sing.)

urbs, urbis f., city

via,-ae f., way/road/street
virgō, virginis f., virgin/maiden
vīs, vīs f., force; pl., strength

Review Work Sheet: Chapters I–XII

I. Using a paradigm format indicating case and number, decline the following.

     1. vis magna
     2. tempus malum
     3. civis felix

II. Conjugate the following verbs in the Present, Imperfect, and Future Tenses. (No English translations required.)

     1. sum, esse, fui, futurus
     2. possum, posse, potui
     3. debeo, debere, debui, debitum
     4. incipio, incipere, incepi, inceptum

III. Form the Imperatives of the following verbs.

     1. curro, currere, cucurri, cursum
     2. deleo, delere, delevi, deletum
     3. facio, facere, feci, factum
     4. iuvo, iuvare, iuvi, iutum
     5. duco, ducere, duxi, ductum
     6. venio, venire, veni, ventum
     7. dico, dicere, dixi, dictum

IV. Translate the following.

     1. veniebant
     2. in illā urbe
     3. cuius amici?
     4. eo tempore
     5. ducit
     6. nostra historia
     7. suum laborem
     8. e civitate
     9. reges quos

     10. cum cive forti
     11. scribetisne?
     12. puella quae
     13. cum honore
     14. has insidias
     15. vestro regi
     16. Incipite!
     17. vi
     18. quibus artibus?

NB: Every few chapters you will now be coming upon Review Work Sheets. These are optional, for additional review and/or grammar clarification. There is a Key at the back of the book with answers for a self-check.

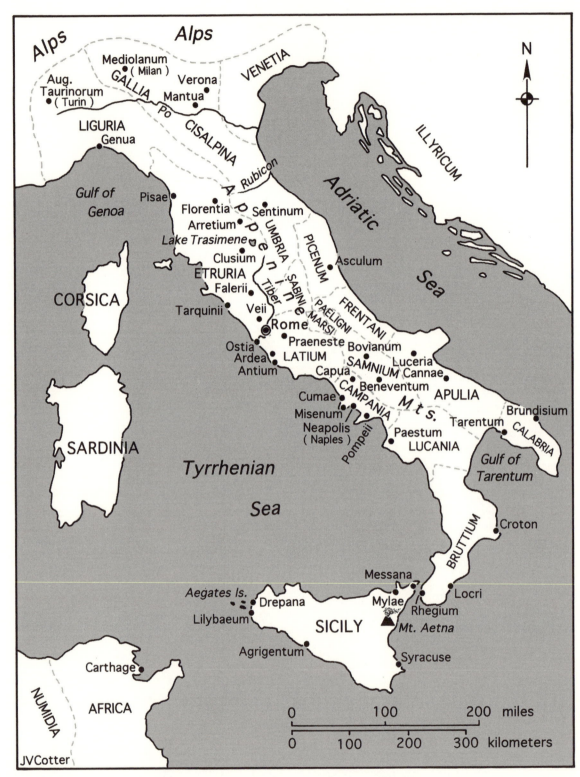

Roman Italy. (Map by John Cotter, reproduced courtesy of Paul A. Zoch)

Perfect Active System, All Verbs
Perfect Indicative
Pluperfect Indicative
Future Perfect Indicative

Objectives

To enable you to:
1. distinguish the Present System from the Perfect Active System;
2. recognize, translate, and form the Perfect Active Indicative Tense;
3. recognize, translate, and form the Pluperfect Active Indicative Tense;
4. recognize, translate, and form the Future Perfect Active Indicative Tense.

Perfect Active System, All Verbs

You are already familiar with the **Present System**, which is formed from the **First Two Principal Parts** of a Regular Verb and is composed of the **Present, Imperfect,** and **Future Tenses**. The **Perfect Active System** is derived from the **Third Principal Part** of a Regular Verb and is composed of the **Perfect, Pluperfect,** and **Future Perfect Tenses**.

So you now know that the Romans divided time into six specific tenses reflecting chronological occurrence. If you will agree to accept that time is a straight line running left to right, I can demonstrate on a chart how this works.

Time Before   **Present Time**   Time After

| Pluperfect | Perfect | | Future Perfect | Future → |

Imperfect

Perfect by literal definition means something that has been done or completed. Notice in the chart above that the **Imperfect Tense** falls below the line; that is because it is used for **incomplete** or **ongoing past action**; *imperfect* literally means something that is not complete. The **Imperfect Tense** is also (and mostly) used for **general description of events of the past**.

Now to clearly define the tense uses of the **Perfect Active System.** The **Perfect Tense** is used for a completed action; the **Pluperfect Tense** is used for an action completed before a Perfect action; the **Future Perfect Tense** is used to indicate an action to be completed by a certain time in the future. All the tenses of the Perfect Active System are formed from the **Third Principal Part of the Verb.** To find the stem for the Perfect Active Tenses, drop the *-i* from the Third Principal Part of the Verb and add the appropriate tense endings.

The Perfect endings (in **bold** below) are the only new forms to be learned, and these must be thoroughly committed to memory *subito* (i.e., immediately, if not sooner). The Pluperfect and Future Perfect (except for 3rd Plural) endings are tense forms of the verb *sum, esse,* with which you are already familiar.

voco, vocare, ***vocavi****, vocatum*

Perfect		**Pluperfect**		**Future Perfect**	
vocāv**ī**	*I called, did call, have called*	vocāv**eram**	*I had called*	vocāv**erō**	*I will have called*
vocāv**istī**		vocāv**erās**		vocāv**eris**	
vocāv**it**		vocāv**erat**		vocāv**erit**	
vocāv**imus**		vocāv**erāmus**		vocāv**erimus**	
vocāv**istis**		vocāv**erātis**		vocāv**eritis**	
vocāv**ērunt**		vocāv**erant**		vocāv**erint**	

Be sure to note that the Perfect Active Indicative has three possible translations *but* there is only one possible translation for the Pluperfect Tense and there is only one possible translation for the Future Perfect Tense.

Perfect Indicative

vocāvī	vīdī	mīsī	cēpī	scīvī
vocāvistī	vīdistī	mīsistī	cēpistī	scīvistī
vocāvit	vīdit	mīsit	cēpit	scīvit
vocāvimus	vīdimus	mīsimus	cēpimus	scīvimus
vocāvistis	vīdistis	mīsistis	cēpistis	scīvistis
vocāvērunt*	vīdērunt*	misērunt*	cepērunt*	scīvērunt*

*Perfect Stem + *ēre* represents an alternate 3rd Plural Perfect form:

vocavēre	vidēre	misēre	cepēre	scivēre

Pluperfect Indicative

vocāveram	vīderam	mīseram	cēperam	scīveram
vocāverās	vīderās	mīserās	cēperās	scīverās
vocāverat	vīderat	mīserat	cēperat	scīverat
vocāverāmus	vīderāmus	mīserāmus	cēperāmus	scīverāmus
vocāverātis	vīderātis	mīserātis	cēperātis	scīverātis
vocāverant	vīderant	mīserant	cēperant	scīverant

Future Perfect Indicative

vocāverō	vīderō	mīserō	cēperō	scīverō
vocāveris	vīderis	mīseris	cēperis	scīveris
vocāverit	vīderit	mīserit	cēperit	scīverit
vocāverimus	vīderimus	mīserimus	cēperimus	scīverimus
vocāveritis	vīderitis	mīseritis	cēperitis	scīveritis
vocāverint	vīderint	mīserint	cēperint	scīverint

Vocabulary

brevis,-e brief
cārus,-a,-um dear
difficilis,-e difficult

Asia,-ae f., Asia
caelum,-i n., sky/heaven
fēmina,-ae f., woman
Caesar, Caesaris m., Caesar
Cicero, Cicerōnis m., Cicero
lībertās, lībertātis f., liberty/freedom

committō, committere, commīsī, commissum to commit/entrust
exspectō (1) to await/expect
iaciō, iacere, iēcī, iactum to throw/hurl
mūtō (1) to change/alter
timeō, timēre, timuī to fear/be afraid

diū adv., for a long time
inde adv., thence
inter + acc. among/between
itaque adv., and so
quoniam since

Exercises

A. Form the **Present Active System** and the **Perfect Active System** of the verbs below. Give the English translation of 3rd Person Plural for each tense.

    1. timeo, timere, timui
    2. iacio, iacere, ieci, iactum
    3. sum, esse, fui, futurus

B. Form the Singular and Plural Imperatives of:

    1. muto, mutare, mutavi, mutatum
    2. committo, committere, commisi, commissum

C. Using paradigm formats indicating cases and numbers, decline:

    1. difficilis femina
    2. breve tempus

D. Translate the following verb forms.

    1. didicerant
    2. dixerit
    3. habuisti
    4. dederam
    5. ducent
    6. docet
    7. docuerant
    8. invenimus
    9. monuerimus
    10. nescivit

E. Translate the following phrases into the correctly <u>declined</u> Latin forms.

    1. for a dear friend
    2. difficult seas
    3. in blessed peace
    4. of Cicero himself
    5. swift Caesar
    6. of wretched labors
    7. with true liberty
    8. pretty skies
    9. in wretched times
    10. blessed Asia

F. Sentence translations.

    1. Ira furor brevis est. (Horace)
      furor furoris = m., madness
    2. Ars est longa, vita brevis. (Hippocrates)
    3. In triumpho Caesar ostendit hunc titulum: Veni, vidi, vici! (Suetonius)
      triumphus,-i = m., triumph
      ostendo, ostendere, ostendi, ostentum = to exhibit
      titulus,-i = m., placard
    4. Vixit, dum vixit, bene. (Terence)
      bene = adv., well
    5. Non ille diu vixit sed diu fuit. (Seneca)

6. Amici Pythagorae in disputationibus saepe dixerunt: "Ipse dixit." 'Ipse'
   autem erat Pythagoras; nam huius auctoritas etiam sine ratione valuit.
   (Cicero)

   Pythagoras,-ae = m., Proper Noun, a Greek philosopher who founded a school in
   southern Italy

   autem = conj., however

   disputatio, disputionis = f., debate

   auctoritas, auctoritatis = f., authority

7. Fugere non potes necessitates, eas potes vincere. (Seneca)

   necessitas, necessitatis = f., necessity

8. Homines vitia sua et amant simul et oderunt. (Seneca)

   et . . . et = both . . . and

   simul = at the same time

   odi, odisse = to hate

9. Levis est fortuna; id cito reposcit quod dedit. (Publilius Syrus)

   levis,-e = fickle

   cito = adv., quickly

   reposco, reposcere = to demand back

10. In principio Deus creavit caelum et terram, et Deus aquas maria appellavit.
    (Genesis)

    aqua,-ae = f., water

    principium,-i = n., beginning

    creo (1) = to create

Text Translation

This is a continuation of the Roman foundation myths recorded by Livy that we began in chapter X. Numitor is the older brother from whom Amulius stole the rule. Romulus and Remus are the twin sons born to Rea Silva and the god Mars.

Romulus[1] et Remus,[2] iam[3] iuvenes,[4] in latrones[5] impetos[6] faciebant, praedamque[7] cum pastoribus[8] dividebant.[9] Sed tandem[10] latrones Remum insidiis ceperunt et eum ad Amulium traxerunt. Amulius Remum ad Numitorem[11] mittit quod impetus accidit[12] in terrā Numitoris. Numitor autem[13] Remum cognoverat: paraverunt[14] consilium.[15] Romulus cum pastoribus et Remus cum amicis Numitoris Amulium occidunt.[16] Tandem Numitor est rex. Posterea[17] Romulus Remusque statuunt[18] condere[19] urbem in eis locis ubi pueri vixerant. Sed gemini[20] erant. Quis appellabit[21] urbem? Quis erit rex? Tandem statuerunt auguria[22] capere. Remus primus[23] sex[24] vultures[25] vidit, sed Romulus duodecim[26] viderat. Inde altercatio[27] est, deinde[28] rixa[29] et Romulus suum fratrem[30] occidit. Sic[31] Romulus solus erat rex; suam novam urbem Romam appellavit.

(*Ab Urbe Condita* Bk. I, vi, vii)

1. **Romulus,-i** m., legendary founder and first king of Rome
2. **Remus,-i** m., twin brother of Romulus
3. **iam** adv., now/already
4. **iuvenis,-e** young (men)
5. **latro, latronis** m., robber
6. **impetus,-i** m., attack/raid
7. **praeda,-ae** f., booty/plunder
8. **pastor, pastoris** m., shepherd
9. **divido, dividere, divisi, divisum** to divide
10. **tandem** adv., at last
11. **Numitor, Numitoris** m., legal heir to throne of Alba Longa; older brother of Amulius
12. **accido, accidere, accidi** to happen
13. **autem** however
14. **paro (1)** to prepare
15. **consilium,-i** n., plan
16. **occido, occidere, occidi, occisum** to kill
17. **posterea** adv., afterward
18. **statuo, statuere, statui, statutum** to decide
19. **condo, condere, condidi, conditum** to found
20. **geminus,-i** m., twin
21. **appello (1)** to name
22. **augurium,-i** n., augury/observation and interpretation of omens
23. **primus,-a,-um** first
24. **sex** six
25. **vultur, vulturis** m., vulture
26. **duodecim** twelve
27. **altercatio,-onis** f., altercation/dispute
28. **deinde** adv., then
29. **rixa,-ae** f., fight/brawl
30. **frater, fratris** m., brother
31. **sic** adv., so

Personal Pronouns
Reflexive Pronouns

Objectives

To enable you to:
1. recognize and decline Personal Pronouns;
2. recognize and decline Reflexive Pronouns;
3. understand the difference in translation of a Personal Pronoun and a Reflexive Pronoun.

Personal Pronouns

Since the Romans indicated pronoun subjects with personal endings added to a verbal stem, they had little need for pronouns in the Nominative Case except for <u>emphasis</u>, and this is the only reason Personal Pronouns in the Nominative Case are ever used in Latin. The good news is that Latin Personal Pronouns are fairly easy to learn as a group because of the repetitive forms and, of course, you already know the 3rd Person *is, ea, id*.

	1st Person		2nd Person		3rd Person (Chapter VI)	
Nom.	*ego*	I	*tū*	you	*is, ea, id*	he, she, it
Gen.	*meī**	of me	*tuī**	of you	*eius, eius, eius*	his/hers/its
Dat.	*mihi*	to/for me	*tibi*	to/for you	*eī, eī, eī*	to/for him/her/it
Acc.	*mē*	me	*tē*	you	*eum, eam, id*	him/her/it
Abl.	*mē*	by/with/ from me	*tē*	by/with/ from you	*eō, eā, eō*	by/with/ from him/her/it
Nom.	*nōs*	we	*vōs*	you	*eī, eae, ea*	they, these, those
Gen.	*nostrum/ nostrī**	of us	*vestrum/ vestrī**	of you	*eōrum, eārum, eōrum*	their/of them
Dat.	*nōbīs*	to/for us	*vōbīs*	to/for you	*eīs, eīs, eīs*	to/for them
Acc.	*nōs*	us	*vōs*	you	*eōs, eās, ea*	them
Abl.	*nōbīs*	by/with/ from us	*vōbīs*	by/with/ from you	*eīs, eīs, eīs*	by/with/from, them

The Romans used **Possessive Adjectives** (chapter X) to indicate **possession**. The **Genitive forms** of the **Personal Pronouns** (marked with asterisks* above) are **never used to show possession**. These forms are reserved for **Special Genitive Usages**, one of which will be covered in chapter XXXV.

Reflexive Pronouns

Reflexive Pronouns "reflect" (i.e., refer to) the subject of the verb. Reflexive Pronouns for 1st and 2nd Persons Singular and Plural are identical in form to the Personal Pronouns (above), <u>except</u> that the Nominative forms are missing. This is because Reflexive Pronouns "reflect" the subject of the verb.

1st Person Reflexive

	sing.		pl.	
Nom.	—		—	
Gen.	*meī*	of myself	*nostrum/nostrī*	of ourselves
Dat.	*mihi*	to/for myself	*nōbīs*	to/for ourselves
Acc.	*mē*	myself	*nōs*	ourselves
Abl.	*mē*	by/with/from myself	*nōbīs*	by/with/from ourselves

2nd Person Reflexive

	sing.		pl.	
Nom.	—		—	
Gen.	*tuī*	of yourself	*vestrum/vestrī*	of yourselves
Dat.	*tibi*	to/for yourself	*vōbīs*	to/for yourselves
Acc.	*tē*	yourself	*vōs*	yourselves
Abl.	*tē*	by/with/from yourself	*vōbīs*	by/with/from yourselves

3rd Person Reflexive

This is a **new Pronoun** that is used only for 3rd Person and only in a Reflexive situation. There is only one form which is used both for the singular and the plural.

Nom.	—	
Gen.	*suī*	of himself/herself/itself/themselves
Dat.	*sibi*	to/for himself/herself/itself/themselves
Acc.	*sē*	himself/herself/itself/themselves
Abl.	*sē*	by/with/from himself/herself/itself/themselves

NB: When *cum* is used with the Ablative forms of the Personal and Reflexive pronouns, it is attached to the end of the pronoun:

mēcum, tēcum, sēcum, nōbīscum, vōbīscum

Summary of New Terminology

1. Pronouns: *pro* in Latin means "in place of"; pronouns take the place of nouns
2. Personal Pronouns: designate the person (I, you, he, she, it, we, you, they) saying or doing something, the person spoken to or receiving an action, or the person or thing spoken about
3. Reflexive Pronouns: pronouns referring to the subject of the verb

Vocabulary

ego, meī I
tū, tuī you (sing.)
nōs, nostrum we
vōs, vestrum you (pl.)
—, suī 3rd Per Reflexive Pronoun, himself/herself/itself/themselves

frāter, frātris m., brother
māter, mātris f., mother
pāter, pātris m., father
soror, sorōris f., sister
nōmen, nōminis n., name

iungō, iungere, iūnxī, iūnctum to join
sentiō, sentīre, sēnsī, sēnsum to feel/perceive/think
autem moreover/however
bene adv., well
per + acc. through

Exercises

A. Using paradigm formats, decline:

1. noster frater
2. tuum nomen
3. mea soror
4. suus pater

B. Translate the following phrases into English.

1. tecum
2. cum sua sorore
3. ad me
4. vestris patribus
5. per vos
6. post nos
7. vobiscum
8. propter te
9. ante se
10. alter ego *alter,-tera,-terum* = another

C. Form the Present Active System and then the Perfect Active System of the following verbs in the Person listed.

1. iungo, iungere, iunxi, iunctum
    in 2nd Person Singular
2. sentio, sentire, sensi, sensum
    in 3rd Person Singular

D. Fill in the blank with the appropriately declined Pronoun or Adjective and then translate the sentence.

1. _____ amo _____. Amo _____ amicos.
    I   you (sing.)   our

2. _____ amas _____. Amas _____ amicas.
    You   yourself   your (sing.)

3. _____ amat _____. Amat _____ amicos.
    He   himself   his

4. _____ amant _____. Amant _____ amicos.
    They   themselves   their

5. _____ amatis _____. Amatis _____ amicas.
    You   yourselves   your

6. Amo _____. Amo _____ amicos.
        myself   my

7. _____ mittet _____ ad _____.
    He   me   you

8. _____ laudabimus _____; non laudabimus _____.
    We   them   ourselves

9. _____ remanebit cum _____; non remanebit _____.
    She   them   with you

10. _____ servaverunt _____.
   They themselves   themselves

E. Sentence translations.

1. Nec tecum possum vivere nec sine te. (Martial)

   nec . . . nec = neither . . . nor

2. Tu nobiscum vivere non potes, quod tu et tui de exituo totius civitatis cogitatis. (Cicero)

   exituus,-i = m., destruction

3. Animus ipse se alit. (Seneca)

   alo, alere, alui, altum = to nourish

4. Ipsi nihil per se sine eo facere potuerunt. (Cicero)

5. Ipse ad eos contendit equitesque ante se misit. (Caesar)

   contendo,-tendere,-tendi,-tensum = to hasten

   eques, equitis = m., horseman

6. Quisque ipse se diligit nam quisque per se sibi carus est. (Cicero)

   diligo ,diligere, dilexi, dilectum = to esteem

   quisque, quidque = each one/each thing

7. Homo doctus in se semper divitias habet. (Phaedrus)

   doctus,-a,-um = learned/educated

   divitiae, divitiarum = f., wealth/riches

8. Filii mei fratrem meum diligebant, me fugiebant; meam mortem exspectabant. Nunc autem mores meos mutavi et filios ad me traho. (Terence)

9. Magna pars mei mortem vitabit. (Horace)

10. Turbam vita. Cum his vive qui te meliorem facere possunt; illos admitte quos tu potes facere meliores. (Seneca)

   turba,-ae = f., crowd

   melior, melioris = m./f., better

   *admitto,-mittere,-misi,-miss*um = to receive/admit

Text Translation

Marcus Tullius Cicero (106–43 BC) is considered the greatest of all Roman orators. He was not a member of the aristocratic class, but he did secure political advancement as a successful advocate in political trials. The following excerpt is from the *Pro Archia*, a famous case in which Cicero represented a well-known poet/lecturer whose influence and stimulus Cicero claimed had been pivotal to his (Cicero's) own success.

Archias was now an old man and was faced with the possibility of deportation for failing to register as a Roman citizen. He had registered, but there was no evidence, as the records had been destroyed in a fire. Cicero successfully makes the point that it really did not matter whether Archias had registered or not, as it was to Rome's advantage to have literary figures such as Archias writing about the great men of the age, a service all nations always had appreciated and sought.

Et si quis[1] minorem[2] copiam gloriae putat[3] e Graecis litteris quam[4] ex

Latinis, errat. Quod Graecae litterae leguntur[5] in omnibus fere[6] gentibus,[7]

dum Latinae litterae in suis exiguis[8] finibus[9] remanent. In illa loca ubi

nostra tela[10] venerunt, etiam[11] nostram gloriam famamque penetrare[12]

cupere[13] debemus, quod litterae faciunt gentes amplas.[14] Quam multos

scriptores[15] factorum[16] suorum magnus ille Alexander secum habuit! Is

tamen[17] ante tumulum[18] Achillis[19] quondam stetit:[20] "Fortunate,"[21] inquit,[22]

"adulescens,[23] quod Homerum[24] laudatorem[25] tuae virtutis invenisti." Et

vere![26] Nam sine Iliade[27] illā, tumulus, qui corpus eius obruerat, nomen

eius etiam obruere[28] potuit.

(*Pro Archia Poeta* X, xiii, xiv)

1. **si quis** if anyone
2. **minor, minoris** less
3. **puto (1)** to think
4. **quam** than
5. **lego, legere, legi, lectum** to read; lego**ntur** pass., "is read"
6. **fere** adv., almost
7. **gens, gentis** f., nation
8. **exiguus,-a,-um** narrow
9. **finis,-is** m., boundary; pl. = territory
10. **telum,-i** n., weapon
11. **etiam** conj, also/even
12. **penetro (1)** to penetrate/extend
13. **cupio, cupere, cupivi, cupitum** to desire
14. **amplus,-a,-um** great/important/eminent
15. **scriptor, scriptoris** m., writer
16. **factum,-i** n., deed
17. **tamen** conj., yet/nevertheless
18. **tumulus,-i** m., tomb
19. **Achilles, Achillis** m., Proper Noun, a Greek warrior
20. **sto, stare, steti, statum** to stand

21. **fortunatus,-a,-um** fortunate
22. **inquit** defective verb, he said; occurs after one or more words of a direct quotation
23. **adulescens, adulescentis** m., youth
24. **Homerus,-i** m., Proper Noun, Homer, author of the <u>Iliad</u>
25. **laudator, laudatoris** m., praiser
26. **vere** adv., truly/indeed
27. **Ilias, Iliadis** f., <u>Iliad</u>, an epic poem by Homer
28. **obruo, obruere, obrui, obrutum** to bury

Review Work Sheet: Chapters XIII–XIV

A. Using paradigm formats labeling cases, decline:

    1. libertas cara   2. nomen difficile

B. Form the **Present System** and then the **Perfect System** of *traho, trahere, traxi, tractum.* Give the English translation of 1st Person Plural for each tense.

C. Provide the correctly declined Latin Pronoun or Reflexive Pronoun.

    1. me   6. us
    2. with you (pl.)   7. himself
    3. for us   8. we
    4. he   9. with me
    5. to you (sing.)   10. themselves

D. Provide the appropriate conjugated Latin verb for:

    1. they had thrown   6. I am changing
    2. we sensed   7. he will learn
    3. Did you consider?   8. she had been able
    4. it remained   9. you have been
    5. you will have expected   10. I did understand

E. Render the following sentences into Latin.

    1. Did my brother join your father in the city?
    2. Why do such men always praise themselves?
    3. He had not been in Asia for a long time.
    4. They were expecting difficult seas at that time of year.
    5. He will have expected his own troops.

Active Voice
Passive Voice
Ablative of Agent
Present Passive System Formation
Passive Infinitives

Objectives

To enable you to:
1. recognize, conjugate, and translate the Present, Imperfect, and Future
   <u>Passive</u> Indicative of all conjugations of Latin verbs;
2. recognize and translate Ablatives of Agent;
3. recognize, form, and translate Passive Infinitives.

Active Voice

The following are Active Statements because each has Direct Objects that receive the action of the verb.

1. I love the girl | *I* | = Subject
   Amo puellam | *love* | = Active Verb
   | *girl* | = Direct Object

2. You saw the men. | *you* | = Subject
   Vidisti viros. | *saw* | = Active Verb
   | *men* | = Direct Object

3. He will send the book. | *he* | = Subject
   Mittet librum. | *will send* | = Active Verb
   | *book* | = Direct Object

Passive Voice

Now I am going to convert the sentences above into Passive Statements in which the Subject of the verb receives the action (i.e., there is no Direct Object).

1. The girl is loved by me.

girl	= Subject
is loved	= Passive Verb
by me	= Ablative of Agent*

2. The men were seen by you.

men	= Subject
were seen	= Passive Verb
by you	= Ablative of Agent*

3. The book will be sent by him.

book	= Subject
will be sent	= Passive Verb
by him	= Ablative of Agent*

* See discussion of Ablative of Agent that follows.

Ablative of Agent

An Ablative of Agent occurs only with Passive Verbs and tells by whom an action was done. An Ablative of Agent is preceded by **ab** or **ā,** followed by a noun or a pronoun in the Ablative Case.

Present Passive System Formation

The Passive Voice of the Present System is formed uniformly for all conjugations. To make a Latin verb Passive, simply replace the Active Endings *-o/m,-s,-t,-mus,-tis,-nt* with the Passive Endings **-r,-ris,-tur,-mur,-mini,-ntur**. What you actually do is add an **-r** to the 1st Person Singular Active and then replace the other endings with **-ris,-tur,-mur,-mini,-ntur**.

ama**r**	*I am loved*	amā**mur**	*we are loved*
amā**ris**	*you are loved*	amā**minī**	*you are loved*
amā**tur**	*he, she, it is loved*	ama**ntur**	*they are loved*

1. The girl is loved by me.   Puella ama**tur** a me.
2. The men were seen by you.   Viri videba**ntur** a te.
3. The book will be sent by him.   Liber mitte**tur** ab eo.

Present Passive System

Present Tense

amor	videor	mittor	capior	scior
amāris	vidēris	mitteris*	caperis*	scīris
amātur	vidētur	mittitur	capitur	scitur
amāmur	vidēmur	mittimur	capimur	scimur
amāminī	vidēminī	mittiminī	capiminī	sciminī
amantur	videntur	mittuntur	capiuntur	sciuntur

Imperfect Tense

amābar	vidēbar	mittēbar	capiēbar	sciēbar
amābāris	vidēbāris	mittēbāris	capiēbāris	sciēbāris
amābātur	vidēbātur	mittēbātur	capiēbātur	sciēbātur
amābāmur	vidēbāmur	mittēbāmur	capiēbāmur	sciēbāmur
amābāminī	vidēbāminī	mittēbāminī	capiēbāminī	sciēbāminī
amābantur	vidēbantur	mittēbantur	capiēbantur	sciēbantur

Future Tense

amābor	vidēbor	mittar	capiar	sciar
amāberis*	vidēberis*	mittēris	capiēris	sciēris
amābitur	vidēbitur	mittētur	capiētur	sciētur
amābimur	vidēbimur	mittēmur	capiēmur	sciēmur
amābiminī	vidēbiminī	mittēminī	capiēmini	sciēminī
amābuntur	vidēbuntur	mittentur	capientur	scientur

* The Romans apparently did not like the sound of *-iris*, accounting for these consistent irregularities.

Passive Infinitives

Just as conjugated verbs can be rendered in the Passive Voice by altering the endings, Active Infinitives can be converted to Passive Infinitives by employing the following steps.

1. For 1st, 2nd, and 4th Conjugation verbs, change the final **-e** to **-ī**:

	Active		Passive	
1st	*vocare*	= to call	*vocari*	= to be called
2nd	*videre*	= to see	*videri*	= to be seen
4th	*scire*	= to know	*sciri*	= to be known

2. For 3rd and 3rd-*io* verbs, change the final *-ere* to *-ī*:

	Active	Passive
3rd	*mittere* = to send	*mitti* = to be sent
3rd-*io*	*capere* = to capture	*capi* = to be captured

Vocabulary

amīcitia,-ae f., friendship
cōnsilium,-ī n., plan/advice
factum,-ī n., deed
vēritās, vēritātis f., truth

subitus,-a,-um sudden

dīligō, dīligere, dīlēxī, dīlēctum to esteem
moveō, movēre, mōvī, mōtum to move/arouse
videor, videri, visus sum* to seem/appear

aut or
aut . . . aut either . . . or
ferē adv., almost

* Passive forms of *video, videre, vidi, visum* very often mean "to seem/to appear."

Exercises

A. Form the Active and then the Passive of the <u>Present System</u> of ***diligo, diligere, dilexi, dilectum***. Give the English translation of 1st Person Singular in each tense.

Column Format:

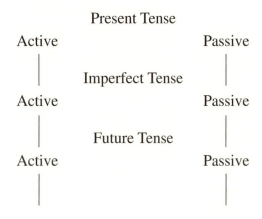

Present Tense

Active   Passive

Imperfect Tense

Active   Passive

Future Tense

Active   Passive

B. Form the Passive Infinitives and then give the English translation of the Passive Infinitives of the following verbs.

1. diligo, diligere, dilexi, dilectum
2. moveo, movere, movi, motum
3. sentio, sentire, sensi, sensum
4. muto, mutare, mutavi, mutatum
5. iacio, iacere, ieci, iactum

C. Form the Singular and then the Plural Imperatives of the following verbs.

1. diligo, diligere, dilexi, dilectum
2. moveo, movere, movi, motum
3. sentio, sentire, sensi, sensum
4. muto, mutare, mutavi, mutatum
5. iacio, iacere, ieci, iactum

D. Translate the following verb forms.

1. movemus
2. movemur
3. diliges
4. diligeris
5. muto

6. mutor
7. iaciebant
8. iaciebantur
9. audiunt
10. audiuntur

E. Render the following verbs forms into Latin.

1. you sense
2. it used to be felt
3. we will discover
4. he will be discovered
5. I used to possess

6. I will be possessed
7. You (pl.) know
8. You are known
9. She used to see
10. She is seen

F. Sentence translations.

1. Etiam stultus qui tacebit sapiens ducetur. (Proverbs)

    taceo, tacere, tacui, tacitum = to be silent

    sapiens, sapientis = wise

    duco, ducere, duxi, ductum = to consider

2. Diligemus eum qui pecuniā non movetur. (Cicero)

3. Malum est consilium quod mutari non potest. (Publilius Syrus)

4. Bona mens nec commodatur nec emitur. (Seneca)

    commodo (1)= to loan

    emo, emere, emi, emptum = to buy

5. Tempus mutat nos et mutamur in illis. (Ovid)

6. Omnes mutantur; omnia fluunt; quod fuimus aut sumus cras non erimus.
    (Ovid)

    fluo, fluere, fluxi, fluctum = to flow

    cras = adv., tomorrow

7. De eo cui multum datur multum requiritur. (Luke 12:48)

    requiro,-quirere,-quisivi,-quisitum = to require/demand

8. Amor misceri cum timore non potest. (Publilius Syrus)

    misceo, miscere, miscui, mixtum = to mix

    timor, timoris = m., fear

9. Etiam fortes viri subitis periculis terrentur. (Terence)

    terreo, terrere, terrui, territum = to terrify

10. Fas est ab hoste doceri. (Virgil)

    fas = n., indeclinable noun, right

    hostis,-is = m., enemy

Text Translation

In addition to the actual war campaigns, the *Commentaries* of Julius Caesar (100–44 BC) on the Gallic War contain descriptions of the Gallic people, their religion, and their countryside (present-day France). The Druids were unique to Gaul and Britain and were of supreme importance to the peoples living in these regions.

In omni Galliā[1] eorum hominum qui in honore[2] habentur, genera[3] sunt

duo:[4] Druides[5] equitesque.[6] Plebs[7] fere in loco servorum[8] habetur et ob[9]

magnitudinem[10] tributorum[11] se in servitutem[12] nobilibus[13] dant. Druides

cum divinis[14] intersunt;[15] ad hos magnus adulescentium[16] numerus

disciplinae[17] causā[18] venit: magnique hi inter eos in honore habentur.

Druides in fere omnibus controversis[19] publicis[20] privatisque[21] constituunt[22]

et si facinus[23] committitur aut si de hereditate[24] aut de finibus[25]

controversia est, decernunt,[26] et praemia[27] poenasque constituunt. Dum

equites semper in bello versantur,[28] Druides de bello eximuntur.[29]

(Bk. VI, xiii, xiv)

1. **Gallia,-ae** f., Gaul
2. **honor, honoris** m., honor/esteem
3. **genus, generis** n., type
4. **duo** two
5. **Druides, Druidum** m., Druids
6. **eques, equitis** m., horse soldier (a noble in Gallic society)
7. **plebs, plebis** f., common people
8. **servus,-i** m., slave
9. **ob + acc.** on account of
10. **magnitudo, magnitudinis** f., magnitude
11. **tributus,-i** m., tribute
12. **servitus, servitutis** f., slavery
13. **nobilis,-e** noble
14. **divinus,-a,-um** divine
15. **intersum,-esse,-fui,-futurus** to be concerned with
16. **adulescens, adulescentis** m., youth
17. **disciplina,-ae** f., learning
18. **gen. + causā** for the sake of/for the purpose of
19. **controversia,-ae** f., controversy/dispute
20. **publicus,-a,-um** public
21. **privatus,-a,-um** private
22. **constituo,-stituere,-stitui,-stitum** to decide/determine
23. **facinus, facinoris** n., crime
24. **hereditas, hereditatis** f., inheritance
25. **finis,-is** m., border; pl., territory
26. **decerno, decernere, decrevi, decretum** to decide/judge
27. **praemium,-i** n., reward
28. **verso (1)** to engage
29. **eximo, eximere, exemi, exemptum** to exempt

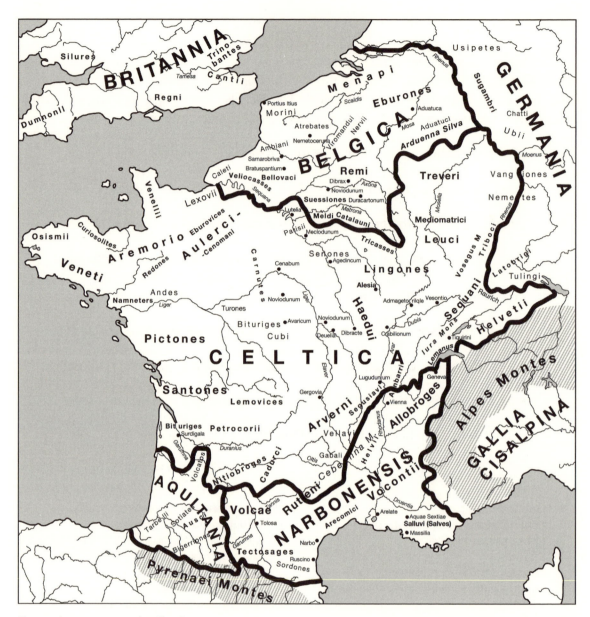

Caesar's conquests in Gaul

4th Principal Part of Verbs
Perfect Passive System, All Conjugations
Synopsis of Verbs

XVI

Objectives

To enable you to:
  1. recognize, translate, and form the Perfect, Pluperfect, and Future Perfect Passive Indicative of all conjugations of Latin verbs;
  2. to form a Synopsis of Active and Passive Indicative Tenses of Regular Verbs.

4th Principal Part of Verbs

At last you will find out the purpose of the 4th Principal Part of the verb; as you will see, it is the basis of the Perfect Passive System, which includes the Perfect, Pluperfect, and Future Perfect Tenses.

The 4th Principal Part of a verb is the Perfect Passive Participle; Participles are Verbal Adjectives and like all Adjectives have case, number, and gender. In the cause of brevity, only the Nominative Singular Neuter Form is given, but in reality the Perfect Passive Participle is a 1st–2nd Declension Adjective following the same declension pattern as *bonus,-a,-um* and means "having been _____."

voc, vocāre, vocāvī, ***vocātum***	= *vocātus,-a,-um*	→ having been called
vide, vidēre, vīdī, ***vīsum***	= *vīsus,-a,-um*	→ having been seen
mitt, mittere, mīsī, ***missum***	= *missus-,a,-um*	→ having been sent
capi, capere, cēpī, ***captum***	= *captus,-a,-um*	→ having been captured
sci, scīre, scīvī, ***scītum***	= *scītus,-a,-um*	→ having been known

Perfect Passive System, All Conjugations

The Perfect Passive System is formed by combining the Present, Imperfect, and Future Tenses of the verb ***sum, esse*** with the Perfect Passive Participle to form a Compound Verb. The gender and number of the subject is indicated by the Participle Part of the Verb and theoretically can be masculine, feminine, or neuter singular or plural. The conjugated paradigms that follow are only those for 1st Conjugation verbs; on pages 298–99 there is a complete chart of the Passive Forms for all conjugations.

Perfect Passive Indicative *(Perfect Passive Participle + **sum**)*

vocātus,-a,-um sum	*I have been called/was called*
vocātus,-a,-um es	*you have been called/were called*
vocātus,-a,-um est	*he, she, it has been called/was called*
vocātī,-ae,-a sumus	*we have been called/were called*
vocātī,-ae,-a estis	*you have been called/were called*
vocātī,-ae,-a sunt	*they have been called/were called*

Pluperfect Passive Indicative *(Perfect Passive Participle + **eram**)*

vocātus,-a,-um eram	*I had been called*
vocātus,-a,-um erās	*you had been called*
vocātus,-a,-um erat	*he, she, it had been called*
vocāti,-ae,-a erāmus	*we had been called*
vocāti,-ae,-a erātis	*you had been called*
vocāti,-ae,-a erant	*they had been called*

Future Perfect Passive Indicative *(Perfect Passive Participle + **ero**)*

vocātus,-a,-um ero	*I will have been called*
vocātus,-a,-um eris	*you will have been called*
vocātus,-a,-um erit	*he, she, it will have been called*
vocātī,-ae,-a erimus	*we will have been called*
vocātī,-ae,-a eritis	*you will have been called*
vocātī,-ae,-a erunt	*they will have been called*

Synopsis of Verbs

A verb **Synopsis** is an abbreviated way of rendering all the verb tenses, active and passive, singular and plural, in a format that permits less error <u>and</u> at the same time saves your hand from becoming numb from so much writing.

As you know, "synopsis" by definition means a shortened rendering of something. By listing all the tenses vertically and labeling columns as Active and Passive, it is possible to render a complete conjugation of a verb in a particular person. When forming a synopsis, <u>always</u> list the four Principal Parts of the verb.

Present System	Perfect Active System	Perfect Passive System
vocō, vocāre	*vocāvī*	*vocātum*

A **Synopsis** of this verb in **3rd Person Singular Masculine** would look like this:

	Present Active System			Present Passive System	
Pres.	*vocat*	he calls		*vocatur*	he is called
Imp.	*vocābat*	he was calling		*vocābātur*	he was being called
Fut.	*vocābit*	he will call		*vocābitur*	he will be called
Perf.	*vocāvit*	he has called		*vocātus est*	he has been called
Plup.	*vocāverat*	he had called		*vocātus erat*	he had been called
FutP.	*vocāverit*	he will have called		*vocātus erit*	he will have been called

A Synopsis of *scio, scire, scivi, scitum* in 3rd Person Plural Feminine would look like the paradigm below. Be sure to note the Principal Parts used for the formation of each system.

sciō, scīre

Pres.	*sciunt*	they know		*sciuntur*	they are known
Imp.	*sciēbant*	they knew		*sciēbantur*	they were known
Fut.	*scient*	they will know		*scientur*	they will be known

scīvī   *scītum*

Perf.	*sciverunt*	they have known		*scītae sunt*	they have been known
PluP.	*scīverant*	they had known		*scītae erant*	they had been known
FutP.	*scīverint*	they will have known		*scītae erunt*	they will have been known

NB: 1. In forming the compound verbs of the Perfect Passive System, only the nominative forms of the Participles are used. Also, subjects can be implied by the Participle and Verb Endings.

She had been moved.	=	*Ea mota erat.*	or	*Mota erat.*
They had been moved.	=	*Ei moti erant.*	or	*Moti erant.*

2. The masculine, feminine, and neuter forms (*-us,-a,-um*) are listed as theoretical possibilities, but we know that "I", "you," and "we" necessarily reflect a masculine or feminine gender. This means neuter forms can only occur in 3rd Person.

It had been moved.	=	*Id motum erat.*	or	*Motum erat.*
They had been moved.	=	*Ea mota erant.*	or	*Mota erant.*

Vocabulary

certus,-a,-um certain
incertus,-a,-um uncertain
senex, senis adj./noun, old

gēns, gentis f., nation/gens/clan
Graecia,-ae f., Greece
iūdicium,-ī n., judgement/decision/court
mundus,-ī m., world/universe
studium,-ī n., study/eagerness/zeal

legō, legere, lēgī, lēctum to read/choose
neglegō, neglegere, neglēxī, neglēctum to neglect/disregard
parō (1) to obtain/prepare

at but
atque or **ac** and/and also/and even

Exercises

A. Form the Perfect, Pluperfect, and Future Perfect <u>Passive</u> Indicative of **lego, legere, legi, lectum**. Give the English translations of 2nd Person Plural of each tense.

B. Using a paradigm format indicating tenses and voices, give a Synopsis with English translations of the following verbs in the Person listed.

    1. **paro (1)** in 3rd Pers. Pl. F.   2. **sum, esse, fui, futurus** in 3rd Pers. Sing.

C. Translate the following verb forms.

    1. paravit
    2. paratum est
    3. neglegebant
    4. neglecti erant
    5. movebis
    6. motus eris
    7. diligo
    8. diligor
    9. lecti sunt
    10. lectae erunt

D. Provide the Latin conjugated verb form for:

    1. he chooses
    2. he had chosen
    3. he will be chosen
    4. we are chosen
    5. we will have chosen
    6. they were preparing
    7. they were prepared
    8. they have prepared
    9. you (pl.) will have moved
    10. you (pl.) will have been moved

E. Render the following sentences into Latin.

    1. The books had been read often by the old man.
    2. In uncertain times the arts are always neglected.
    3. The Greek world was joined by the sea.
    4. After many years of war, peace was obtained by the Romans.
    5. Can liberty be obtained without many and certain risks?

Text Translations

Lucretius was a 1st century BC Roman poet and philosopher. His *About the Nature of Things* is a didactic poem meant to abolish superstitions by explaining the nature and cause of change in the world.

Augescunt[1] **aliae**[2] gentes, **aliae** minuuntur;[3] inque brevi spatio[4] mutantur

saecla[5] animantium,[6] et, quasi[7] cursores,[8] vitae facem[9] tradunt.[10]

(*De Rerum Naturā* II, 79)

1. **augesco,-ere** to grow/increase	6. **animans,-antis** adj., living beings
2. **aliae . . . aliae** some . . . others	7. **quasi** just as
3. **minuo,-uere,-ui,-utum** to diminish	8. **cursor,-oris** m., runner
4. **spatium,-i** n., space/period of time	9. **fax, facis** f., torch
5. **saeclum,-i** n., generation	10. **trado,-dere,-dui,-ditum** to pass on

Sophocles was a famous 5th century BC Greek playwright. In his essay about old age, **Cicero** uses Sophocles as an example of an old person retaining all his mental faculties.

Sophocles ad summam[1] senectutem tragoedias[2] scripsit; propter hoc

studium neglegere familiam[3] videbatur[4] et ab filiis in iudicium vocatus est.

Tum senex *Oedipum Coloneum*,[5] tragoediam quam proxime[6] scripserat,

iudicibus[7] recitavit[8] et sententiis iudicum liberatus est.[9]

(Cicero's *De Senectute* 7:22)

1. **summus,-a,-um** extreme	6. **proxime** adv., most recently
2. **tragoedia,-ae** f., tragedy	7. **iudex, iudicis** m., judge
3. **familia,-ae** f., family	8. **recito (1)** to recite
4. Passive of *video* to seem	9. **libero (1)** to free
5. *Oedipus Coloneus* Oedipus at Colonus	

In the first line of his *Commentaries*, **Julius Caesar** describes ancient Gaul.

Omnis Gallia[1] divisa[2] est in partes tres,[3] quarum unam incolunt[4]

Belgae,[5] aliam Aquitani,[6] tertiam[7] qui in linguā[8] suā vocantur

Celtae,[9] in linguā nostrā Galli.[10]

(*Bellum Gallicum*, Bk. 1, 1)

126

1. **Gallia,-ae** f., Gaul
2. **divido, dividere, divisi, divisum** to divide
3. **tres** three
4. **incolo, incolere, incolui** to inhabit
5. **Belgae,-arum** Belgians
6. **Aquitanus,-a,-um** Aquitanian; from southwest part of Gaul
7. **tertius,-a,-um** third
8. **lingua,-ae** f., language/tongue
9. **Celtae,-arum** m., Celts
10. **Galli,-orum** m., Gauls

Vocabulary: Chapters XIII–XVI

amīcitia,-ae f., friendship
Asia,-ae f., Asia
at but
atque/ac and/and also/and even
aut or
aut . . . aut either . . . or
autem moreover/however

bene adv., well
brevis,-e brief

caelum,- ī neut., sky/heaven
Caesar, Caesaris m., Caesar
cārus,-a,-um dear
certus,-a,-um certain
Cicero, Ciceronis m., Cicero
committō, committere, commīsī, commissum to commit/entrust
cōnsilium,- ī neut., plan

difficilis,-e difficult
dīligō, dīligere, dīlēxī, dīlēctum to esteem
diū adv., for a long time

ego, meī I
exspectō (1) to expect/await

factum,-i neut., deed
fēmina,-ae f., woman
ferē adv., almost
frāter, frātris m., brother

gēns, gentis f., nation/gens/clan
Graecia,-ae f., Greece

iaciō, iacere, iēcī, iactum to throw/hurl
incertus,-a,-um uncertain
inde adv., thence

inter + acc. between/among
itaque adv., and so
iūdicium,- ī neut., judgment/decision/court
iungō,iungere,iūnxī,iūnctum to join

legō, legere, lēgī, lēctum to read/choose
lībertās, lībertātis f., liberty/freedom

māter, mātris f., mother

miser, misera, miserum miserable/wretched
moveō, movēre, mōvī, mōtum to move/arouse
mundus,- ī m., world/universe
mūtō (1) to change/alter
neglegō, neglegere, neglēxī, neglēctum to neglect/disregard
nōmen, nōminis neut., name
nōs, nostrum we

parō (1) to obtain/prepare
pāter, pātris m., father
per + acc. through

quoniam since

senex, senis adj./noun old
sentiō, sentīre, sēnsī, sēnsum to feel/perceive/think
soror, sorōris f., sister
studium,- ī neut., study/eagerness/zeal
subitus,-a,-um sudden
———,suī 3rd Per. Refl. Pron., himself, herself, itself

timeō, timere, timuī to fear/to be afraid
tū, tuī you (sing.)

vēritās, vēritātis f., truth
vōs, vestrum you (pl.)

Interrogative Pronouns *quis, quid*
Ablative of Separation

Objectives
To enable you to:
1. recognize, translate, and decline Interrogative Pronouns *quis, quid;*
2. recognize and translate Ablatives of Separation.

Interrogative Pronouns quis, quid

You are already familiar with the nominative singular forms of the Interrogative Pronoun *quis* (who?) and *quid* (what?). Be sure to notice in the paradigm below that:

1. the masculine and feminine singular have the same form;
2. the masculine, feminine, and neuter plural forms are the same as the Interrogative Adjective masculine, feminine, and neuter plural forms;
3. the English translation of the singular forms is the same for the plural forms.

	Singular				Plural		
	m./f.		n.		m.	f.	n.
Nom.	*quis*	who?	*quid*	what?	*quī*	*quae*	*quae*
Gen.	*cuius*	whose?	*cuius*	of what	*quōrum*	*quārum*	*quōrum*
Dat.	*cui*	to/for whom?	*cui*	to/for what?	*quibus*	*quibus*	*quibus*
Acc.	*quem*	whom?	*quid*	what?	*quōs*	*quās*	*quae*
Abl.	*quō*	by/with/ from whom?	*quō*	by/with/ from what?	*quibus*	*quibus*	*quibus*

The difference between the Interrogative Pronoun (*who?* or *what?*) and the Interrogative Adjective (*which?*) is clearly distinct in translation.

1. Who did this?	*Quis fecit hoc?*
2. Which man did this?	*Qui vir fecit hoc?* or *Qui fecit hoc?*
3. What is this?	*Quid est hoc?*
4. Which names were chosen?	*Quae nomina lecta sunt?*

Ablative of Separation

The Romans had a peculiar perspective regarding verbs of **freeing, lacking,** or **depriving.** While in English we say someone has no money (i.e., is "broke"), a Roman would more euphemistically say:

> *Caret pecuniā suā.*   He is separated from (lacks) his money.
> ***careo, carere, carui, cariturus*** = to lack/to be separated from

Pecuniā suā is in the Ablative Case because the verb *careo* is always followed by an Ablative of Separation. The following verbs also take an Ablative of Separation: ***libero*** (1) = to free/liberate; ***privo*** (1) = to deprive.

> *Liberabit eos servitute.*   He will free them from slavery.
> *Privavit eos libertate.*   He has deprived them of freedom.

Vocabulary

careō, carēre, caruī, caritūrus + abl. **of sep** to lack/be deprived of
contineō, continēre, continuī, contentum to contain/hold together
iubeō, iubēre, iussī, iussum to order/command
liberō (1) to free/liberate
prīvō (1) to deprive
rapiō, rapere, rapuī, raptum to seize/carry away/snatch
causa,-ae f., cause/reason/case;
      genitive + *causā* for the sake of/on account of

fīnis,-is m., end/limit/boundary; pl. territory

quis? quid? interr. pron., who? what?

communis,-e common

iam adv., now/already
ita adv., so/thus

Exercises

A. Using paradigm formats indicating tenses, give a synopsis of the Active and Passive forms of the following verbs in the persons indicated.

    1. rapio, rapere, rapui, raptum in 3rd Sing. M.
    2. iubeo, iubere, iussi, iussum in 1st Pl. F.

B. Form the Passive Infinitives with the English translations of the following verbs.

    1. libero, liberare   4. rapio, rapere
    2. contineo, continere   5. invenio, invenire
    3. neglego, neglegere   6. timeo, timere

C. Form the Singular and Plural Imperatives.

    1. iacio, iacere
    2. venio, venire
    3. teneo, tenere
    4. lego, legere
    5. libero, liberare

D. Fill in the blank with the correct declined form of the Interrogative Pronoun then translate the sentence.

    1. _____ est ille?   6. _____ causā venerunt?
       Who   Of whom (sing.)

    2. _____ amici sunt?   7. _____ liberati sunt?
       Whose (pl.)   From whom

    3. In _____ continebatur id?   8. A _____ videbaris?
         what   whom

    4. De _____ currebant?   9. _____ sunt ei?
         whom   Who (pl.)

    5. _____ haec dixisti?   10. _____ hoc factum est?
       To whom   For whom

E. Translate the following according to their declined meanings.

    1. beatus finis   6. quibuscum?
    2. gravia vitia   7. litterae quibus?
    3. laus cuius?   8. iudicium grave
    4. fines communes   9. in mundo incerto
    5. pacis causā   10. graves causae

F. Identify the particular Ablative Constructions (underlined below) then render each sentence into Latin.

    1. He freed the citizens <u>from perpetual dangers</u>.
    2. His plans were carried out <u>by the citizens</u>.
    3. <u>At that time</u> we were lacking money.
    4. <u>By means of great strength</u> of character he had contained his anger.
    5. Who will have been <u>in the city</u> at that time?
    6. He had been called to Rome <u>by Caesar</u>.
    7. We had been <u>away from the state</u> for many years.
    8. You wrote the letter <u>with great care</u>.
    9. They had come into the city <u>with many friends</u>.
    10. To whom and <u>by whom</u> had these things been said?

G. Sentence translations.

    1. Prima virtus est vitio carere. (Quintilian)
       primus,-a,-um = first
    2. Oedipus oculis se privavit.
    3. Quis eum quem timet amare potest? (Cicero)
    4. Nullus accusator caret culpā; omnes peccavimus. (Seneca)
       accusator,-oris = m., accusor
       pecco (1) = to sin
    5. Nulla pars vitae officio liberari potest.
    6. Vale, puella, iam Catullus valet, nec te requirit nec rogabit puellam invitam et tu dolebis cum rogaberis nulla. Quis nunc ad te veniet? Cui videberis bella? Quem nunc amabis? Cuius esse diceris? (adapted from Catullus VIII)
       doleo, dolere, dolui = to grieve/suffer
       invitus,-a,-um = unwilling
       requiro,-quirere,-quisivi,-quisitum = to require
       rogo (1) = to ask
    7. Omnia promittis, cum tota nocte bibisti;
       mane nihil praestas. Pollio, mane bibe. (Martial, <u>Epigrams</u>, Bk. XII, xii)
       bibo, bibere, bibi, bibitum = to drink
       mane = adv., in the morning
       Pollio, Pollionis = m., Proper Noun
       praesto,-stare,-stiti,-stitum = to be responsible for
       promitto,-mittere,-misi,-missum = to promise/undertake
    8. Septima iam, Phileros, tibi conditur uxor in agro.
       Plus nulli, Phileros, quam tibi, reddit ager. (Martial, <u>Epigrams</u>, Bk. X, xliii)
       condo,-dere,-didi,-ditum = to put away/bury
       Phileros,-otis = m., Proper Noun
       plus = more
       quam = than
       reddo,-dere,-didi,-ditum = to return/pay back/grant
       septimus,-a,-um = seventh
       uxor, uxoris = f., wife

Text Translation

The Rape of the Sabine Women as a means of obtaining wives for the male inhabitants of Romulus's new city is a famous story.

Romulus, primus[1] rex Romae, bene regnabat.[2] Quod erant pauci viri, Romam fecit urbem asyli.[3] Ad hoc asylum multi, liberi servique,[4] fugerunt. Quod nullae feminae in urbe erant, legatos[5] ad finitimas[6] gentes misit. In nullo loco, legati benigne[7] accepti[8] sunt. Ita Romulus patresque consilium fecerunt. Multi novam urbem videre cupiunt;[9] ita Romani finitimos[10] suos ad ludos[11] invitaverunt.[12] Cum Romulus signum[13] dedit, virgines Sabinorum[14] raptae sunt. Paucis annis, Sabini et socii[15] cum Romanis bellum gesserunt, sed feminae puellaeque, nunc uxores[16] Romanorum, inter tela[17] cucurrerunt. Ita pax facta est et unam civitatem quam Romam appellaverunt et unum populum, Romanos, fecerunt.

(*Ab Urbe Condita* Bk. I, ix–xii)

1. **primus,-a,-um** first
2. **regno (1)** to rule
3. **asylum,-i** n., refuge
4. **servus,-i** m., slave
5. **legatus,-i** m., legate/ambassador
6. **finitimus,-a,-um** neighboring
7. **benigne** adv., kindly
8. **accipio,-ere,-cepi,-ceptum** to receive
9. **cupio, cupere, cupivi, cupitum** to desire
10. **finitimus,-i** m., neighbor
11. **ludus,-i** m., game
12. **invito (1)** to invite
13. **signum,-i** n., signal
14. **Sabini,-orum** m., Sabine
15. **socius,-i** m., ally
16. **uxor, uxoris** wife
17. **telum,-i** n., weapon

4th Declension Nouns
Irregular Pronoun *nemo*

Objectives

To enable you to:
1. recognize, translate, and decline 4th Declension Nouns;
2. recognize, translate, and decline the Irregular *Noun nemo, neminis*

4th Declension Nouns

4th Declension Nouns are characterized by the letter *u,* as is abundantly clear in the following declension paradigms.

	m./f.		*exercitus, exercitūs* = m., army	
Nom.	-us	-s	exercitus	exercitūs
Gen.	-ūs	-uum	exercitūs	exercituum
Dat.	-uī	-ibus	exercituī	exercitibus
Acc.	-um	-ūs	exercitum	exercitūs
Abl.	-ū	-ibus	exercitū	exercitibus

	n.		*cornū, cornūs* = n., horn	
Nom.	-ū	-ua	cornū	cornua
Gen.	-ūs	-uum	cornūs	cornuum
Dat.	-ū	-ibus	cornū	cornibus
Acc.	-ū	-ua	cornū	cornua
Abl.	-ū	-ibus	cornū	cornibus

While most 4th Declension Nouns are masculine, there is an occasional neuter and a few feminine forms of which **manus** is the most common.

manus, manūs = <u>**f.**</u>, hand/handwriting/troops.

Irregular Pronoun nēmō, nēminis = *m./f., no one*

Captain Nemo, as everyone knows, was really Captain "No One." However, I doubt very much that Jules Verne would have chosen this name had the English language required declension of nouns.

Nom.	**nēmō**	
Gen.	**nēminis**	
Dat.	**nēminī**	**No Plural**
Acc.	**nēminem**	
Abl.	**nūllō/nūllā**	

Please note in the examples below that **nemo** can also be used as a negative adjective.

Noun usage:	*Nemo hoc sciebat.*	No one knew this.
Negative Adjective usage:	*Nemo humanus hoc fecit.*	No human did this.

Vocabulary

cornū, cornūs n., horn
exercitus,-ūs m., army
fructus,-ūs m., profit/fruit
ignis,-is m., fire
lēx, lēgis f., law
manus,-ūs f., hand/handwriting/band of men
metus,-ūs m., fear
scelus, sceleris n., crime/sin
senātus,-ūs m., senate
versus,-ūs m., verse/line

nēmō, nēminis indef. pron./adj., no one
tollō, tollere, sustulī, sublātum to raise/destroy/lift up

Exercises

A. Using paradigm formats indicating cases and numbers, decline:

1. gravis metus
2. stultus versus
3. bella manus
4. magnum cornu

B. Fill in the blank with the correct declined form of **nemo** and then translate the sentence.

1. _____ vidi.
    No one

2. A _____ videbatur.
    no one

3. Amicus _____ est.
    of no one

4. Haec _____ dicta sunt.
    to no one

5. _____ hoc legere potest.
    No one

C. Using a paradigm format give a synopsis, Active and Passive, and translate each conjugated form in 2nd Pers. Pl. M. of *tollo, tollere, sustuli, sublatum*.

D. Translate the following phrases into Latin.

1. He lacked fear.
2. The city was destroyed by fire.
3. His crimes were known by the senate.
4. Which armies will be carried away?
5. The verses had been written by hand and with great care.

E. Sentence translations.

1. Reges Romam a principio habuerunt; libertatem Lucius Brutus Romanis dedit.
    principium,-i = n., beginning (Tacitus)
    Lucius Brutus, Lucii Brutii = m., Brutus, the first consul of the Roman Republic
2. Demosthenes multos versus uno spiritu pronuntiabat. (Cicero)
    Demosthenes,-is = m., Demosthenes, a famous 4th-century BC Athenian orator
    spiritus,-us = m., breath
    pronuntio (1) = to recite
3. Iste communi sensu caret. (Horace)
    sensus,-us = m., sense
4. Cornua cervum a periculis defendunt. (Martial)
    cervus,-i = m., stag
    defendo, defendere, defendi, defensum = to defend
5. Magno metu me liberabis si ex urbe manum tuam tecum duces. (Cicero)

6. Iussu Caesaris ancorae sublatae sunt. (Caesar)

> *iussū* = by the order
>
> *ancora,-ae* = f., anchor
>
> *Caesar, Caesaris* = Julius Caesar

7. Civitas nostra eo tempore fructibus pacis libertatisque caruit.

8. Colosseum est magnum amphitheatrum quod etiam nunc stat. Hīc Romani ludos spectabant. Gladiatores aut contra homines aut contra animalia ibi pugnabant. Multi gladiatores liberabantur quod bene pugnaverant.

> *amphitheatrum,-i* = n., amphitheater
>
> *sto, stare, steti, statum* = to stand
>
> *hīc* = adv., here
>
> *ludus,-i* = m., game
>
> *specto* (1) = to watch
>
> *gladiator,-oris* = m., gladiator
>
> *contra* = against
>
> *pugno* (1) = to fight

Text Translations

This account is based on Livy and others who affirm that Rome had a total of seven kings.

Post Romulum, Numa Pompilius factus est rex Romanorum. Hic pacem amavit et Romanis leges multas bonasque dedit. Aedificia[1] templaque[2] quoque[3] a Numā facta sunt. Tullius Hostilius erat tertius[4] rex Romae et multa bella gessit. Denique (post trigenta[5] duo annos belli!) Juppiter[6] Tullium cum fulmine[7] percussit.[8] Ancus Martius, nepos[9] Numae, erat proximus[10] rex. Janiculum[11] collem[12] non solum muro[13] sed etiam ponte[14] urbi iunxit. Tum Tarquinius Priscus Romanos regnavit;[15] aedificavit[16] Circum[17] Maximum ubi Romani cursus[18] cum curribus[19] habebant. Servius Tullius, proximus rex, colles Romae ad septem[20] augebat.[21] Circum[22] colles murum et circum murum fossas[23] fecit. Ultimus[24] rex Romanorum erat Tarquinius Superbus et bene diuque regnavit sed quod is et filius suus crudeles[25] erant, Romani regnum[26] regum deposuerunt.[27]

1. **aedificium,-i** n., building
2. **templum,-i** n., temple
3. **quoque** adv., also
4. **tertius,-a,-um** third
5. **trigenta duo** thirty-two
6. **Juppiter** m., Jupiter, chief of the gods
7. **fulmen, fulminis** n., thunderbolt
8. **percutio,-cutere,-cussi,-cussum** to strike
9. **nepos, nepotis** m., grandson
10. **proximus,-a,-um** next
11. **Janiculum,-i** hill west of Rome on right bank of Tiber
12. **collis,-is** m., hill
13. **murus,-i** m., wall
14. **pons, pontis** m., bridge
15. **regno (1)** to reign/rule
16. **aedifico (1)** to build
17. **Circus Maximus** m., the great racetrack at Rome
18. **cursus,-us** m., race
19. **currus,-us** m., chariot
20. **septem** seven
21. **augeo, augere, auxi, auctum** to increase
22. **circum** adv., around
23. **fossa,-ae** f., ditch
24. **ultimus,-a,-um** last
25. **crudelis,-is** cruel
26. **regnum,-i** n., rule
27. **depono,-ponere,-posui,-positum** to lay aside

Review Work Sheet: Chapter XVIII

I. Provide the missing Principal Parts.

     1. disco
     2. contineo
     3. gero
     4. neglego
     5. muto
     6. iacio
     7. tollo
     8. iungo
     9. traho
   10. sentio

II. Provide the appropriate conjugated Latin verb for:

     1. they had thrown
     2. we sensed
     3. Did you consider?
     4. you remained
     5. they had been expected
     6. we were terrified
     7. you (pl.) will be deprived
     8. she had been able
     9. he will be seized
   10. he neglected

5th Declension Nouns
Irregular Pronoun *idem, eadem, idem*

Objectives
To enable you to:
1. recognize, translate, and decline 5th Declension Nouns;
2. recognize, translate, and decline the Irregular 2nd Declension Noun *deus,-i;*
3. recognize, translate, and decline the Irregular Pronoun *idem, eadem, idem.*

5th Declension Nouns

You will be glad to know that the 5th declension represents the last declension of Latin nouns. Most 5th Declension Nouns are feminine, with the exception of *diēs, diēī* = m., day.

	m./f.		*rēs, reī* = f., thing	
Nom.	**-ēs**	**-ēs**	**rēs**	**rēs**
Gen.	**-eī**	**-ērum**	**reī**	**rērum**
Dat.	**-eī**	**-ēbus**	**reī**	**rēbus**
Acc.	**-em**	**-ēs**	**rem**	**rēs**
Abl.	**-ē**	**-ēbus**	**rē**	**rēbus**

There are three short Latin words beginning with the letter "**d**," completely unrelated but often confused, that I want to clearly distinguish:

	*deus,-ī** = m., god		*diēs,-ēī* = m., day		*diū* = adv., for a long time
Nom.	de**us**	de**i** <u>or</u> d**ī**	di**ēs**	di**ēs**
Gen.	de**ī**	de**ōrum**	di**ēī**	di**ērum**
Dat.	de**ō**	de**is** <u>or</u> d**īs**	di**ēī**	di**ēbus**
Acc.	de**um**	de**ōs**	di**em**	di**ēs**
Abl.	de**ō**	de**is** <u>or</u> d**īs**	di**ē**	di**ēbus**

*2nd Declension Noun with possible Irregular forms in the Plural.

Irregular Pronoun idem, eadem, idem

The Irregular Pronoun *īdem, eadem, idem* represents a combination of the Personal Pronoun *is, ea, id* (he, she, it, this, that) plus the indeclinable suffix *-dem* (the same). The spelling changes are phonetic: *m* before *d* always changes to *n*; double *d* is redundant and thus not used; the Romans could not decide on *s* plus *d* and consequently deleted it in some instances and retained it in others.

idem, eadem, idem = the same

	Sing.			Pl.		
	m.	f.	n.	m.	f.	n.
Nom.	īdem	eadem	idem	eidem	eaedem	eadem
Gen.	eiusdem	eiusdem	eiusdem	eōrundem	eārundem	eōrundem
Dat.	eīdem	eīdem	eīdem	eīsdem	eīsdem	eīsdem
Acc.	eundem	eandem	idem	eōsdem	eāsdem	eadem
Abl.	eōdem	eādem	eōdem	eīsdem	eīsdem	eīsdem

Vocabulary

deus,-ī m., god
diēs, diēī m., day
fidēs,-eī f., faith/trust
genus, generis n., class/kind
lūdus,-ī m., school/game
rēs,reī f., thing
rēs pūblica, reī pūblicae f., republic
spēs,-eī f., hope

īdem, eadem, idem the same

alō, alere, aluī, altum to support/nourish/sustain
ēripiō, ēripere, ēripuī, ereptum to rescue/take away
terreō, terrēre, terruī, territum to frighten/terrify

unde whence/from which
utrum . . . an whether . . . or

Exercises

A. Using a paradigm format that indicates cases and number, decline:

    1. res publica   3. omnis spes
    2. idem dies   4. eadem fides

B. Translate the following according to their declined meaning.

    1. eodem tempore   6. eundem deum
    2. communi spe   7. perpetuorum dierum
    3. eadem scelera   8. eiusdem fidei
    4. eisdem ludis   9. communia genera
    5. eādem nocte   10. eosdem metus

C. Using paradigm formats that indicate tenses and voices, give a synopsis Active and Passive with English translations of the following verbs in the persons indicated.

    1. terreo, terrere, terrui, territum in 1st Pers. Sing. M.
    2. eripio, eripere, eripui, ereptum in 3rd Pl. F.

D. Form the Passive Infinitives with the English translation of the following verbs.

    1. tollo, tollere   4. libero, liberare
    2. terreo, terrere   5. alo, alere
    3. eripio, eripere   6. contineo, continere

E. Render the following verbs forms into Latin.

    1. we will have been rescued
    2. they had been sustained
    3. you were terrified
    4. it will nourish
    5. I have terrified

F. Sentence translations.

    1. Dum vita est, spes est. (Cicero)
    2. Carpe diem! *carpo, carpere, carpsi, carptum* = to seize/use (Horace)
    3. Et mihi res subiungam non me rebus. (Horace)
        subiungo,-iungere,-iunxi,-iunctum = to subject
    4. Est modus in rebus. Sunt certi fines ultra quos virtus non potest esse. (Horace)
        ultra + acc. = beyond
    5. Felix est qui potest causas rerum intellegere; et fortunatus ille qui deos diligit.
       (Virgil)
        fortunatus,-a,-um = fortunate
        intellego, intellegere, intellexi, intellectum = to understand

6. Civi et rei publicae. (Motto of the University of Oklahoma)

7. Amicus certus in re incertā decernitur. (Cicero)

   decerno,-cernere,-crevi,-cretum = to discern

8. Stoicus noster, "Vitium," inquit, "non est in rebus sed in animo ipso." (Seneca)

   stoicus,-i = m., stoic

   inquit = (he) says

9. Fuerunt quondam in hāc re publicā viri magnae virtutis et antiquae fidei.
   (Cicero)

10. Res publica consiliis meis eo die ex igne atque ferro erepta est. (Cicero)

    ferrus,-i = m., sword/iron

Text Translation

Pliny the Younger (AD 61–112) states in a letter to the historian Tacitus that he was eighteen years old when Vesuvius erupted (79 AD) and obliterated the towns of Pompeii, Herculaneum, and Stabiae. Pliny was in Misenum visiting his uncle Pliny the Elder, who was in charge of the Roman fleet in the Bay of Naples. When the elder Pliny saw the unusual cloud over Vesuvius, he immediately set out to investigate. He lost his life as a result of the poisonous fumes.

Eramus Miseni[1] ubi avunculus[2] meus classem[3] imperio[4] regebat.[5] Horā fere septimā[6] mater mea vidit nubem inusitatam[7] et in magnitudine[8] et in specie.[9] Ille qui in lecto[10] studuerat,[11] rogavit[12] soleas[13] suas et ascendit[14] locum ex quo videre poterat. Incertum erat ex quo monte[15] nubes (candida[16] nunc, nunc sordida[17] et maculosa[18] ut[19] terram an[20] cinerem[21] portabat[22]) veniebat. Properat[23] ad illum locum unde alii fugiebant. Iam in navibus[24] cineres; iam pumices[25] atque ignis lapides;[26] iam vadum[27] subitum ruinaque[28] montis ubi ante fuerat litus.[29] Nautae terrebantur. Gubernator[30] cupivit[31] rotare[32] navem. Sed meus avunculus, "Fortes," inquit,[33] "fortuna iuvat: litus pete!"[34]

(*C. Plinii Caecilii Secundi: Epistularum* Bk. VI, xvi)

1. **Misenum,-i** n., Misenum, translate "at Misenum"
2. **avunculus,-i** m., uncle
3. **classis,-is** f., fleet
4. **imperium,-i** n., official authority
5. **rego, regere, rexi, rectum** to direct
6. **septimus,-a,-um** seventh
7. **inusitatus,-a,-um** unusual
8. **magnitudo,-inis** f., magnitude
9. **species,-ei** f., appearance
10. **lectus,-i** m., couch
11. **studeo, studere, studui** to be studying
12. **rogo (1)** to ask for
13. **solea,-ae** f., sandal
14. **ascendo,-cendere,-cendi,-censum** to go up
15. **mons, montis** m., mountain
16. **candidus,-a,-um** shining white
17. **sordidus,-a,-um** dirty
18. **maculosus,-a,-um** stained
19. **ut + indic. verb** as
20. **an** or
21. **cinis, cineris** m., ash
22. **porto (1)** to carry
23. **propero (1)** to hasten
24. **navis,-is** f., ship
25. **pumex, pumicis** m., pumice
26. **lapis, lapidis** m., stone
27. **vadum,-i** n., shallow
28. **ruina,-ae** f., ruin
29. **litus, litoris** n., shore
30. **gubernator,-oris** m., navigator
31. **cupio, cupere, cupivi, cupitum** to desire
32. **roto (1)** to turn around
33. **inquit** said
34. **peto, petere, petivi, petitum** to seek

Latin Abbreviations Used in English

A.B.	(*artium baccalaureus*)	Bachelor of Arts
AD	(*anno domini*)	in the year of the Lord
ad lib	(*ad libitum*)	in accordance with one's wishes
aet.	(*aetate, aetatis*)	in the age, of age
a.m.	(*ante meridiem*)	before noon
AM	(*artium magister*)	Master of Arts
ca.	(*circa*)	around
cf.	(*confer*)	compare
e.g.	(*exempli gratia*)	for example
et al.	(*et alii, et alia*)	and other, and other things
etc.	(*et cetera*)	and other things
et seq.	(*et sequitur*)	and it follows; a logical inference
ibid.	(*ibidem*)	in the same place
id.	(*idem*)	the same author
i.e.	(*id est*)	that is
JD	(*iuris doctor*)	Doctor of Law
lb.	(*libra*)	pound
loc. cit.	(*loco citato*)	in the place cited
ms.	(*manu scriptum*)	manuscript
N.B.	(*nota bene*)	note well
no.	(*numero*)	number
non seq.	(*non sequitur*)	it does not follow logically
ob.	(*obiit*)	he/she died
op. cit.	(*opere citato*)	in the work cited
percent	(*per centum*)	by the hundred
PhD	(*philosophiae doctor*)	Doctor of Philosophy
p.m.	(*post meridiem*)	after midday
pro tem.	(*pro tempore*)	for the time being
p.s.	(*postscriptum*)	written afterward, postscript
Q.E.D.	(*quod erat demonstrandum*)	which was to be demonstrated
q.v.	(*quod vide*)	which see
sc.	(*scire licet*)	it is permitted to know/namely
v.	(*vide*)	see
viz.	(*videre licet*)	it is permitted to see/namely
vs.	(*versus*)	against

Participles:
Participle Formation,
Declension of Participles,
Translation of a Participle

Objectives

To enable you to:
1. understand that Participles are Verbal Adjectives that are formed from verbs;
2. recognize, translate, form, and decline Participles.

Participles

Participles are Verbal Adjectives and represent an ingenious sort of shorthand, which involves making Adjectives from Verbs. The use of Participles also renders smoother and more easily understood speech. I will show you what I mean.

Without Participles:

Caesar was loved by the crowd; he was leading his army; he was about to receive the rule; he was deserving to be praised; he was happy. (twenty-seven words)

With Participles (underlined words):

Caesar, <u>loved</u> by the crowd, <u>leading</u> his army, <u>deserving to be praised</u>, and <u>about to receive</u> the rule, was happy. (twenty words)

Using Participles, the Romans can say the same thing in <u>eleven words</u>!

Caesar amatus a vulgo, ducens exercitum, laudandus, accepturus regnum, erat felix.
vulgus,-i = m., crowd   *regnum,-i* = n., rule

Participle Formation

Every regular Latin verb has four Participles, two Active and two Passive. Here are the steps to form them:

1. For the **Present Active Participle** for 1st, 2nd, and 3rd Conjugation verbs, drop the final two letters from the Active Infinitive and add *–ns* for the Nominative Singular, *-ntis* for the Genitive Singular; for 3rd-*io* and 4th Conjugations, drop the final three letters from the Active Infinitive and add *-iens,-ientis.*

2. The fourth Principal Part of a regular verb is the **Perfect Passive Participle.**

3. To form the **Future Active Participle**, replace the *–us,-a,-um* of the Perfect Passive Participle with *-urus,-ura,-urum.*

4. For the **Future Passive Participle,** drop the final two letters from the Active Infinitive and add *–ndus,-nda,-ndum* (for 1st, 2nd, and 3rd Conjugation verbs); drop the final three letters from the Active Infinitive and add *-iendus, -ienda,-iendum* (for 3rd-*io* and 4th Conjugations.)

Participle Endings for 1st, 2nd, and 3rd Conjugation verbs

	Active	Passive
Present	*-ns* (nominative) *-ntis* (genitive)	—
Perfect	—	*-us,-a,-um*
Future	*-ūrus,-a,-um*	*-ndus,-a,-um*

Participle Endings for 3rd-*io* and 4th Conjugations

	Active	Passive
Present	*-iens* (nominative) *-ientis* (genitive)	—
Perfect	—	*-us,-a,-um*
Future	*-ūrus,-a,-um*	*-iendus,-a,-um*

Participles of *ago, agere, egi, actum* (to do)

	Active	Passive
Present	*agēns, agentis* = adj, doing	—
Perfect	—	*āctus,-a,-um* = adj, (having been)* done
Future	*āctūrus,-a,-um* = adj., about to do	*agendus,-a,-um* = adj., (fit/deserving)* to be done

* The words in parentheses are not generally rendered in translation.

Declension of Participles of ago, agere, egi, actum

Present Active Participle

	\multicolumn{2}{c}{Sing.}	\multicolumn{2}{c}{Pl.}
	m./f.	n.	m./f.	n.
Nom.	agens	agens	agentēs	agentia
Gen.	agentis	agentis	agentium	agentium
Dat.	agentī	agentī	agentibus	agentibus
Acc.	agentem	agens	agentēs	agentia
Abl.	agente*	agente	agentibus	agentibus

* The Ablative ends in -ī only when an essential part of the personality, i.e., by a loving father = *ab amantī patre.*

Perfect Passive Participle

	\multicolumn{3}{c}{Sing.}	\multicolumn{3}{c}{Pl.}
	m.	f.	n.	m.	f.	n.
Nom.	āctus	ācta	āctum	āctī	āctae	ācta
Gen.	āctī	āctae	āctī	āctōrum	āctārum	āctōrum
Dat.	āctō	āctae	āctō	actīs	āctīs	āctīs
Acc.	āctum	āctam	āctum	āctōs	āctās	ācta
Abl.	āctō	āctā	āctō	āctīs	āctīs	āctīs

Future Active Participle

	\multicolumn{3}{c}{Sing.}	\multicolumn{3}{c}{Pl.}
	m.	f.	n.	m.	f.	n.
Nom.	āctūrus	āctūra	āctūrum	āctūrī	āctūrae	āctūra
Gen.	āctūrī	āctūrae	āctūrī	āctūrōrum	āctūrārum	āctūrōrum
Dat.	āctūrō	āctūrae	āctūrō	āctūrīs	āctūrīs	āctūrīs
Acc.	āctūrum	āctūram	āctūrum	āctūrōs	āctūrās	āctūra
Abl.	āctūrō	āctūra	āctūrō	āctūrīs	āctūrīs	āctūrīs

Future Passive Participle

	\multicolumn{3}{c}{Sing.}	\multicolumn{3}{c}{Pl.}
	m.	f.	n.	m.	f.	n.
Nom.	agendus	agenda	agendum	agendī	agendae	agenda
Gen.	agendī	agendae	agendī	agendōrum	agendārum	agendorum
Dat.	agendō	agendae	agendō	agendīs	agendīs	agendīs
Acc.	agendum	agendam	agendum	agendōs	agendās	agenda
Abl.	agendō	agendā	agendō	agendīs	agendīs	agendīs

Translation of a Participle

A Participle can be translated literally as a Verbal Adjective or as a conjugated verb employing English conjunctions such as *when, since, although, because, after*. The easiest and best plan for a beginning Latin student at your current level is to translate Participles literally.

Literal Translation:

1. *Videns suum amicum, vir erat felix.*
   Seeing his friend, the man was happy.
   When, since, after he saw his friend,*

2. *Visurus suos amicos, vir erat felix.*
   About to see his friends, the man was happy.
   Because, since he was about to see his friends,*

3. *Iutus ab amicis suis, vir erat felix.*
   Having been helped by his friends, the man was happy.
   After, since he had been helped by his friends,*

4. *Laudandus a senatu, vir erat felix.*
   Deserving to be praised by the senate, the man was happy.
   Because, since he was to be praised by the senate,*

* Using Conjunctions and Conjugated Verbs.

You will get the hang of all this with a little practice. And the **exercises** that follow **are designed to identify, resolve, and clarify all the questions** you ever thought you might have regarding Participles.

Vocabulary

cupiō, cupere, cupīvī, cupītum to wish/desire
petō, petere, petīvī, petītum to seek/petition
premō, premere, pressī, pressum to press/pursue/press hard
vertō, vertere, vertī, versum to turn

fātum,-ī n., fate
iustitia,-ae f., justice
ōrātor, ōrātōris m., orator
scientia,-ae f., knowledge
servus,-ī m., slave
signum,-ī n., sign/seal
victor, victōris m., victor

Exercises

A. Using **peto**, **petere**, **petivi**, **petitum**:

1. give a synopsis (paradigm format) in 3rd Sing. M. with the English translation of each conjugated form;
2. form the Participles, declining them completely into the m., f., and n. sing. and pl. forms.

B. Using a paradigm format listing tenses and voices, form the Participles (Nom and Gen. Sing. of Pres. Act., Nom. Sing. forms of rest) of the following verbs.

1. premo, premere, pressi, pressum
2. cupio, cupere, cupivi, cupitum
3. ago, agere, egi, actum
4. laudo, laudare, laudavi, laudatum

C. Using a paradigm format indicating cases and number, decline:

1. movens orator
2. signum dandum
3. poeta incepturus
4. amata puella

D. Translate the following into Latin.

1. the written words
2. the army about to turn the war
3. driving fates
4. of the desired slave
5. to the turning orator
6. for those seeking peace
7. a people fit to be helped
8. having been pressed
9. about to be victors
10. the petitioned knowledge

E. Identify the case and translate the following Participles into English.

1. premendos
2. scripturus
3. cupientes
4. petentis
5. videndorum
6. facienda
7. dicens
8. petitis
9. versuris
10. laudato

F. Render the following sentences into Latin, being sure to use participles for the underlined words.

1. For those <u>seeking</u> justice, the <u>written</u> law is never neglected.
2. <u>After learning</u> these things, we sought new knowledge.
3. The men <u>about to petition</u> the orator were seized by those <u>fearing</u> the army.
4. Not all books are <u>fit to be read</u>.
5. Can a person <u>neglecting</u> small things accomplish great things?
6. Praise <u>sustained</u> by truth is not able to be destroyed.

G. Translations.

1. Territi ex illā re publicā fugerunt.
2. Timeo Graecos dona ferentes.
    ferens,-ntis = bearing
3. Graecia capta ferum victorem cepit. (Horace)
    ferus,-a,-um = wild/uncultured
4. Aptissima arma senectutis sunt artes exercitationesque virtutum quia
    memoria vitae bene actae multorumque bene factorum iucunda est. (Cicero)
    aptissimus,-a,-um = most effective/most apt
    exercitatio,-ionis = f., exercise
    quia = because
    iucundus,-a,-um = pleasant
5. Is qui timens vivet, liber non erit umquam. (Horace)
    umquam = adv., ever
6. Non is est miser qui iussus aliquid facit, sed is qui invitus facit. (Seneca)
    aliquis, aliquid = someone, something
    invitus,-a,-um = unwilling
7. Cura oratoris dicturi eos audituros delectat. (Quintilian)
    delecto (1) = to delight
8. Saepe stilum verte, bonum librum scripturus. (Horace)
    stilus,-i = m., stylus
9. Thais habet nigros, niveos Laecania dentes. Quae ratio est? Emptos haec
    habet, illa suos. (Martial)
    Thais = f., Proper Noun
    Laecania = f. Proper Noun
    dens, dentis = m., tooth
    niger,-gra,-grum = black
    niveus,-a,-um = snowy
    emo, emere, emi, emptum = to buy
10. Vox audita perit, littera scripta manet.
    vox, vocis = f., voice
    perire = to perish

Text Translation

Between 46 and 44 BC Cicero (106–43 BC) wrote most of his philosophical works. The following excerpt on justice is adapted from book II of his *De Officiis*.

Quis non diligit splendorem[1] et pulchritudinem[2] virtutis et maxime[3] iustitiam ex quā virtute viri boni appellantur?[4] Etiam solitario[5] homini agenti vitam in agro, opinio[6] iustitiae necesse[7] est, eique magis,[8] quod si hanc opinionem non habet, iniustus[9] ducitur[10] et victima[11] erit multorum malorum. Atque eis vendentibus[12] et ementibus[13] iustitia ad <u>rem gerendam</u>[14] necesse est. <u>Ne</u>[15] viri <u>quidem</u> mali vivere possunt sine ullā iustitiā ut[16] dicuntur esse leges etiam apud[17] latrones.[18] Si iustitia tantam[19] vim habet apud latrones, tantum magis habet in legibus et iudiciis in constitutā[20] re publicā. Eis cupientibus gloriam et nomen bonum, officia requisita[21] iustitiae primum[22] debent geri.

1. **splendor,-oris** m., splendor
2. **pulchritudo,-inis** f., beauty
3. **maxime** adv., especially
4. **appello (1)** to call/name
5. **solitarius,-a,-um** solitary
6. **opinio,-onis** f., reputation
7. **necesse** indeclinable adj., necessary
8. **magis** adv., more
9. **iniustus,-a,-um** unjust
10. **duco, ducere** to consider
11. **victima,-ae** f., victim
12. **vendo, vendere, vendidi, venditum** to sell
13. **emo, emere, emi, emptum** to buy
14. **res gerenda** "business"
15. **ne . . . quidem** not even
16. **ut + indic. verb** as
17. **apud + acc.** among
18. **latro, latronis** m., thief
19. **tantus,-a,-um** so much/so great
20. **constitutus,-a,-um** arranged/"constitutional"
21. **requiro, requirere, requisi, requisitum** to require
22. **primum** adv., first

Review Work Sheet: Chapters XVIII–XX

I. Using the verb ***verto***, ***vertere***, ***verti***, ***versum***:

1. give a synopsis in 3rd Plural Neuter of all passive and active tenses using a paradigm format identifying tenses and voices;
2. form the participles (nominative case only); using a paradigm format identifying tenses and voices;
3. form the imperatives.

II. Using paradigm formats identifying cases and number, decline:

1. premens exercitus
2. dies cupiendus
3. alta spes
4. manus scriptura

III. Render the following participial phrases into Latin.

1. the woman about to speak
2. for a people seeking peace
3. in a republic lacking serious fears
4. of known crimes
5. the thing to be sought

IV. Render the following sentences into Latin, being sure to make the participle agree in case, number, and gender with the noun it modifies.

1. We seized the men terrifying the state.
2. Terrifying the state, the army of the tyrant was at last contained.
3. The petitioned peace was supported by a senate fearing war.
4. Hope had not been destroyed in those about to flee.
5. Will the same crimes and the same faults destroy our new republic?
6. The orator about to speak was recognized by no one.
7. Will we now be able to live in peace and without serious fears?

Vocabulary: Chapters XVII-XX

alō, alere, aluī, altum to support/nourish/sustain

careō, carēre, caruī, caritūrus
   + abl. of sep to lack/be separated from/deprive
causa,-ae f., cause/reason/case
commūnis,-e common
contineō,-tinēre,-tinuī,-tentum to contain/hold
   together
cupiō, cupere, cupīvī, cupītum to wish/desire

deus,-ī m., god
diēs,-ēī m., day

ēripiō, ēripere, ēripuī, ēreptum to rescue/take
   away
exercitus,-ūs m., army

fātum,-ī neut., fate
fidēs,-eī f., faith/trust
fīnis,-is m., end/boundary; pl. = territory
frūctus,-ūs m., profit/fruit

genus, generis neut., class/kind
gravis,-e heavy/serious/grave

iam adv., now/already
īdem, eadem, idem the same
ignis,-is m., fire
ita adv., so
iubeō, iubēre, iussī, iussum to order/command
iustitia,-ae f., justice
lēx, lēgis f., law
līberō (1) to free/liberate
lūdus,-ī m., game/school

manus,-ūs f., hand/handwriting/military
   detachment
metus,-ūs m., fear
modus,-ī m., measure/bound

ōrātor, ōrātōris m., orator

petō, petere, petīvī, petītum to seek/petition
premō, premere, pressī, pressum to
   press/pursue/press hard
prīvō (1) to deprive
quis? quid? interr. pron., who? what?

rapiō, rapere, rapuī, raptum to seize/carry
   away/snatch
rēs pūblica, reī pūblicae f., republic
scelus, sceleris neut., crime/sin
scientia,-ae f., knowledge
senātus,-ūs m., senate
servus,-ī m., slave
signum,-ī neut., sign/seal/signal
spēs,-eī f., hope

terreō, terrēre, terruī, territum to frighten/terrify
tollō, tollere, sustulī, sublātum to raise/destroy/lift
   up

unde whence/from which
utrum . . . an whether . . . or

versus,-ūs m., verse/line
vertō, vertere, vertī, versum to turn
victor, victōris m., victor

154

Vocabulary: Chapters I–XX

ab (ā) + abl. from/away from
ācer, ācris, ācre sharp/fierce/keen
adv. + acc. toward/to (with verbs of motion)
aetās, aetātis f., age
ager, agrī m., field/farm
agō, agere, ēgī, āctum to do/lead/act/drive
agricola,-ae m., farmer
alius, alia, aliud another/other
alo, alere, aluī, altum to support/nourish/sustain
amīca,-ae f., friend
amīcitia,-ae f., friendship
amīcus,-ī m., friend
amō (1) to love
amor, amōris m., love
animal, animalis neut., animal
animus,-ī m., soul/spirit
annus,-ī m., year
ante + acc. before
antīquus,-a,-um old/ancient
arma, armōrum neut., weapons/arms
ars, artis f., art/skill
Asia,-ae f., Asia
at but
atque *or* **ac** and/and also/and even
audeō, audēre, ausus sum to dare
audiō, audīre, audīvī, audītum to hear/to listen to
aut or
aut . . . aut either . . . or
autem moreover/however
auxilium,-ī neut., help/aid

beātus,-a,-um blessed/happy
bellum,-ī, neut., war
bellus,-a,-um pretty
bene adv., well
bonus,-a,-um good
brevis,-e brief

caelum,-ī neut., sky/heaven
Caesar, Caesaris m., Caesar
capiō, capere, cēpī, captum to capture/seize
careō, carēre, caruī, caritūrus + abl. of sep. to lack/deprive
cārus,-a,-um dear
causa,-ae f., cause/reason/case; gen. + **causā** for the sake of
celer, celeris, celere swift/quick/rapid
certus,-a,-um certain
Cicerō, Cicerōnis m., Cicero
cīvis, cīvis m., citizen

cīvitās, cīvitātis f., state
cōgitō (1) to think/understand/consider
cognōscō,-nōscere,-nōvī,-nitum to know/be acquainted with
committō,-mittere,-mīsī,-missum to commit/entrust
commūnis,-e common
cōnsilium,-ī neut., plan
contineō,-tinēre,-tinuī,-tentum to contain/hold together
cōpia,-ae f., abundance/supply; pl., troops/forces/supplies
corpus, corporis neut., body
cornū,-ūs neut., horn
culpa,-ae f., fault/blame
culpō (1) to blame
cum + abl. with
cum + indic. verb when
cupiō, cupere, cupīvī, cupītum to wish/desire
cūr why?
cūra,-ae f., care/anxiety
currō, currere, cucurrī, cursum to run

dē + abl. about/from
dēbeō, dēbēre, dēbuī, dēbitum to ought/owe
deleo, delere, delevi, deletum to destroy/delete/wipe out
dēnique adv., finally
deus,-ī m., god
dīcō, dīcere, dīxī, dictum to say/tell
diēs, diēī m., day
difficilis,-e difficult
dīligō, dīligere, dīlēxī, dīlēctum to esteem
discō, discere, didicī to learn
diū adv., for a long time
dō, dare, dedi, datum to give
doceō, docere, docuī, doctum to teach
dōnum,-i neut., gift
dūcō, dūcere, dūxī, ductum to lead
dulcis,-e sweet/pleasant/agreeable
dum adv. and conj., while
dūrus,-a,-um hard/harsh

ego, meī I
ergō adv., therefore
ēripiō, ēripere, ēripuī, ēreptum to rescue/take away
errō (1) to err/go astray
et and
etiam even/also

ex/ē + abl. out of/from
exemplar, exemplaris neut., example/model
exercitus,-ūs m., army
exspectō (1) to expect/await

faciō, facere, fēcī, factum to make/do
factum,-i neut., deed
fāma,-ae f., fame/rumor
fatum,-i neut., fate
fēlix, fēlīcis happy/lucky
fēmina,-ae f., woman
ferē adv., almost
festīnō (1) to hasten
fidēs,-eī f., faith/trust
filia,-ae f., daughter
filius,-ī m., son
fīnis,-is m., end/limit/boundary; pl., territory
fōrma,-ae f., shape/form/beauty
fortis,-e strong/brave
fortūna,-ae f., fortune/luck
frāter, frātris m., brother
frūctus,-ūs m., profit/fruit
fugiō, fugere, fūgī, fugitūrus to flee

gēns, gentis f., gens, clan
genus, generis neut., class/kind
gerō, gerere, gessī, gestum to carry on/conduct/accomplish
glōria,-ae f., glory
Graecia,-ae f., Greece
Graecus,-a,-um Greek
gravis,-e heavy/serious/severe

habeō, habēre, habuī, habitum to have/hold/possess
hic, haec, hoc this/the latter
historia,-ae f., story/history
homō, hominis m., human being/man
honor,honōris m., honor/office
hōra,-ae f., hour

iaciō, iacere, iēcī, iactum to throw/hurl
iam adv., now/already
ibi adv., there
īdem, eadem, idem the same
igitur adv., therefore/then
ignis,-is m., fire
ille, illa, illud that/the former
in + abl. in/on + **acc.** into
incertus,-a,-um uncertain
incipiō, incipere, incēpī, inceptum to begin
inde adv., thence

insidiae,-ārum f., plots,treachery
inter + acc. between/among
inveniō, invenīre, invēnī, inventum to discover/come upon
ipse, ipsa, ipsum himself/herself/itself
īra,-ae f., anger
is, ea, id, he, she, it, this, that
iste, ista, istud such
ita adv., so
Italia,-ae f., Italy
itaque adv., and so
iubeō, iubēre, iussī, iussum to order/command
iūdicium,-ī neut., judgment/decision
iungō, iungere, iūnxī, iūnctum to join
iūs, iūris neut., right/law
iustitia,-ae f., justice
iuvō, iuvāre, iūvī, iūtum to help/aid

labor, labōris m., labor/work/task
laudō (1) to praise
laus, laudis f., praise
legō, legere, lēgī, lēctum to read/choose
lentē adv., slowly
lēx, lēgis f., law
liber, lībera, līberum free
liber, librī m., book
līberō (1) to free/liberate
lībertās, lībertātis f., liberty/freedom
littera,-ae f., letter of alphabet; pl., epistle/literature
loca, locōrum neut., region
locus,-i m., place/passage in literature
longus,-a,-um long
lūdus,-i m., school/game

magister,-trī m., teacher
magnus,-a,-um great
malus,-a,-um bad/evil
manus,-ūs f., hand/handwriting/band of men
mare, maris neut., sea
māter, mātris f., mother
memoria,-ae f., memory
mens, mentis f., mind
metus,-ūs m., fear
meus,-a,-um my
miser, misera, miserum miserable/wretched
mittō, mittere, mīsī, missum to send
modus,-i m., model/mode/bound
moneō, monēre, monuī, monitum to advise/warn
mora,-ae f., delay
mors, mortis f., death
mōs, mōris m., custom/habit; pl., character
moveō, movēre, mōvī, mōtum to move/arouse

multus,-a,-um much/many
mundus,-ī m., world/universe
mūtō (1) to change/alter

nam for
natiō, natiōnis f., nation
natura,-ae f., nature
nauta,-ae m., sailor
neglegō,-legere,-lēxī,-lēctum to neglect/disregard
nesciō, nescīre, nescīvī, nescītum to not know
nihil or **nil** neut., indecl. noun, nothing
nimis (also **nimium**) indecl. adj./adv., too
    much/very much
nōmen, nōminis neut., name
nōn adv., not
nōs, nostrum we
noster,-tra,-trum our
novus,-a,-um new
nox, noctis f., night
nūbēs, nūbis f., cloud
nūllus,-a,-um none/no
numerus,-ī m., number
numquam adv., never
nunc adv., now

obtineō, obtinēre, obtinuī, obtentum to
    hold/possess/obtain
oculus,-ī m., eye
officium,-ī neut., duty/office
omnis,-e every; pl. all
ōrātor, ōrātōris m., orator
ōtium,-ī neut., leisure

parō (1) to obtain/prepare
pars, partis f., part/share
parvus,-a,-um small
pāter, pātris m., father
patria,-ae f., country/homeland
pauci,-ae,-a few
pāx, pācis f., peace
pecūnia,-ae f., money
per + acc. through
perīculum,-ī neut., danger
perpetuus,-a,-um perpetual
petō, petere, petīvī, petītum to seek/petition
philosophia,-ae f., philosophy
poena,-ae f., penalty/punishment
poeta,-ae m., poet
populus,-ī m., people/nation
porta,-ae, f., gate
possum, posse, potuī to be able
post + acc. after

premō, premere, pressī, pressum to
    press/pursue/press hard
prīvō (1) to deprive
propter + acc. on account of/because of
puella,-ae f., girl
puer,-ī m., boy
pulcher, pulchra, pulchrum beautiful/handsome

quam adv. and conj., how
quī? quae? quod? interr. adj., which?/what?
quī, quae, quod rel. pron., who/which/what/that
quis?quid? interr. pron., who? what?
quod because
quondam adv., once
quōniam since

rapiō, rapere, rapuī, raptum to seize/carry away
ratiō, ratiōnis f., reason/judgement
(re)maneō,-manēre,-mānsī,-mānsum to
    remain/stay behind
rēs pūblica, rēi pūblicae f., republic
rēs, reī f., thing
rēx,rēgis m., king
Rōma,-ae f., Rome
Rōmānus,-a,-um Roman

saepe adv., often
salveō, salvēre (only two Principal Parts) to be in
    good health
sapientia,-ae f., wisdom
satis enough (indecl. noun, adj. and adv.)
scelus, sceleris neut., crime/sin
scientia,-ae f., knowledge
sciō, scīre, scīvī, scītum to know
scrībō, scribere, scrīpsī, scrīptum to write
sed but
semper adv., always
senātus,-ūs m., senate
senectūs, senectūtis f., old age
senex, senis adj./noun old
sententia,-ae f., feeling/thought
sentiō, sentīre, sēnsī, sēnsum to feel/perceive/think
servō (1) to save/preserve
servus,-i m., slave
sī if
signum,-ī neut., sign/seal
sine + abl. without
sōlus,-a,-um alone/only
soror, sorōris f., sister
spēs,-eī f., hope
studium,-ī neut., study/eagerness/zeal
stultus,-a,-um foolish

sub under
subitus,-a,-um sudden
————**,suī** 3rd pers. refl. pron., himself, herself, itself
sum, esse, fuī, futūrus to be
superō (1) to surpass/overcome
suus,-a,-um his own/her own/its own

tempestās, tempestātis f., storm/wind
tempus, temporis neut., time
teneō, tenēre, tenuī, tentum to hold/keep/possess
terra,-ae f., land
terreō, terrēre, terruī, territum to frighten/terrify
timeō, timere, timuī to fear/to be afraid
tolerō (1) to tolerate/endure
tollō, tollere, sustulī, sublātum to raise/destroy/ lift up
tōtus,-a,-um whole/entire
trahō, trahere, trāxī, tractum to derive/draw/drag/get
trāns + acc. across
tum adv., then
tū, tuī you (sing.)
tuus,-a,-um your (sing.)
tyrannus,-ī m., tyrant/absolute ruler

ubi adv., when/where
ūllus,-a,-um any

unde adv., whence/from which
ūnus,-a,-um one
urbs, urbis f., city

valeō, valēre, valuī, valitūrus to be strong
veniō, venīre, vēnī, ventum to come
verbum,-ī neut., word
vēritās, vēritātis f., truth
versus,-ūs m., verse/line
vertō, vertere, vertī, versum to turn
vērus,-a,-um true/real/proper
vester, vestra, vestrum your (pl.)
via,-ae f., way/road/street
victor, victōris m., victor
videō, vidēre, vīdī, vīsum to see/understand
vincō, vincere, vīcī, victum to conquer
vir,-ī m., man
virgo, virginis f., virgin/maiden
virtūs, virtūtis f., courage/character/virtue
vis, vis f., force; pl., strength
vita,-ae f., life
vitium,-ī neut., vice/fault
vītō (1) to avoid/shun
vīvō, vivere, vīxī, vīctum to live
vocō (1) to call
vōs, vestrum you (pl.)

Grammar Review: Chapters I–XX:

Review Sheet I: Nouns

I.   Latin declined nouns have six possible cases. List the cases and identify the grammatical usage of each case.

II. List the genitive singular endings determining each of the five declensions.

III. Using paradigm formats indicating case and number, decline the following nouns. Give the English translation of each declined form of *gloria,-ae.*

      1. gloria,-ae   5. oculus,-i

      2. officium,-i   6. lex, legis

      3. nomen, nominis   7. mare, maris

      4. senatus,-us   8. res publica, rei publicae

IV. Fill in the blanks with the appropriate form of the Latin <u>declined</u> noun.

    1. _____ of good grades is hard work.
      The cause

    2. The power _____ is great.
            of friendship

    3. We praise _____.
          courage

    4. The letter _____ was written _____.
         for the king   by a slave

    5. I saw the king _____.
           among the people

    6. He gave _____ _____.
          gifts   to the leaders

    7. _____ of success is a powerful _____.
      Love   force

Review Sheet II: Verbs

I.   Grammatically, a conjugated verb indicates five things:

    1.   2.   3.   4.   5.

II.   Verbs are divided into four major categories based on the spelling of the _____.

III.   Identify the conjugation of each of the following verbs.

    1. scio, scire   4. erro, errare
    2. cupio, cupere   5. peto, petere
    3. video, videre

IV.   Form the Singular and Plural Imperatives of the following verbs.

	Sing.	Pl.
1. *venio, venire*	_____	_____
2. *audeo, audere*	_____	_____
3. *laudo, laudare*	_____	_____
4. *facio, facere*	_____	_____
5. *vivo, vivere*	_____	_____
6. *fugio, fugere*	_____	_____

V.   List the Active and then the Passive Personal Endings for conjugated verbs followed by the English pronoun equivalents.

VI.   Using a paradigm format listing tenses, give a synopsis of the following verbs in the person indicated. Give the English translation of each conjugated <u>form.</u>

    1. *sum, esse, fui, futurus* in 3rd Person Singular Feminine
    2. *possum, posse, potui* in 3rd Person Plural

VII.   The general Future Tense sign for 1st and 2nd Conjugation verbs is:_____; the general Future Tense sign for 3rd, 3rd-*io,* and 4th Conjugation verbs is: _____; the Imperfect Tense sign for all verbs is: _____.

VIII.   Using paradigm formats indicating tense and voice, give a synopsis of the verbs below in the person indicated

    1. *teneo, tenere, tenui, tentum*   1st Pers. Pl. M. (Give English translations)
    2. *do, dare, dedi, datum*   3rd Pers. Pl. Neut.
    3. *scio, scire, scivi, scitum*   3rd Pers. Pl. F.
    4. *lego, legere, legi, lectum*   2nd Pers. Pl. M.
    5. *cupio, cupere, cupivi, cupitum*   2nd Pers. Pl. F.

Review Sheet III: Adjectives

I. An Adjective must agree with the Noun it modifies in:

    1. _____ 2. _____ 3. _____

II. Using paradigm formats indicating case, number and gender, decline the following adjectives.

    1. *multus,-a,-um*
    2. *felix, felicis*
    3. *fortis,-e*
    4. *celer, celeris, celere*

III. Fill in the chart with the required possessive adjective.

	Sing.	Pl.
1st Pers.	_____	_____
2nd Pers.	_____	_____
3rd Pers. (refl.)	_____	_____

IV. Using a paradigm format decline completely *qui, quae, quod.*

V. Participles are _____. Using paradigm formats indicating tense and voice, form the Singular Nominative Cases of the Participles of the verbs below.

    1. *deleo, delere, delevi, deletum* (Give the English translations.)
    2. *voco* (1)
    3. *facio, facere, feci, factum*
    4. *invenio, invenire, inveni, inventum*
    5. *peto, petere, petivi, petitum*

VI. Fill in the blank with the required declined adjective.

    1. _____ pueri
       loving

    2. _____ poetam
       great

    3. _____ irae
       your (sing.)

    4. _____ rebus?
       for which?

    5. _____ urbes
       your (pl.)

    6. virum _____
       about to speak

    7. puella _____
       having been called

    8. res (pl.) _____
       to be done

    9. _____ amici
       my

    10. _____ liber?
        which?

Review Sheet IV: Pronouns

I. Using paradigm formats indicating case and number, decline:

    1. hic, haec, hoc
    2. ille, illa, illud

II. Decline the Personal Pronouns. Give the English translation of each declined form.

<table>
<tr><td></td><td>Sing.</td><td>Pl.</td></tr>
<tr><td>1st Pers.</td><td>_____</td><td>_____</td></tr>
<tr><td>2nd Pers.</td><td>_____</td><td>_____</td></tr>
<tr><td>3rd Pers.</td><td>_____</td><td>_____</td></tr>
</table>

III. Nominative forms of Latin Personal Pronouns are used for _____. The Intensive Pronoun _____, _____, _____, which means _____, _____, _____ is used for the same purpose.

   Reflexive Pronouns always refer back to the _____ of the verb. The Reflexive Pronouns for 1st and 2nd Persons are identical to the Personal Pronouns except they do not have a _____ case.

IV. Using a paradigm format denoting cases, decline the Reflexive Pronoun for 3rd Person Singular and Plural.

V. Fill in the blank with appropriate underlined Latin form.

    1. Viri _____ viderunt _____.
          themselves   him

    2. _____ dedi pecuniam _____ viris.
          I   to those same ← *tricky!*

    3. _____ laudas _____ ; _____ laudat _____.
          You   yourself   he   himself

    4. Cleopatra _____ laudavit _____.
                   herself   herself

    5. Romani laudaverunt _____.
                            themselves

    6. Populus nescivit _____ vitia.
                          his

VI. Using a paradigm format listing cases, gender, and number, decline the Interrogative Pronoun.

VII. Fill in the blank with the appropriate Latin <u>declined</u> form for the underlined words.

1. The girl <u>who</u> lives next door . . .	1. _____
2. <u>Which</u> days are available?	2. _____
3. <u>Whom</u> are you seeking?	3. _____
4. The men *whose* boats are sinking...	4. _____
5. <u>What</u> are you doing?	5. _____
6. <u>To whom</u> was the letter written?	6. _____
7. <u>By which</u> road will he arrive?	7. _____
8. The cities <u>that</u> you destroyed . . .	8. _____
9. The teacher <u>for whom</u> you slave . . .	9. _____
10. <u>Who</u> is dedicated, responsible, and in medias res? (A <u>Latin</u> student!)	10. _____

The Flavian Amphitheater (Colosseum)

Ablative Absolutes

Objectives
To enable you to:
1. Recognize Ablative Absolutes;
2. Translate Ablative Absolutes.

Ablative Absolutes

An Ablative Absolute is a type of Participial Phrase. **An Ablative Absolute consists of a Noun or a Pronoun in the Ablative Case accompanied by an agreeing Participle.** Simple Participial Phrases modify a Noun or a Pronoun in the Main Clause of a Complex Sentence. **An Ablative Absolute cannot modify a Noun or a Pronoun in the Main Clause of a Complex Sentence.** With this in mind, decide whether the following underlined phrases are Simple Participial Phrases or Ablative Absolutes.

1. The orator <u>praising that man</u> is my brother.
2. <u>Since the laws were known</u>, the punishment was clear.
3. <u>Understanding the danger</u>, the soldiers fled.
4. <u>With Caesar holding the command</u>, I will not fear.
5. <u>About to overcome the enemy,</u> the citizens were happy.
6. <u>Although the danger was great</u>, the men did not flee.

Now, let's see what the Latin renditions look like, agreeing that the phrases in sentences 1, 3, and 5 are Simple Participial Phrases, i.e., the Participles modify (and agree in case number and gender with) the Subject of the Main Clause.

1. The orator praising that man is my brother.
   Orator laudans illum virum est meus frater.
3. Understanding the danger, the soldiers fled.
   Videntes periculum, milites fugerunt.
5. About to overcome the enemy, the citizens were happy.
   Victuri hostem, cives erant felices.

LATIN ALIVE AND WELL

The phrases in sentences **2, 4** and **6** are **Ablative Absolutes**, i.e., Participial Phrases that do not modify a Noun or a Pronoun in the main clause. To render these phrases in Latin, the Noun in the phrase must be declined in the Ablative Case and the Participle declined to agree with this noun in Case, Number, and Gender. You can use English conjunctions such as "when, since, although, after" to translate an Ablative Absolute (as in sentences 2 and 6), but notice these conjunctions do not appear in the Latin format. For that reason it may be a better option to stick to a **more literal Ablative Absolute translation**, at least until you become familiar with the Latin format. **A near fail-proof way of getting to a basic translation of an Ablative Absolute is to use this formula: _"with"_ + the meaning of the Noun + the literal meaning of the Participle** (as in sentence 4).

2. Since the laws were known, the punishment was clear.
   Iuribus scitis, poena erat clara.
4. With Caesar holding the command, I will not fear.
   Caesare tenente imperium, non timebo.
6. Although the danger was great, the men did not flee.
   Periculo magno*, viri non fugerunt.

NB: Two nouns or a noun and adjective in the Ablative Case can compose an Ablative Absolute. The reason for this is that although the verb _sum, esse_ has only one Participle (_futūrus,-a,-um_), Present and Perfect Participle translations can be <u>assumed</u> through context (but only with the verb **sum, esse**).

Summary of New Terminology

1. Clauses (see chapter XII).
2. Complex Sentence: A sentence consisting of a main clause and one or more dependent clauses.
3. Participial Phrase: A sequence of words containing a participle and possibly a direct object of the participle.

Vocabulary

dīvitiae, dīvitiārum f., wealth/riches
dux, ducis m., leader/general
imperium,-ī n., absolute power/command
navis,-is f., ship
telum,-i n., weapon/spear/javelin

expellō, expellere, expulī, expulsum to expel/drive out
inquit defective verb, he says/said; occurs after one or more words of a direct quotation
ostendō, ostendere, ostendī, ostentum to show/exhibit
pellō, pellere, pepulī, pulsum to beat/strike

tandem adv., finally/at last
circā (alternate form for _circum_) adv., around

166

Exercises

A. Give a Synopsis in 3rd Sing. M. of **pello, pellere, pepuli, pulsum**.

B. Using a chart paradigm indicating Tense and Voice, form the Participles (Nom. and Gen. Sing. of Pres., Nom. Sing. forms of rest) of **duco, ducere, duxi, ductum**, followed by their English translations.

C. Decline the following Participle and Noun combinations.

    1. amans amica   2. dux territus

D. Translate the following phrases as Ablative Absolutes using this formula: "with" + the meaning of the noun + the literal meaning of the Participle + D.O. of the Participle (if one).

    Examples: Auxilio misso   *With help having been sent*
                       Exercitu capturo urbem   *With the army about to capture the city*

    1. Duce pulso
    2. Imperio obtento
    3. Donis ostentis
    4. Servis imperium tenentibus
    5. Duce servum pulsuro
    6. Caesare imperium tenente
    7. Tyrannis expulsis
    8. Illis mala expellentibus
    9. Duce pellendo
    10. Donis ostendendis

E. Render the following sentences into Latin, making sure the underlined phrases are all <u>Ablative Absolutes</u>.

    1. <u>With the king leading the men</u>, the citizens were not afraid.
    2. <u>With the men having been led by the king</u>, the citizens were not afraid.
    3. <u>Since the king was about to lead the men</u>, the citizens were not afraid.
    4. <u>Because the men were to be led by the king</u>, the citizens were not afraid.
    5. <u>Since the danger was great</u>, the state sent help.
    6. <u>When the army was seen</u>, the people began to run.

F. Sentence translations

    1. "Solus stultus," inquit, "divitias suas ostendit."
    2. "O Cives, cives," inquit stultus, "Petite divitias ante omnia."
    3. Divitiis ostentis, servi dona sua legerunt.
    4. "Vivo Caesare," inquit, "res publica est in periculo."
            vivus,-a,-um = living/alive

5. Audentes fortuna iuvat.
6. Lex videt iratum virum; iratus legem non videt. (Publilius Syrus)
   iratus,-a,-um = angry
7. Divitiis inveniendis, periculum e mentibus eorum expulsum erat.
8. Insidiis scitis, periculum remansit.

Text Translation

Julius Caesar (100–44 BC) was the embodiment of Roman military and administrative genius. I have chosen this excerpt which follows not only to provide a notion of Caesar's audacity and self-confidence, but also because in it Caesar describes the inhabitants of Britain for the first time.

Solā parte aestatis[1] relictā[2], Caesar iubet naves parari. Britanni[3] in omnibus fere Gallicis[4] bellis auxilium hostibus[5] nostris dederant. Caesar in Porto[6] Itio erat; huc[7] naves undique[8] venire iubet. Exspectans in illo loco multos dies, tandem secundum[9] ventum[10] accipit;[11] naves circā vigiliā[12] tertiā[13] solvit.[14]

Ipse horā circa diei quartā[15] cum primis[16] navibus Britanniam[17] tangit.[18] Ibi armatas[19] hostium copias in omnibus collibus[20] expositas[21] vidit. Haec erat loci natura et populi: mare altis[22] montibus[23] continebatur; tela ex locis superioribus[24] in litus[25] iaci poterant: omnes Britanni non solum se vitro[26] inficiunt[27] sed etiam capillum[28] habent longum et omnem corporis partem praeter[29] caput[30] et labrum[31] superius[32] radunt.[33] Hic nequaquam[34] idoneus[35] locus esse videbatur et ad nonam[36] horam reliquas[37] naves in ancorā[38] exspectavit. Tandem, cognitis omnibus rebus, Caesar iubet tolli ancoras.

(*Bellum Gallicium*, Bk. IV, 20–23)

1. **aestas, aestatis** f., summer
2. **relinquo,-ere,-liqui,-lictum** to leave
3. **Britanni,-orum** m., Britons
4. **Gallicus,-a,-um** Gallic
5. **hostis,-is** m., enemy
6. **Portus Itius, Porti Itii** m., (name of port)
7. **huc** adv., hither
8. **undique** adv., from all over
9. **secundus,-a,-um** favorable
10. **ventus,-i** m., wind
11. **accipio, accipere** to receive/get
12. **vigilia,-ae** f., watch
13. **tertius,-a,-um** third
14. **solvo,-ere, solvi, solutum** to loosen/untie
15. **quartus,-a,-um** fourth
16. **primus,-a,-um** first
17. **Britania,-ae** f., Britain
18. **tango,-ere, tetigi, tactum** to touch
19. **armo (1)** to arm/provide with arms
20. **collis,-is** m., hill
21. **expono,-ere,-posui,-positum** to exhibit
22. **altus,-a,-um** high
23. **mons, montis** m., mountain
24. **superior, superioris** adj., higher
25. **litus, litoris** n., beach/seashore
26. **vitrum,-i** n., woad, a blue dye
27. **inficio,-ficere,-feci,-fectum** to dye
28. **capillus,-i** m., hair

169

29. **praeter** adv., except
30. **caput, capitis** n., head
31. **labrum,-i** m., lip
32. **superius** upper
33. **rado, radere, rasi, rasum** to shave
34. **nequaquam** adv., not at all

35. **idoneus,-a,-um** suitable
36. **nonus,-a,-um** ninth
37. **reliquus,-a,-um** remaining
38. **ancora,-ae** f., anchor

Review Work Sheet: Chapter XXI

I. Give the word order of a typical <u>simple</u> Latin sentence.

    _____ _____ _____ _____ _____ _____

II. Identify the conjugation of the following verbs and then form the Passive Infinitives.

    1. supero, superare   _____   _____
    2. moveo, movere   _____   _____
    3. iacio, iacere   _____   _____
    4. mitto, mittere   _____   _____
    5. scio, scire   _____   _____

III. Participles are verbal adjectives. As adjectives, Participles have_____, _____, _____; as verbs, Participles have _____ and _____.

IV. Ablative Absolutes are participial phrases that do not modify a noun or a pronoun in the main clause of a sentence. An Ablative Absolute is composed of a _____ or a _____ in the Ablative Case with a _____ agreeing.

V. In translating Participial Phrases into English, conjunctions are sometimes employed for smoothness and/or clarity. List four English conjunctions used to translate participial phrases.

    1. _____ 2. _____ 3. _____ 4. _____

VI. Identify the following underlined phrases as SP (Simple Participial Phrases) or AA (Ablative Absolutes).

    1. <u>Eum imperium tenentem</u> timeo.   1. _____
        I fear him holding the command.

    2. <u>Eo tenente imperium</u> non timebo.   2. _____
        Since he is holding the command, I will not fear.

    3. <u>Audiens has res</u> fugi.   3. _____
        Hearing these things, I fled.

    4. <u>Scitis his rebus</u> fugi.   4. _____
        With these things having been known, I fled.

    5. <u>Capturus urbem</u> rex erat felix.   5. _____
        About to capture the city, the king was happy.

    6. <u>Captā urbe</u>, rex erat beatus.   6. _____
        Since the city was captured, the king was happy

VII. List the nine Common Ablative Constructions covered thus far. Give <u>examples in Latin</u> of each.

    1.

    2.

    3.

    4.

    5.

    6.

    7.

    8.

    9.

VIII. Using the verb *lego, legere, legi, lectum* and additional vocabulary from the vocabulary to date, render into Latin the English sentences below. Follow these steps:
    A. using the paradigm below, form the Participles (declension identifying cases only) of *lego,* followed by the English translation of each;
    B. underline the Participle in each sentence;
    C. render the English sentences into Latin, being sure to incorporate the correct form of the Participle required.

Participle Paradigm: Act.   Pass.
                                Pres.
                                Perf.
                                Fut.

    1. Present Active Participle Usage
       I know the man reading the book.
       Rendered in Latin:

    2. Perfect Passive Participle Usage
       After the books had been read, the students were happy.
       Rendered in Latin:

                                            discipulus,-i = m., student

    3. Future Active Participle Usage
       We helped the citizens about to petition the senate.
       Rendered in Latin:

    4. Future Passive Participle Usage
       The women were called by the tasks/labors to be done.
       Rendered in Latin:

Passive Periphrastic
Dative of Agent

XXII

Objectives

To enable you to:
1. recognize a Passive Periphrastic Construction;
2. understand the Usage and Translation of Passive Periphrastic;
3. recognize and be able to translate Dative of Agent.

Passive Periphrastic

The Passive Periphrastic is a special conjugation that the Romans used to indicate necessity or obligation. Just as the Perfect Passive System is formed by a combination of the Perfect Passive Participle (4th Principal Part of regular verbs) plus various forms of *sum, esse*, the Passive Periphrastic Conjugation is a combination of the Gerundive (another name for the Future Passive Participle) plus whatever form of the verb *sum, esse* is required.

Passive Periphrastic: Future Passive Participle (Gerundive) + *sum, esse*

1. *Hoc faciendum est.*   This has to be/must be done.
2. *Haec facienda erant.*   These things had to be done.
3. *Hi labores faciendi erunt.*   These tasks will have to be completed.
4. *Urbs delenda est.*   The city has to be/must be destroyed.

Dative of Agent

Apparently the Romans wanted no question to arise as to *who was supposed to do* whatever *had to be done,* and to emphasize this point they used **Dative of Agent** with Passive Periphrastic rather than the usual ablative case to indicate agent.

1. *Hoc faciendum est **mihi.***   This has to be done/must be done **by me.**
2. *Haec facienda erant **Caesari.*** These things had to be done **by Caesar.**
3. *Populus servandus erit **nobis.*** The people will have to be saved **by us.**

173

Vocabulary

aliquis, aliquid someone/something
quisque, quidque each one/each thing
cupiditās, cupiditātis f, desire/passion/avarice
iūcundus,-a,-um pleasant
praeteritus,-a,-um past

accipiō, accipere, accēpī, acceptum to take/accept
narrō (1) to tell/narrate
quaerō, quaerere, quaesīvī, quaesītum to seek/ask/inquire
recipiō, recipere, recēpī, receptum to receive/regain/take back
relinquō, relinquere, relīquī, relictum to relinquish/abandon/leave
rideō, ridēre, rīsī, rīsum to laugh

umquam adv., ever

Exercises

A. Form a synopsis of **quaero, quaerere, quaesivi, quaesitum** in 3rd Plural Masculine. Give the English translation of each conjugated form.

B. Using a paradigm format indicating tenses and voices, form the Participles (Nom. and Gen. Sing. of Pres., Nom. Sing. forms of rest) of **accipio, accipere, accepi, acceptum.**

C. Translate the following verb forms.

1. accipiunt
2. accepti erant
3. pellendi sunt
4. relinquent
5. quaerenda erunt

6. rident
7. relinque
8. pulsi erunt
9. ostenderunt
10. quaerebant

D. Using a paradigm format labeling cases, decline **quisque, quidque** into all singular forms. (The rarely seen Plural follows the same declension of the Relative Pronoun.)

E. Give the declined meaning of the following pronoun forms.

1. alicui
2. quemque
3. cuique
4. aliquem
5. alicuius

6. cuiusque
7. aliquid
8. quoque
9. quisque
10. aliquo

F. Render the following sentences into Latin.

1. Since truth and virtue were sought, our state is strong.
2. What has to be done is not always pleasant.

G. Sentence translations.

1. Spes nostrae civitatis malis viris non delendae sunt.
2. Eidem casus iterandi sunt illis populis qui historiae non student.
   casus,-us = m., misfortunes/tragedies
   itero (1) = to repeat
   studeo, studere + dat. = to study
3. De gustibus non est disputandum! (Horace)
   gustus,-us = taste
   disputo (1) = to discuss/argue
4. Hoc est quod erat demonstrandum.
   demonstro (1) = to demonstrate
   q.e.d. = a formula in geometry
5. Neque imperia semper petenda sunt neque semper accipienda sunt. (Cicero)
   neque . . . neque = neither . . . nor

175

6. Cur fabulam meam rides? Nomine mutato, de te fabula narratur. (Horace)

    fabula,-ae = f., story

7. Bonis viris imperium tenentibus, res publica valebit.

8. Veritas virtusque omnibus viris semper quaerendae sunt.

9. Difficile est primum quidque. (Cicero)

    primus,-a,-um = first

10. Suum cuique decus posteritas rependit. (Tacitus)

    decus,-oris = n., honor/glory/distinction

    posteritas,-atis = f., posterity

    rependo,-pendere,-pendi,-pensum = to repay/make up for

Text Translation

Phaedrus was a freedman of Augustus, perhaps from Macedonia. Five incomplete books of his variously amusing and/or terse and satiric fables survive. In this poem he explains why we are able to see others faults so quickly but are blind to our own.

Vitia

Peras[1] imposuit[2] Iuppiter[3] nobis duas:[4]

Propriis[5] (unam) repletam[6] vitiis post tergum[7] dedit,

Alienis[8] (vitiis) ante pectus[9] suspendit[10] aliam gravem.

Hāc re nostra mala videre non possumus;

Alii simul[11] delinquunt[12] censores[13] sumus.

(Liber IV, x)

1. **pera,-ae,** f., bag/wallet
2. **impono,-ponere,-posui,-positum** to put/place
3. **Iuppiter, Iovis** m., the supreme god among the Romans
4. **duae,-arum** f., two
5. **proprius,-a,-um** one's own
6. **repleo,-plere,-plevi,-pletum** to fill up/fill
7. **tergus,-i** n., back
8. **alienus,-a,-um** belonging to another
9. **pectus,-oris** n., chest
10. **suspendo,-pendere,-pendi,-pensum** to suspend/hang
11. **simul** adv., as soon as
12. **delinquo,-linquere,-liqui,-lictum** to commit a crime/fail
13. **censor, censoris** m., judge/censor

177

Infinitives of Indirect Statement

> ## Objectives
> To enable you to:
> 1. understand that Infinitives are the verb forms used for Latin Indirect Statements;
> 2. form the Present, Past, and Future Infinitives of Indirect Statement;
> 3. recognize and translate Latin Indirect Statements.

Indirect Statement

The following are **Direct Statements**.

Active	*Passive*
1. He is doing this.	1. This is being done by him.
2. She did this.	2. This was done by her.
3. They will do this.	3. This will be done by them.

The following are **Indirect Statements**.

Active	*Passive*
1. They say (that) he is doing this.	1. They say (that) this was done by him.
2. They know (that) she did this.	2. They know (that) this was done by her.
3. He thinks (that) they will do this.	3. He thinks (that) this will be done by them.

Latin Indirect Statement

Just as in English, Latin Indirect Statement is **introduced** by verbs of *saying, knowing, thinking,* and *perceiving.* Common verbs used to introduce Indirect Statement include:

1. saying: ***dīcō, negō, ait, nūntiō, narrō, scribō, doceō, ostendō***
2. knowing: ***sciō, nesciō, intellegō, memoriā teneō***
3. thinking: ***credō, putō, sperō***
4. perceiving: ***audiō, videō, sentiō***

178

In Latin, the verb forms required for Indirect Statement are Infinitives and the Subject of the Indirect Statement is in the Accusative Case. The **translation** of Present, Perfect and Future Active and Passive **Infinitives of Indirect Statement is relative to the time of the Introductory Verb.** The sentence examples will demonstrate this, but the first step is to learn how to form Infinitives of Indirect Statement.

Infinitives of Indirect Statement

	Active	*Passive*
Present (Same time as Introductory Verb)	**Present Active Infinitive**	**Present Passive Infinitive**
Perfect (Time before Introductory Verb)	**Perfect Stem + -*isse***	**Perfect Passive Participle + *esse***
Future Time after Introductory Verb)	**Future Active Participle + *esse***	[Supine*]

* The Future Passive Infinitive is considered Supine (i.e., dead, on its back, face up), and therefore there is no reason for a beginning Latin student to be concerned with it.

Relative time relationships will present no difficulty if our time chart is kept in mind.

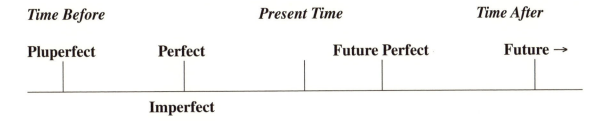

Now, with the above information, let's render into Latin the examples of English Indirect Statement at the beginning of this chapter, remembering that the:

1. **Subject of the Indirect Statement** must be in the **Accusative Case**;
2. **Infinitives are the verb forms in Indirect Statement**;

Infinitives of Indirect Statement of *faciō, facere, fēcī, factum*

Time Relationship to Introductory Verb	Active	Passive
Same Time/Present	***facere***	***faci***
Time Before/Perfect	***fecisse***	***factus,-a,-um esse***
Time After/Future	***factūrus,-a,-um esse***	

1. They say (that) <u>he</u> is doing this. *Dicunt <u>eum</u> facere hoc.*
   eum = **Accusative Case,** because it is the Subject of the Indirect Statement
   facere = **Present Infinitive,** because the action is occurring at the **Same Time as** the tense of the **Introductory Verb**
   hoc = **Accusative Case,** because it is the Direct Object of the Infinitive
2. They say he is doing this. *Dicunt eum facere hoc.*
3. They know (that) <u>she</u> did this. *Sciunt <u>eam</u> fecisse hoc.*
4. He thinks (that) <u>they</u> will do this. *Putat **eos** factur**os*** esse hoc.*
   *Putat **eas** factur**as*** esse hoc.*

* The Participle portion of the compound Infinitive must be Accusative in order to agree with the Accusative Subject.

5. He knows <u>he</u> will find the dog. *Scit <u>se</u>* inventurum esse canem.*
   (canis,-is = c., dog)

* A **Reflexive Pronoun** is used to indicate that the Subject of the Indirect Statement is the same as the Subject of the Introductory Verb.

6. They said she had done it. *Dixerunt eam fecisse id.*
7. She knew that he would do it. *Ea sciebat eum facturum esse id.*

Now, let's try the Passive Voice and use the Infinitives of ***iuvo, iuvare, iuvi, iutum.***

8. They say she is being helped by him. *Dicunt eam iuvari ab eo.*
9. They say she was helped by him. *Dicunt eam iutam esse ab eo.*
10. They said she was helped by him. *Dixerunt eam iuvari ab eo.*

Summary of New Terminology

1. Indirect Statement: a statement that occurs after verbs of *saying, knowing, thinking,* or *perceiving.*
2. Latin Indirect Statement grammatical construction: the subject of the Indirect Statement is Accusative; the verb form is an Infinitive.

Vocabulary

adulēscens, adulēscentis m., youth/adolescent
hostis,-is m., enemy
iūs iūrandum, iūris iūrandī n., oath

fidēlis,-e faithful/loyal
hūmānus,-a,-um human
immortālis,-e immortal
mortālis,-e mortal

ait, aiunt defective verb; he says/they say
crēdo, crēdere, crēdidī, crēdītum* to believe/give trust to
intellego, intellegere, intellēxī, intellēctum to understand
memoriā teneō to remember
negō (1) to deny
nūntiō (1) to report/announce
putō (1) to judge/imagine/suppose/think
spērō (1) to hope

hīc adv., here
prō + abl for/instead of/in front of
quia because

* *credo, credere, credidi, creditum*
        + dat. = to (give) trust (to)/believe
        + acc. (Indirect Statement) = to believe

Exercises

A. Form a synopsis in 1st Pers. Pl. M. of *dico, dicere, dixi, dictum*.

B. Using paradigm formats indicating tenses and voices, form the Participles (Nominative forms) and then the Infinitives of Indirect Statement of:

1. credo, credere, credidi, creditum.
2. quaero, quaerere, quaesivi, quaesitum
3. narro (1)
4. teneo, tenere, tenui, tentum
5. accipio, accipere, accepi, acceptum

C. Translate the Indicative and Imperative forms; identify Infinitives by tense and voice.

1. nuntia
2. credunt
3. pulsos esse
4. sentiebat
5. recepisse

6. teneri
7. quaesiturum esse
8. ostendi
9. dicti sunt
10. ait

D. Using a paradigm indicating cases and number, decline *humana cupiditas*.

E. Translate the following sentences into English.

1. Negant eum facere hoc.
2. Memoriā teneo eum fecisse id.
3. Vidimus te venturum esse.
4. Sperat eas venturas esse.
5. Sentio id faciendum esse.
6. Credisne te debere laudari?
7. Negavistis dona accepta esse.

F. Render the following sentences into Latin.

1. He said he would report the youth.
2. The enemy thought we would be here.
3. You denied that you had done these things.

G. Translations.

1. Possunt quia posse videntur. (Virgil)
2. Aiunt metum esse initium sapientiae.
    initium,-i = n., beginning
3. Errant qui in prosperis rebus putant se fugisse omnes impetus fortunae. (Cicero)
    impetus,-us = m., onslaught
    prosperus,-a,-um = prosperous/fortunate

4. Socrates putabat se esse civem totius mundi. (Cicero)
5. Negant quemquam esse bonum nisi sapientes. (Cicero)
   quisquam, quaequam, quidquam = anyone/anything

   nisi = except

   sapiens, sapientis = m., philosopher
6. Adulescens sperat se diu victurum esse; senex potest dicere se diu vixisse.
   (Cicero)
   diu = adv., for a long time
7. Nego mortem timendam esse. (Cicero)
8. Hannibal fecit ius iurandum patri suo numquam se in amicitiā cum Romanis
   futurum esse. (Cornelius Nepas)
9. Adulescens putat se immortalem esse.
10. Credo Pyrrhum semper memoriā tenuisse Romanos.
    Pyrrhus,-i = m., Proper Noun, a famous Hellenistic mercenary
11. Dic, hospes, Spartae te nos hic iacentes vidisse, patriae fideles. (Epigram at
    Thermopylae, Cicero)
    hospes,-itis = stranger

    Sparta,-ae = f., Sparta

    iaceo (2) = to lie dead

Text Translation

The Sabines, having lost their *virgines* to the Romans, eventually come back to claim their daughters. Livy describes the treachery of Tarpeia; how the Sabine women save Rome, and how Romulus's rule ends.

Spurius Tarpeius Romanae praeerat[1] arci[2]. Huius filiam, Tarpeiam, auro[3] corrumpit[4] Tatius, rex Sabinorum[5]. Dicunt Sabinos habuisse aureas[6] armillas[7] magni ponderis[8] in suis bracchiis[9] sinistris.[10] Tarpeia amans aureas armillas dixit se accepturam esse armatos[11] in arcem. Sed Sabini pro aureis donis scuta[12] in eam iecerunt quae in sinistris manibus habebant. Ita oppressa[13] scutis, Tarpeia periit[14] et Sabini arcem ceperunt. Die proximo,[15] magnum proelium[16] erat. Denique Sabinae mulieres[17] ex urbe inter tela volabant.[18] Exclamant[19] se filias esse <u>alterius</u>[20] populi uxores[21] <u>alterius</u>. Ita pax facta est et una civitas ex duabus.[22] Aliquot[23] annos erant duo reges, Romulus Tatiusque. Sed uno die Tatius faciens publicum[24] sacrificium[25] subito[26] interfectus[27] est. Dicunt Romulum accepisse eam rem minus[28] cum aegre[29] quam[30] dignum[31] erat. Romulus solus multos annos regnabat.[32] Sed quondam cum rex exercitum in campo[33] vocaverat, subito tempestas[34] magno cum fragore[35] accessit;[36] Romulus denso[37] nube celatus[38] est; cum lux[39] revenit,[40] milites[41] vacuam[42] sedem[43] regiam[44] viderunt. Multi crediderunt Romulum deum deo natum[45] ad caelum reventum esse; alii tamen[46] putabant regem a patribus esse interfectum.

(*Ab Urbe Condita* I, xii–xvi)

1. **praesum,-esse,-fui + dat.** to be over/in charge of
2. **arx, arcis** f., citadel/stronghold
3. **aurum,-i** n., gold
4. **corrumpo,-rumpere,-rupi,-ruptum** to bribe/break

5. **Sabini,-orum** Sabines
6. **aureus,-a,-um** golden
7. **armilla,-ae** f., bracelet
8. **pondus, ponderis** n., weight
9. **bracchium,-i** n., arm
10. **sinister,-tra,-trum** left

184

11. **armo (1)** to arm
12. **scutum,-i** n., shield
13. **opprimo,-primere,-pressi,-pressum** to crush
14. **pereo, perire, perii, peritum** to perish
15. **proximus,-a,-um** next
16. **proelium,-i** n., battle
17. **mulier, mulieris** f., woman
18. **volo (1)** to fly
19. **exclamo (1)** to exclaim
20. **alter . . . alter** one . . . another
21. **uxor, uxoris** f., wife
22. **duo, duae, duo*** two
23. **aliquot** several
24. **publicus,-a,-um** public
25. **sacrificium,-i** n., sacrifice
26. **subito** adv., suddenly
27. **interficio,-ficere,-feci,-fectum** to kill
28. **minus** adv., less
29. **aegre** adv., difficulty
30. **quam** than
31. **dignus,-a,-um** deserving/worthy
32. **regno (1)** to rule/reign
33. **campus,-i** m., field/level field for military meetings
34. **tempestas, tempestatis** f., storm
35. **frago, fragoris** m., thunder crash
36. **accedo, accedere, accessi, accessum** to approach
37. **densus,-a,-um** dense/thick
38. **celo (1)** to conceal/hide
39. **lux, lucis** f., light
40. **revenio,-venire,-veni,-ventum** to return
41. **miles, militis** m., soldier
42. **vacuus,-a,-um** empty
43. **sedes,-is** f., seat
44. **regius,-a,-um** regal
45. **natus,-a,-um** born
46. **tamen** nevertheless

NB: Irregular declension of duo, duae, duo:

Nom.	duo	duae	duo
Gen.	duōrum	duārum	duōrum
Dat.	duōbus	duābus	duōbus
Acc.	duōs	duās	duo
Abl.	duōbus	duābus	duōbus

Comparative and Superlative Adjectives
quam as a Conjunction

Objectives

To enable you to:

1. form Comparative and Superlative Adjectives from Positive Adjectives;
2. recognize and translate Comparative and Superlative Adjectives;
3. recognize that **quam** after a Comparative is a conjunction meaning "than"; **quam** before a Superlative means "as . . . as possible."

Comparative and Superlative Adjectives

The Adjectives we have learned so far are known as Positives. **Positive** Degree Adjectives indicate basic qualities such as *pretty, ugly, foolish, famous*. But in order to say something or someone is *prettier* or *uglier* or *more foolish* or *more famous* than something or someone else (i.e., comparing two nouns), a **Comparative** Adjective must be employed. When you are comparing more than two persons or objects (i.e., more than two nouns), a **Superlative** Adjective must be used that indicates the *prettiest, ugliest, most foolish, most famous*. Regular Comparative and Superlative Degree Adjectives are formed from the base of Positives.

Comparative Adjectives

Comparative Adjectives are 3rd Declension. **To form the Nominative Case** of a Comparative Adjective, add **-ior** (m./f.) or **-ius** (n.) to the **base of the Positive**. **To form the Genitive Case**, add **-iōris** (m./f./n.) to the **base of the Positive**.

     bellus,-a,-um (pretty)   →   *bellior, bellius* (*prettier*)

bellior, bellius

| | m./f | | n. | |
	Sing.	Pl.	Sing.	Pl.
Nom.	**bellior**	**belliōrēs**	**bellius**	**belliōra**
Gen.	**belliōris**	**belliōrum**	**belliōris**	**belliōrum**
Dat.	**belliōrī**	**belliōribus**	**belliōrī**	**belliōribus**
Acc.	**belliōrem**	**belliōrēs**	**bellius**	**belliora**
Abl.	**belliōre**	**belliōribus**	**belliōre**	**belliōribus**

Superlative Adjectives

To form **Superlative Adjectives**, add *-issimus,-a,-um* to the **base of the Positive**.

Positive	Comparative	Superlative
bellus,-a,-um	*bellior, bellius*	*bellissimus,-a,-um*
(pretty)	(prettier/**too** or **rather** pretty*)	(prettiest/**very** pretty*)
turpis,-e	*turpior, turpius*	*turpissimus,-a,-um*
(ugly)	(uglier/**too** or **rather** ugly*)	(ugliest/**very** ugly*)

* Alternate Translations for Comparatives and Superlative Adjectives.

Quam *As a Conjunction*

After a Comparative, *quam* means "than" and acts as a conjunction joining the two things compared. The illustrations below represent correct English and at the same time illustrate the point that the thing or things compared must always agree in case.

1. She is prettier than I.   *Ea est bellior quam ego.*
2. He is stronger than she.   *Is est fortior quam ea.*
3. These books are clearer than those.   *Hi libri sunt clariores quam illi.*
4. We think that these books are more clear than those.   *Putamus hos libros esse clariores quam illos.*

Before a Superlative, *quam* means "as . . . as possible."

1. She is as happy as possible.   *Ea est quam felicissima.*
2. It is as disgraceful as possible.   *Id est quam turpissimum.*

Vocabulary

auctor, auctōris m., author
lūx, lūcis f., light
remedium,-ī n., remedy

quīdam, quaedam, quiddam indef. pron./adj., someone/ something; a certain one/thing
acerbus,-a,-um harsh/bitter
clārus,-a,-um clear/famous
turpis,-e ugly/base/disgraceful

quam + comparative than
quam + Superlative as . . . as possible

coepi, coepisse, coeptum* Defective Verb, began

* Only the Perfect Tenses of this verb exist; the regular verb *incipio* is used to form the Present System.

Exercises

A. Form the Nominative Cases of the Comparative and Superlative Adjectives (followed by the English translations) from these Positives:

    1. gravis,-e   2. clarus,-a,-um

B. Using a paradigm format, decline ***acerbius remedium***.

C. Translate the following according to the declined forms.

    1. clarissimus auctor   6. immortalia iura iuranda
    2. clarissimae lucis   7. humanissimus adulescens
    3. gravioribus hostibus   8. fideliorum amicorum
    4. graviora remedia   9. humani metus
    5. turpe vitium   10. turpissima tela

D. Give a synopsis of ***intellego, intellegere, intellexi, intellectum*** with English translations of each conjugated form in 3rd Pl. M.

E. Using paradigm formats, form the <u>Participles</u> (Nom. and Gen. Sing. of Pres., Nom. Sing. forms of rest) and then the <u>Infinitives</u> of:

    1. vito (1)   2. intellego, intellegere, intellexi, intellectum

F. Sentence translations.

    1. Quaedam remedia graviora sunt quam ipsa pericula. (Seneca)
    2. Qui imperia accipit, partem acerbissimam servitutis vitat. (Seneca)
        servitus, servitutis = f., slavery
    3. Mens quieta, vires, prudens simplicitas, amici—haec vitam beatiorem faciunt. (Marshal)
        quietus,-a,-um = quiet
        prudens,-ntis = prudent
        simplicitas,-tatis = f., simplicity
    4. Non tam praeclarum est scire Latinam quam turpe nescire. (Cicero)
        praeclarus,-a,-um = noteworthy
        "linguam" = understood (*lingua,-ae* = f., language)
    5. Quid turpius quam fraudare amicum?
        fraudo (1) = to deceive
    6. Sentimus nos vitas iucundissimas agere.
    7. Estne hic auctor clarior quam ille?
    8. Turpiores culpae acerbiores poenae.
    9. Vita turpe; pete bonum; age vitam moderatam et eris beatior.
        moderatus,-a,-um = moderate
    10. Speravimus nos vitavisse turpissimum bellum.

Text Translation

Martial (ca. AD 40–103) was a writer of epigrams, short witty poems or sayings. In the poem that follows, Martial chastises his friend Posthumus about his pro<u>cras</u>tination.

Cras[1] te victurum[2] (esse), cras dicis, Postume,[3] semper.

Dic mihi, cras istud,[4] Postume, quando[5] venit?

Quam longe[6] est cras istud? ubi est? aut unde[7] petendum?

Numquid[8] apud[9] Parthos[10] Armeniosque latet[11]?

Iam cras istud habet Priami[12] vel[13] Nestoris[14] annos.

Cras istud....dic mihi potest emi[15]?

Cras vives? Hodie[16] iam vivere, Posthume, serum[17] est:

Ille sapit[18] quisquis,[19] Posthume, vixit heri.[20]

(<u>Epigrams</u>, Book V, lviii)

1. **cras** adv./indeclinable n. noun, tomorrow
2. **vivo, vivere, vixi, victum**
3. **Postumus,-i** m., Proper Noun
4. **iste, ista, istud** that _____ of yours
5. **quando** when?
6. **longe** adv., far away
7. **unde** adv., whence/where?
8. **numquid** neg. interr.; expected answer "no"
9. **apud** among
10. **Parthi,-orum; Armenii,-orum** ancient Eastern civilizations
11. **lateo, latere** to lie hidden
12. **Priamus,-i** aged king of Troy
13. **vel** or
14. **Nestor, Nestoris** oldest man participating in Trojan War
15. **emo, emere, emi, emptum** to buy
16. **hodie** *hō(c) die* adv., today
17. **serus,-a,-um** late
18. **sapio, sapere** to be wise
19. **quisquis, quidquis** whoever/whatever
20. **heri** adv., yesterday

Vocabulary: Chapters XXI–XXIV

accipiō, accipere, accēpī, acceptum to take/accept
acerbus, -a, -um harsh/bitter
adulēscēns, adulēscentis m., youth/adolescent
ait, aiunt defective verb; he says/they say
aliquis, aliquid someone/something
auctor, auctōris m., author

circā adv., around
clārus, -a, -um clear/famous
coepi, coepisse, coeptum defective verb, began
crēdō, crēdere, crēdidī, crēditum to believe/trust
cupiditās, cupiditātis f., desire/passion/avarice

divitiae, divitiārum f., wealth/riches
dūx, dūcis m., leader

expellō, expellere, expulī, expulsum to expel/drive
  out

fidēlis, -e faithful/loyal

hīc adv., here
hostis, -is m., enemy
hūmānus, -a, -um human

immortālis, -e immortal
imperium, -ī neut., absolute power/command
inquit defective verb, he says/said; occurs after one
  or more words of a direct quotation
intellegō ,intellegere, intellēxī, intellēctum to
  understand
iūcundus, -a, -um pleasant
iūs iūrandum, iūris iūrandī neut., oath

lūx, lūcis f., light

memoriā teneō to remember
mortālis, -e mortal

narrō (1) to tell/narrate
navis, -is f., ship
negō (1) to deny
nūntiō (1) to report/announce

ostendō, ostendere, ostendī, ostentum to
  show/exhibit

pellō, pellere, pepulī, pulsum to beat/strike
praeteritus, -a,-um past
prō + abl for/instead of
putō (1) to judge/imagine/suppose/think

quaerō, quaerere, quaesīvī, quaesītum to
  seek/ask/inquire
quam + comparative than;
  + **Superlative** as . . . as possible
quia because
quīdam, quaedam, quiddam someone/something;
  certain one/thing
quisque, quidque each one/each thing

recipiō, recipere, recēpī, receptum to
  receive/regain/take back
relinquō, relinquere, relīquī, relictum to
  relinquish/abandon/leave behind
remedium, -ī neut., remedy
rideō, ridēre, rīsī, rīsum to laugh

spērō (1) to hope

tandem adv., finally/at last
telum, -i neut., spear/weapon
turpis, -e ugly/base/disgraceful

umquam adv., ever

Irregular Comparative and Superlative Adjectives

Objectives

To enable you to:
1. form and recognize the most common Irregular Adjectives;
2. form and recognize the **-rr-** Superlative of Positive Adjectives with a Masculine Nominative Singular ending in **-er**;
3. form and recognize the **-ll-** Superlative of Positive Adjectives with a Nominative Singular ending in **-lis**.

Irregular Comparative and Superlative Adjectives

The more often a word is used over an extended period of time, the more irregular it becomes—mainly as a result of regional intonations. Many variations simply make phonetic sense and follow a pattern. Others seem to elude logic, following no apparent pattern, and the individual forms simply must be memorized. This is the case for the following **Common Irregular Comparative and Superlative Adjectives**. The good news is that Latin has surprisingly few irregular forms.

Positive	Comparative	Superlative
bonus,-a,-um	*melior, melius*	*optimus,-a,-um*
good	better	best
magnus,-a,-um	*maior, maius*	*maximus,-a,-um*
great	greater	greatest
malus,-a,-um	*peior, peius*	*pessimus,-a,-um*
bad	worse	worst
parvus,-a,-um	*minor, minus*	*minimus,-a,-um*
small	smaller/lesser	smallest/least
superus,-a,-um	*superior, superius*	*summus,-a,-um**
above	higher	highest
multus,a,um	*plūrēs, plūra***	*plūrimus,a,um*
much	more	most

		m./f.	n.	
suprēmus,-a,-um = last	** nom.	*plūrēs*	*plūra*	3rd *i*-stem Adjectives
	gen.		*plurium*	
	dat.		*pluribus*	
	acc.	*plures*	*plura*	
	abl.		*pluribus*	

Positive Adjectives Ending in –*er*

Positive Adjectives ending in -*er* in the Masculine Singular have a double -*rr*- in the Superlative instead of a double -*ss*-. To form the Superlative, add -*rimus,-a,-um* to the masculine singular nominative form. To form the Comparative, follow the standard rule of adding -*ior* or -*ius* to the base of the Positive.

Positive	Comparative	Superlative
ācer, ācris, ācre	*ācrior, ācrius*	*ācerrimus,-a,-um*
sharp	sharper	sharpest
celer, celeris, celere	*celerior, celerius*	*celerrimus,-a,-um*
swift	swifter	swiftest

Positive Adjectives Ending in –*lis*

Six Adjectives ending in -*lis* have a double -*ll*- rather than the regular double -*ss*- in the Superlative:

1. *difficilis,-e*   difficult   4. *facilis,-e*   easy
2. *dissimilis,-e*   dissimilar/unlike   5. *humilis,-e*   humble
3. *similis,-e*   similar/like   6. *gracilis,-e*   slender

To form the superlatives of these adjectives, add -*limus,-a,-um* to the base of the Positive. Follow the standard rule of adding -*ior* or -*ius* to the base of the Positive to form the Comparative.

Positive	Comparative	Superlative
difficilis,-e	*difficilior, difficilius*	*difficillimus,-a,-um*
difficult	more difficult	most difficult
facilis,-e	*facilior, facilius*	*facillimus,-a,-um*
easy	easier	easiest

Vocabulary

dissimilis,-e unlike/different/dissimilar
facilis,-e easy/agreeable
gracilis,-e slender
humilis,-e humble/lowly
similis,-e similar
superus,-a,-um above/higher

appello (1) to call/name
insula,-ae f., island
lītus, lītoris n., shore
maiores, maiōrum m., ancestors
sōl, sōlis m., sun
sapiēns, sapientis adj./noun, wise/wiseman/philosopher

-ve enclitic, or/nor

Exercises

A. Using a paradigm format indicating cases and numbers, decline:

    1. amicus optimus   2. filius maior

B. Give a synopsis of *appello* (1) in 2nd Pers. Sing. M.; then form:

    1. the Imperatives
    2. the Participles (Nom. Sing. forms in paradigm format)
    3. the Infinitives of Indirect Statement (paradigm format)

C. Give the declined English meaning of the following phrases.

1. minima spes	6. minores pueri
2. puellae pulcherrimae	7. civibus pessimis
3. labor difficillimus	8. mare minus
4. civium liberrimorum	9. in mari minore
5. duces meliores	10. peior metus

D. Give the declined Latin forms for the following.

1. more (acc. pl. n.)	6. much (nom. sing. n.)
2. small (nom. sing. f.)	7. easier (acc. sing. n.)
3. greater (dat. pl. m.)	8. smallest (nom. pl. f.)
4. worst (gen. pl. m.)	9. better (nom. sing. m.)
5. best (abl. sing. f.)	10. worse (dat. sing. f.)

E. Render the following sentences into Latin.

    1. They understood that this was true.
    2. They understood that this had been true.
    3. The smallest gifts are often the most dear/expensive.
    4. The task that/which seems the easiest is often the most difficult.
    5. Since these things were understood by all, we knew it had to be done.
    6. Many very famous authors have said that they came from rather humble homes. (*domus, -us* = f., home)
    7. With all things considered, we think that peace will come only after a very long war. (*solum* = adv., only)
    8. It must be understood that we are mortal.

F. Sentence translations.

    1. Sumus sapientiores quam illi quod nos naturam esse optimum ducem scimus. (Cicero)
    2. Quid stultius quam incerta pro certis habere, falsa pro veris? (Cicero)
        falsus,-a,-um = false
    3. Quisque cupit vitam agere quam felicissimam.

4. Quaedam carmina sunt bona; plura sunt mala. (Martial)

    carmen, carminis = n., poem/song

5. Natura minimum petit; naturae autem se sapiens accommodat. (Seneca)

    accommodo (1) = to accommodate

6. Optimum remedium irae mora est. (Seneca)

7. Qui animos vincit et iram continet, eum cum summis viris non comparo sed eum esse simillimum deo dico. (Cicero)

    comparo (1) = to compare

8. Qui plurima habent semper plura petunt.

9. Iracundiam suam qui vincit, hostem suum superat maximum. (Marcus Aurelius)

    iracundia,-ae = f, angry disposition/fury/wrath

10. Maxima pars eorum quae scimus, est minima pars eorum quae nescimus.

Text Translation

Catullus (floruit 60–55 BC) was a talented poet active in Roman literary circles at the time of Julius Caesar and Cicero. He made a visit to Bithynia in 57 BC in the entourage of the governor Memmius. Upon his return to his home in Sirmio, Catullus placed a miniature model of the yacht that had brought him safely home, with this poem attached to it, in his garden.

Phaselus[1] ille, quem videtis, hospites,[2]

ait [se] fuisse navium celerrimum,

neque impetum[3] ullius natantis[4] trabis[5]

potuisse praeterire,[6] <u>sive</u>[7] palmulis[8]

opus[9] fore[10] volare[11] <u>sive</u> linteo.[12]

et hoc negat neque litus minacis[13] Hadriatici[14]

insulae<u>ve</u> Cyclades[15] neque

Rhodusque[16] nobilis[17] horridaque[18] Thracia[19]

trux<u>ve</u>[20] Ponticus[21] sinus,

ubi post phaselus ante fuit

comata[22] silva[23] . . .

sed haec ante fuēre[24]: nunc recondita[25]

senet[26] quiete[27] seque dedicat[28] tibi,

gemelle[29] Castor[30] et gemelle Castoris.

(Catullus 4)

1. **phaselus,-i** m., small sailing ship
2. **hospes, hospites** m., guest
3. **impetus,-i** m., rush
4. **nato (1)** to float
5. **trabs, trabis** f., beam of wood/ship
6. **praetereo,-ire,-ii,-itum** to go by/pass
7. **sive . . . sive** whether . . . or
8. **palmula,-ae** f., blade of oar (diminutive form)
9. **opus, operis** n., task/work
10. **fore** alternate form of *futurum esse*
11. **volo (1)** to fly
12. **linteum,-i** n., sail
13. **minax, minacis** threatening
14. **Hadriaticus,-i** m., Adriatic Sea
15. **Cyclades,-um** f., group of islands in the Aegean Sea
16. **Rhodus,-i** m., Rhodes
17. **nobilis,-e** noble

197

18. **horridus,-a,-um** horrid
19. **Thracia,-ae** f., Thrace
20. **trux, trucis** savage/fierce
21. **Ponticus sinus, Pontici sinus** m., Black Sea
22. **comatus,-a,-um** leafy
23. **silva,-ae** f., forest
24. **fuēre** fuerunt

25. **reconditus,-a, -um** concealed
26. **seneo, senere** to be old
27. **quiete** adv., quietly
28. **dedico (1)** to dedicate
29. **gemellus,-i** m., twin
30. **Castor, Castoris** m., god of the sea

Review Work Sheet: Chapters XXII–XXV

I. Using paradigm formats labeling tenses and voices, form the Infinitives of the following verbs:

    1. sum, esse, fui, futurus
    2. pello, pellere, pepuli, pulsum
    3. recipio, recipere, recepi, receptum

II. Render the following sentences into Latin.

    1. "The enemy will have to be driven out," he said.
    2. With the best leaders chosen, the citizens thought that peace would come soon.
    3. Our ancestors knew that their fathers had done these things.
    4. The authors about to receive the gifts write rather dissimilar books, but they are very good friends.
    5. Since the island was rather agreeable, the men were as happy as possible.
    6. They will remember that this had to be said.
    7. Although the place was unknown, we drove our ships toward the shore.
    8. They felt that we were writing rather brief letters.

Present Subjunctive Formation
Jussive Subjunctive
Optative Subjunctive

Objectives
To enable you to:
1. form and recognize the Present Subjunctive of Regular Verbs;
2. form and recognize the Present Subjunctive of *sum, esse;*
3. recognize and translate Jussive Subjunctive;
4. recognize and translate Optative Subjunctive.

The Subjunctive Mood

The Subjunctive represents the third and last mood in the Latin language. The Imperative Mood is used for commands; the Indicative Mood indicates a fact. The Subjunctive in Latin has different and particular uses, nine of which we will take up chapter by chapter. Each Subjunctive Usage has a particular and specific format and a corresponding particular and specific translation. After learning the Latin Subjunctive, you will better understand modern Romance language Subjunctive as well as English Subjunctive.

Present Subjunctive Formation

The Present Subjunctive in Latin is formed the same way as in modern Romance languages, with *-e-* being the Present Subjunctive Tense sign for 1st Conjugation verbs and *-a-* the Present Subjunctive Tense sign for all other conjugations. Here is how it looks for each of the conjugations.

1st Conjugation: change the **-a-** in the Present Indicative to **-e-**

voco, vocare, vocavi, vocatum

Active		Passive	
vocem	**vocēmus**	**vocer**	**vocēmur**
vocēs	**vocētis**	**vocēris**	**vocēmini**
vocet	**vocent**	**vocētur**	**vocentur**

For all other conjugations the Present Subjunctive Tense Sign is **-a-**.

2nd Conjugation: add an **-a-** to the Present Indicative

video, videre, vidi, visum

Active		Passive	
videam	**videāmus**	**videar**	**videamur**
videās	**videātis**	**videaris**	**videamini**
videat	**videant**	**videatur**	**videantur**

3rd Conjugation: change the **-i-** in the Present Indicative to **-a-**

mitto, mittere, misi, missum

Active		Passive	
mittam	**mittāmus**	**mittar**	**mittamur**
mittās	**mittātis**	**mittaris**	**mittamini**
mittat	**mittant**	**mittatur**	**mittantur**

3rd-*io* and 4th Conjugations: add an **-a-** to the Present Indicative

capio, capere, cepi, captum

Active		Passive	
capiam	**capiāmus**	**capiar**	**capiamur**
capiās	**capiātis**	**capiaris**	**capiamini**
capiat	**capiant**	**capiatur**	**capiantur**

scio, scire, scivi, scitum

Active		Passive	
sciam	**sciāmus**	**sciar**	**sciamur**
sciās	**sciātis**	**sciaris**	**sciamini**
sciat	**sciant**	**sciatur**	**sciantur**

Irregular Present Subjunctive Forms

Sum, esse, fuī, futūrus and ***possum, posse, potuī,*** as you know, are Irregular Verbs and they retain their irregularity in the Present Subjunctive:

sum, esse, fuī, futūrus		possum, posse, potuī	
sim	**sīmus**	**possim**	**possīmus**
sīs	**sītis**	**possīs**	**possītis**
sit	**sint**	**possit**	**possint**

Jussive Subjunctive

The Jussive Subjunctive is a soft or polite command. The positive form is translated "Let"; the negative is translated "Let ——— not"; ***nē*** is used as the negative in Jussive Subjunctive. Jussive Subjunctive represents the major Independent use of the Subjunctive. Jussive Subjunctive occurs regularly in the Present Tense and most frequently in the 3rd person.

1. Let the slaves (students) do this. *Servi faciant hoc.*
2. Let them eat cake! *Edant crustum!* (Marie Antoinette)
    edo, edere = to eat   *crustum,-i* = n., cake
3. Let him speak for himself. *Dicat sibi.*
4. Let us not be enemies. *Ne simus hostes.*

Optative Subjunctive

Optative Subjunctive is also an Independent Subjunctive usage and occurs in expressions of wishing such as those found on tombstones. It is translated "may."

1. May he/she rest in peace! *Requiescat in pace!*
2. May the earth be light to you! *Sit tibi terra levis!*

Vocabulary

cēdō, cēdere, cessī, cessum to yield/withdraw/go by/proceed

creō (1) to beget/make

interficiō, interficere, interfēcī, interfectum to kill

mereō, merēre, meruī, meritum to deserve/earn

requiēsco, requiēscere, requiēvī, requiētum to rest/repose

stō, stāre, stetī, statum to stand/stand firm

levis,-e light/slight

mortuus,-a,-um dead

beneficium,-ī n., favor/kindness/benefit

occāsiō, occāsiōnis f., opportunity/occasion

202

Exercises

A. Conjugate the following verbs in the Present Subjunctive, Active, and Passive Voice:

    1. cedo, cedere, cessi, cessum   2. appello (1)

B. Give a synopsis of the Indicative Tenses of the following verbs in the person requested, then form the Imperatives, Participles (Nom. Sing. forms), and Infinitives using paradigm formats.

    1. interficio,-ficere,-feci,-fectum in 2nd Pl. M.
    2. requiesco,-quiescere,-quievi,-quietum in 3rd Pl. M.

C. Identify the specific grammatical usage then translate the following phrases, most of which are ablatives.

    1. graviore cum metu
    2. multos annos
    3. paucis horis
    4. Viro interfecto,
    5. magnā spe
    6. a humili duce
    7. Relinquente duce imperium,
    8. Civitate recepturā libertatem,

    9. longum tempus
    10. Caremus pessimis sceleribus.
    11. in peiore loco
    12. e levissimo officio
    13. pluribus copiis
    14. beneficio magno
    15. Caesare duce,

D. Sentence translations.

    1. Vivas hunc diem plurimosque quam beatissimus.
    2. His rebus nuntiatis, sensimus nos esse felicissimos.
    3. Qui beneficium dedit, taceat; narret qui accepit. (Seneca)
        taceo, tacere = to be silent
    4. De mortuis nihil nisi bonum dicamus. (Diogenes Laertius)
        nisi = except
    5. Arma togae cedant. (Cicero)
        toga,-ae = f, toga
    6. Ratio ducat non fortuna. (Livy)
    7. Melior vir vincat! (Errol Flynn)
    8. Melius amavisse et amisisse quam numquam amavisse umquam! (Tennyson)
        amitto, amittere, amisi, amissum = to lose
    9. Caveat emptor!
        caveo, cavere = to beware;
        emptor,-oris = m, buyer
    10. Ne sis anxius de crastino die; curae huius diei satis sint hodie. (Adapted from Matthew)
        anxius,-a,-um = anxious
        crastinus dies = tomorrow
        hodie = adv., today

E. The Romans had a firm belief in an afterlife of reward or punishment; however, only proper burial assured entry into the Elysian Fields and peace for the living. So that the shades of the dead (*Manes,-ium* = a group divinity who watched over the home) might be properly appeased, most Roman tombstones began with *Dis Manibus* ("to the shade gods"). Next on the marker was the name of the deceased in the Dative Case followed by the name or names of those erecting the stone in the Nominative Case.

D M = D(is) M(anibus)	To the Shade Gods
Juliae	For Julia Caesar, Well Deserving (it)
Caesari	
Omnes Tui	All Your Lovers
Amatores	
B M F = B(ene) M(erenti) F(ecerunt) Have Erected (this stone)	

Additional information often included:

1. the age (Roman numerals) of the deceased;
2. the cause (abl. of means or abl. of agent) and place (abl. of place where) of death;
3. a fact or wish.

Common tombstone abbreviations and vocabulary:

in aeternum/in perpetuum = forever
ae./aet./aetat. = aetatis (of age)
anno aetatis suae = in the year of his/her age
ob = obiit (he/she died)
hic iacet = here lies
R.I.P. = Requiescat in pace!
in memoriam = to the memory of
A.D. = Anno Domini

Assignment:

Write a tombstone inscription <u>in Latin</u> including at least **six** of the following grammatical constructions.

1. Dative Case
2. Nominative Case
3. Ablative of place where
4. Ablative of agent
5. Ablative of means
6. Indicative Verb
7. Subjunctive Verb
8. Participle

Text Translation

Gaius Valerius Catullus (floruit 60–55 BC) was a native of Verona, sent to Rome to become cultivated and polished. Although a young (possibly twenty) and shy provincial, his poetry soon attracted the attention of Clodia, the beautiful, wealthy, fast-living mistress of a salon for all the great. Although she was by many years his senior, Catullus was completely captivated by Clodia ("Lesbia" in his poems) and pined away brokenhearted after she tired of him.

Catullus documents this tumultous love affair in lyric verse ranging in subject matter from adoring odes to Clodia to raging invectives directed against Clodia, her pet sparrow, and her many lovers, including Julius Caesar and Rufio, one of Caesar's officers.

Vivamus, mea Lesbia, atque amemus,

rumoresque[1] senum severiorum[2]

omnes unius aestimemus[3] assis.[4]

soles occidere[5] et redire[6] possunt:

nobis cum semel[7] occidit brevis lux,

nox est perpetua una dormienda.[8]

da mi[9] basia[10] mille,[11] deinde[12] centum,[13]

dein[14] mille alterum, dein secundum[15] centum,

dein usque[16] altera[17] mille, deinde centum.

(Catullus 5)

1. **rumor, rumoris** m., common talk/judgment
2. **severus,-a,-um** stodgy/rigid/strict
3. **aestimo (1)** to estimate/to appraise to be
4. **as, assis** m., unit of money
5. **occido,-cidere,-cidi,-cisum** to set/die
6. **redeo,-ire,-ii,-itum** to return
7. **semel** adv., once
8. **dormio, dormire** to sleep
9. **mi** mihi
10. **basium,-i** n., kiss
11. **mille** thousand
12. **deinde** adv., then
13. **centum** hundred
14. **dein** deinde
15. **secundus,-a,-um** second
16. **usque** adv., all the way
17. **alter, altera, alterum** another

Subjunctive Sequence of Tenses
Imperfect Subjunctive Formation
Subjunctive Purpose Clauses

Objectives

To enable you to:
1. form and recognize the Imperfect Subjunctive;
2. understand that Subjunctive Verb Tenses are Relative;
3. recognize and translate Subjunctive Purpose Clauses.

While Jussive and Optative Subjunctive are Independent usages, all other Subjunctive usages that we will cover in this book are Dependent, requiring an Independent Introductory Verb. The four tenses of the Subjunctive are employed to show time relationships to the main verb in a sentence containing an Independent Clause and a Dependent Clause. (A clause is a group of words that contain a subject and a verb. Complex sentences contain an Independent Clause and one or more Dependent Clauses.) In Dependent Subjunctive Clauses, **Present Subjunctive Verbs occur after Present or Future Introductory Verbs** to indicate the Same Time as the Introductory Verb; **Imperfect Subjunctive Verbs occur after Past Tense Introductory Verbs** to indicate the **Same Time** as the Introductory Verb.

Subjunctive Sequence of Tenses

Independent Introductory Verb	Dependent Subjunctive Verb		Translate Subjunctive Verb as:
Present or Future	**Present Subjunctive**	→	**Same Time** or Time After
	Perfect Subjunctive	→	Time Before
Any Past Tense	**Imperfect Subjunctive**	→	**Same Time** or Time After
	Pluperfect Subjunctive	→	Time Before

Imperfect Subjunctive Formation

Good news! The Imperfect Subjunctive is wonderfully easy to form and there are no irregular forms. All you do is add the personal endings to the 2nd Principal Part of the verb (Active Infinitive), and you have it.

Imperfect Active Subjunctive

vocārem	vidērem	mitterem	caperem	scīrem
vocārēs	vidērēs	mitterēs	caperēs	scīrēs
vocāret	vidēret	mitteret	caperet	scīret
vocārēmus	vidērēmus	mitterēmus	caperēmus	scīrēmus
vocārētis	vidērētis	mitterētis	caperētis	scīrētis
vocārent	vidērent	mitterent	caperent	scīrent

Imperfect Passive Subjunctive

vocārer	vidērer	mitterer	caperer	scīrer
vocārēris	vidērēris	mitterēris	caperēris	scīrēris
vocārētur	vidērētur	mitterētur	caperētur	scīrētur
vocārēmur	vidērēmur	mitterēmur	caperēmur	scīrēmur
vocārēminī	vidērēminī	mitterēminī	caperēminī	scīrēminī
vocārentur	vidērentur	mitterentur	caperentur	scīrentur

Subjunctive Purpose Clauses

To express purpose (why something was done or is being done), the Romans used Subjunctive verbs in Dependent Clauses prefaced by the conjunction *ut* (in order that) or *nē* (lest/in order that not). In the examples below I will give you several options for correctly translating Subjunctive Purpose Clauses. The **easiest way** is to use **as few words as possible**. This means using an Infinitive to translate Positive Purpose Clauses and *lest* to translate Negative Purpose Clauses.

NB: Translation with **Introductory Verb** in the **Present Tense**
1. He is doing this <u>to save</u> the city/(in order) that he (may) save the city.
    Facit hoc ut servet urbem.
2. He does these things <u>lest</u> the city be destroyed/(in order) that the city (may) not be destroyed.
    Facit haec ne urbs deleatur.

Translation with **Introductory Verb** in a **Past Tense**
1. He did this <u>to save</u> the city/(in order) that he (might) save the city.
    Fecit hoc ut servaret urbem.

2. The army remained <u>lest</u> the city be destroyed/in order that the city (might) not be destroyed.
    Exercitus remansit ne urbs deleretur.

Vocabulary

discēdō, discēdere, discessī, discessum to go away/depart
praestō, praestāre, praestitī, praestitum to excel/exhibit/supply

mīles, mīlitis m., soldier
stēlla,-ae f., star

quidem adv., indeed/certainly
nē . . . quidem not . . . even

ob + acc. on account of
nisi except/unless

ut + indicative verb as
ut + subjunctive verb conjunction
nē + subjunctive verb negative conjunction

Exercises

A. Give a <u>Synopsis</u> of ***praesto, praestare, praestiti, praestitum*** in 1st Pers. Pl. M., Active and Passive Indicative; then form: the <u>Imperatives</u>, the <u>Participles</u> (Nom. Sing. forms), the <u>Infinitives.</u>

B. Form the Present and Imperfect Subjunctive, Active and Passive, of ***disco, discere, didici***.

C. Identify the conjugation of each of the following verbs.

1. creo, creare
2. discedo, discedere
3. rideo, ridere
4. disco, discere
5. vito,vitare

6. requiesco, requiescere
7. interficio, interficere
8. invenio, invenire
9. recipio, recipere
10. quaero, quaerere

D. Identify the tense of the Subjunctive that would follow these introductory words in order to indicate *Same Time*.

1. Facit ut
2. Fecit ut
3. Faciet ut
4. Faciebamus ut
5. Faciebantur ut

6. Faciunt ut
7. Feceramus ut
8. Facio ut
9. Faciamus ut
10. Factum est ut

E. Translate each of the following Indicative verb forms; identify the Subjunctive verb forms by tense, person, and number.

1. discedunt
2. interficiat
3. staremus
4. praestabatis
5. cedes

6. appellantur
7. doceremur
8. requiescit
9. cedamus
10. stent

F. Sentence translations

1. Cur non mitto meos tibi, Pontiliane, libellos? Ne mihi tu mittas, Pontiliane, tuos. (Martial)
   Pontilianus,-i = Proper Noun
   libellus,-i = m., little book
2. Praecepta tua sint brevia ut cito mentes discipulorum ea discant teneantque memoriā fideli. (Horace)
   praeceptum,-i = n., explanation/rule
   cito = adv., quickly
   discipulus,-i = m., student

3. Romani primum enim diem a Sole appellaverunt, qui princeps est omnium stellarum. (Adapted from Isidore)

   enim = indeed

   princeps,-cipis = m., chief/head

   primus,-a,-um = first

4. Viri multa faciunt ut scientiam inveniant.

5. Memoriā teneamus nos non discere Latinam linguam ut declinemus verba et in investigationibus splendeamus sed ut hāc linguā penetremus in regnum magnificum <u>quod incognitum maiori parti hominum remaneat</u>* . . . regnum cogitationis humanae. (René Boylesve)

   cogitatio,-ionis = f., thought

   declino (1) = to conjugate/decline

   incognitus,-a,-um = unknown

   investigatio,-onis = f, exam

   lingua,-ae = f., language

   magnificus,-a,-um = magnificent

   penetro (1) to penetrate

   regnum,-i = n., realm

   splendeo, splendere = to shine

* The verb is in the Subjunctive Mood because that is the mood of the other clauses. Translate it in the same way as an Indicative Relative Clause.

Text Translation

By 55 BC, Julius Caesar (100–44 BC) had successfully subdued Gaul but was faced immediately with the Germanic hordes, who suddenly came pouring across the Rhine. While he was dealing with the Germans, subversions among the Gallic tribes resulted in sporadic revolutions. Caesar learned from captives that inspiration and help for these revolutions were coming from Britain. So he decided upon an immediate invasion of Britain, a land till now *incognita* to the Romans as well as to the rest of the ancient world. In this excerpt, Caesar describes the difficulties his troops had with Britons opposing the initial landfall of the Romans and how the bravery of a certain standard-bearer was the impetus for a successful invasion.

Be sure to follow these steps when translating:
1. go to the punctuation marks, then look to the left until you find the verb;
2. decide the mood and translation of the verb;
3. match the verb with the subject;
4. repeat this process for the entire translation.

NB: If the punctuation mark is a comma and there is no verb in the preceding phrase, then you are dealing with Ablative Absolutes or Simple Participial Phrases.

Erat ob has causas difficultas:[1] naves propter magnitudinem[2] nisi in alto[3] constitui[4] non poterant. Locis autem ignotis,[5] militibusque pressis magno et gravi onere[6] armorum, manibus impeditis,[7] proelium[8] erat pugnandum.[9]

Hostes autem ex aridā[10] terrā aut paulum[11] in aquam[12] venientes, tela iaciebant. Quod ubi Caesar animadvertit,[13] naves[14] longas ad latus[15] apertum[16] hostium constituere iussit ut tormentis[17] tela iacerent. Barbari[18] moti et navium figurā[19] et remorum[20] motu[21] et inusitato[22] genere tormentorum constituerunt et paulum se reduxerunt.[23] Atque nostris militibus maxime[24] propter altitudinem[25] maris cunctantibus[26] subito quidam aquilifer[27] inquit: "Desilite,[28] milites, nisi cupitis aquilam[29] hostibus producere;[30] ego certe[31] meum reipublicae et imperatori[32] officium praestitero." Tum se ex navi iecit in hostem aquilam portare[33] coepit. Tum

nostri tantum[34] dedecus[35] timentes universi[36] ex navibus desiluerunt.

(*The Gallic War* Bk. IV, xxiv–xxv)

1. **difficultas,-atis** f., difficulty
2. **magnitudo,-inis** f., magnitude
3. **altus,-a,-um** deep
4. **constituo,-stituere,-stitui,-stitutum** to draw up
5. **ignotus,-a,-um** unknown
6. **onus, oneris** n., weight
7. **impeditus,-a,-um** impeded/entangled
8. **proelium,-i** n., battle
9. **pugno (1)** to fight
10. **aridus,-a,-um** dry
11. **paulum** a little
12. **aqua,-ae** f., water
13. **animadverto,-vertere,-verti,-versum** to notice
14. **navis longa** f., warship/man-of-war
15. **latus, lateris** n., side
16. **apertus,-a,-um** open
17. **tormentum,-i** n., war engine
18. **barbarus,-a,-um** foreign/uncultivated
19. **figura,-ae** f., form/shape/figure
20. **remus,-i** m., oar
21. **motus,-us** m., motion/movement
22. **inusitatus,-a,-um** unusual
23. **reduco,-ducere,-duxi,-ductum** to lead back
24. **maxime** adv., especially
25. **altitudo,-inis** f., depth
26. **cuncto (1)** to delay
27. **aquilifer, aquiliferi** m., standard-bearer
28. **desilio, desilire, desilui, desultum** to jump/leap
29. **aquila,-ae** f., eagle; refers to the legion standard topped by an eagle. Standards were carried by standard-bearers, who led their units into battle.
30. **produco,-ducere,-duxi,-ductum** to turn over
31. **certe** adv., certainly
32. **imperator, imperatoris** m., commander
33. **porto (1)** to bear/carry
34. **tantus,-a,-um** so much/so great
35. **dedecus, dedecoris** n., disgrace/dishonor
36. **universus,-a,-um** all together

Text Translation

Bella Stellarum

Lucas Caeliambulator[1] multos annos in avunculi[2] sui praedio[3] locato[4] in longinquā[5] stellā viverat et laboraverat . . . et incredibile[6] defatigabatur.[7] Cupivit facta pulchra <u>quae* eum praeter</u>[8] ultimos[9] <u>mundos ad remotas et alienas terras portarent</u>.[10] Lucas autem recepit plus[11] quam rogavit[12] quando[13] invenit mandatum[14] de pulchrā filiā regis captā ab opaco[15] et valido[16] imperatore.[17] Lucas eum non cognovit sed cognovit puellam sibi servandam esse . . . et statim[18] quod tempus fugiebat. Armatus[19] virtute gladioque[20] lucis qui patri suo fuerat, Lucas iactus est inter saevissimum[21] "spatio-bellum"[22] omnium temporum et peragrabat[23] in rectā[24] viā ad periculosum[25] concursum[26] in castris[27] hostilibus appellatis. . . . STELLA MORTIS!

VIS VOBISCUM!!

* Subjunctive Relative Clause of Purpose; answers the question "why?"

1. **ambulator, ambulatoris** m., walker
2. **avunculus,-i** m., uncle
3. **praedium,-i** n., farm
4. **loco (1)** to locate
5. **longinquus,-a,-um** distant
6. **incredibile** adv., incredibly
7. **defatigo (1)** to bore/tire
8. **praeter** adv., beyond
9. **ultimus,-a,-um** farthest
10. **portarent** would carry
11. **plus** adv., more
12. **rogo (1)** to ask
13. **quando** adv., when
14. **mandatum,-i** n., order/command
15. **opacus,-a,-um** dark
16. **validus,-a,-um** powerful
17. **imperator,-oris** m., commander
18. **statim** adv., immediately
19. **armo (1)** to arm
20. **gladius,-i** m., sword
21. **saevus,-a,-um** savage
22. **spatium,-i** n., space
23. **peragro (1)** to travel
24. **rectus,-a,-um** straight
25. **periculosus,-a,-um** dangerous
26. **concursus,-us** m., encounter
27. **castra,-orum** n., camp

Roman Curia (Senate House)

Perfect and Pluperfect Subjunctive Formation
Subjunctive Result Clauses
Result Clauses by Context

Objectives

To enable you to:

1. form and recognize the Perfect and Pluperfect Subjunctive of Regular Verbs;
2. form and recognize the Perfect and Pluperfect Subjunctive of *sum, esse*;
3. form a Verb Synopsis in the Indicative and the Subjunctive;
4. recognize and translate Subjunctive Result Clauses.

The Perfect and Pluperfect Subjunctive tenses are used in Dependent Subjunctive Clauses to indicate action occurring in the Time Before the Main Verb.

Independent	Dependent	
Introductory Verb	Subjunctive Verb	Translate Subjunctive Verb as:
Present or Future Tense	Present Subjunctive →	Same Time or Time After
	Perfect Subjunctive →	**Time Before**
Any Past Tense	Imperfect Subjunctive →	Same Time or Time After
	Pluperfect Subjunctive →	**Time Before**

Perfect and Pluperfect Subjunctive Formation

The formation of the Perfect and Pluperfect Subjunctive is the same for all Regular Verbs. In the examples below, I use the 1st conjugation verb *voco, vocare, vocavi, vocatum*. For a complete picture of all the Subjunctive forms of each of the four conjugations of verbs, turn to pages 299 and 300.

1. To form the **Perfect Active Subjunctive**, go to the **3rd Principal Part** of the verb, drop the **-i,** and add **-eri** + the Active Personal Endings.

vocāverim	vocāverīmus
vocāverīs	vocāverītis
vocāverit	vocāverint

2. The **Perfect Passive Subjunctive** is a compound verb composed of the **Perfect Passive Participle** + the **Present Subjunctive** of *sum, esse*.

vocātus,-a	sim	vocātī,-ae	sīmus
vocātus,-a	sīs	vocāti,-ae	sītis
vocātus,-a,-um	sit	vocātī,-ae,-a	sint

3. To form the **Pluperfect Active Subjunctive**, go to the **3rd Principal Part** of the verb, drop the **-i,** and add **-isse** + the Active Personal Endings.

vocāvissem	vocāvissēmus
vocāvissēs	vocāvissētis
vocāvisset	vocāvissent

4. The **Pluperfect Passive Subjunctive** is a compound verb composed of the **Perfect Passive Participle** + the **Imperfect Subjunctive** of *sum, esse*.

vocātus,-a	essem	vocātī,-ae	essēmus
vocātus,-a	essēs	vocātī,-ae	essētis
vocātus,-a,-um	esset	vocātī,-ae,-a	essent

Complete Synopsis

Now, let's see what a synopsis in 3rd Singular Masculine of *mittō, mittere, mīsī, missum* would be.

	Indicative			Subjunctive	
	Active	Passive		Active	Passive
Pres.	**mittit**	**mittitur**	Pres.	**mittat**	**mittātur**
Imp.	**mittēbat**	**mittēbatur**	Imp.	**mitteret**	**mitterētur**
Fut.	**mittet**	**mittētur**	Perf.	**mīserit**	**missus sit**
Per.	**mīsit**	**missus est**	Plup.	**mīsisset**	**missus esset**
Plu.	**mīserat**	**missus erat**			
Fut. Perf.	**mīserit**	**missus erit**			

A lot of forms—too many for the common person who spends a great part of the time just earning a living. It will all have to be simplified, and simplification is exactly what occurs in modern Romance languages, where the entire Passive Voice is replaced with Reflexive Pronouns.

NB: There are specific tense translations for the Indicative Tenses, but Subjunctive Tenses can only be translated in context.

Subjunctive Result Clauses

To tell what the result of some action was, the Romans employed Cue Words meaning "so" or "so great" (such as ***tam, sīc, ita, tantus,-a,-um***) and Subjunctive Dependent Clauses introduced by ***ut*** (translated "that") for Positive Result Clauses or ***ut nōn, ut nihil, ut nēmō*** for Negative Result Clauses. The translation of Result Clauses always includes the Cue Word in the Independent Clause, rendering the following translation patterns.

Positive Result Clause:
Cue Word + ***ut*** + Subjunctive Verb = "so————that"

Negative Result Clause:
Cue Word + ***ut nōn*** + Subjunctive Verb = "so————that not"
Cue Word + ***ut nihil*** + Subjunctive Verb = "so————that nothing"
Cue Word + ***ut nēmō*** + Subjunctive Verb = "so————that no one"

Be sure to notice the Sequence of Tenses in the following examples.

1. That teacher is so hard that no one is able to make an A.
    Ille magister est <u>tam</u> durus <u>ut nemo</u> possit facere A.
2. That teacher is so hard that no one was able to make an A.
    Ille magister est <u>tam</u> durus <u>ut nemo</u> potuerit facere A.
3. Hercules was so strong that he feared no one.
    Hercules erat <u>ita</u> fortis <u>ut</u> timeret neminem.
4. The benefits were so great that the dangers had not been considered.
    <u>Tanta</u> beneficia erant <u>ut</u> pericula non cogitata essent.

Result Clauses by Context

Some verbs indicate a result by their meaning and are therefore followed by a dependent subjunctive clause. The more common of these verbs include:

accidō, accidere, accīdī	to happen
efficiō, efficere, effēcī, effectum	to bring about
ēvenio, ēvenīre, ēvēnī, eventum	to turn out

217

1. It happened that on the same night there was a storm.
   Accidit ut eādem nocte esset tempestas.
2. Caesar brought it about that all Gaul was under Roman rule.
   Caesar effecit ut omnis Gallia esset sub imperio Romano.
3. It turned out that the war had been brief.
   Evenit ut bellum fuisset breve.

Vocabulary

accido, accidere, accīdī to happen
āmittō, āmittere, āmīsī, āmissum to lose
constituo, constituere, constituī, constitutum to decide/draw up
efficiō, efficere, effēcī, effectum to effect/bring about
ēveniō, ēvenīre, ēvēnī, eventum to turn out/result
nāvigō (1) to sail

ita adv., so/thus
sīc adv, so/thus
tantus,-a,-um so great/so much

nōndum adv., not yet

Exercises

A. Give a Synopsis in 1st Pers. Pl. M. of the Indicative and Subjunctive of *efficio, efficere, effeci, effectum*. Then form:

    1. the Imperatives
    2. the Participles (Nom. Sing. forms)
    3. he Infinitives of Indirect Statement

B. Translate the following Indicative Verbs; identify the Subjunctive Verbs by tense, voice, person, and number.

    1. constituat
    2. eveniet
    3. navigaverit
    4. effectae sint
    5. acciderent

    6. cessus esset
    7. possemus
    8. discam
    9. navigatis
    10. constitutum est

C. Identify the time sequence of the Subjunctive Verb in the following as Same Time or Time Before the Main Verb and then translate the phrase or sentence.

    1. Evenit ut incipiat . . .
    2. Interfecit ut servaret . . .
    3. Accidit ut naves servarentur . . .
    4. Discamus ut teneamus . . .

    5. Naves praestitae sunt ut hostis videret . . .
    6. Tanta mala audiebamus ut fugissemus.
    7. Tam bene navigabat ut constituissent . . .
    8. Discite haec ut navigetis sine periculo.

D. Determining the grammatic form and function of the elements of a sentence is called "parsing." Since Latin has no linear syntax, parsing is the essential first step in translation. Identify the grammatical construction of the underlined words in the sentences below.
    (1) First find the verb and determine the mood and/or special usage.
    (2) If there is no verb in the underlined words, determine whether you are dealing with an Ablative Absolute or a Simple Participial Phrase.
    (3) Fill in the lettered blanks at the right with your decisions.
    (4) Translate each sentence according to your Parsing decision.

    1. Scivimus <u>vos navigare</u>.   _____

    2. Accidit <u>ut non veniret</u>.   _____

    3. <u>Discipuli hoc faciant</u>.   _____

    4. Quid <u>faciendum est</u>?   _____

    5. <u>Navigemus[a] ne amittamus occasionem[b]</u>.   (a) _____

                                          (b) _____

    6. Dicti sumus <u>te venturum esse</u>.   _____

7. <u>Simus semper liberi</u>. _____

8. <u>Spe omni amissā</u>, exercitus discessit. _____

9. Erat tam stultus <u>ut non petivisset auxilium</u>. _____

10. Putaverunt <u>nos interfectos esse</u>. _____

E. Sentence translations.

1. Tanta est vis probitatis ut eam in hoste diligamus. (Cicero)
   probitas, probitatis = f., honesty

2. Omnes scimus metum esse initium sapientiae.
   initium,-i = n., beginning

3. Integer purusque sceleris non eget iaculis neque arcu. (Horace)

   arcus,-us = m., bow   *integer,-gra,-grum* = blameless

   egeo, egere, egrui + abl., = to need   *iaculum,-i* = n., javelin

   purus,-a,-um = pure

4. Orator exemplum petat ab illo Demosthene, in quo tantum studium fuisse dicitur ut impedimenta naturae diligentiā industriāque superaret. (Cicero)

   diligentia,-ae = f., diligence   *impedimentum,-i* = n., impediments

   exemplum,-i = n., example   *industria,-ae* = f., industry

5. Difficile est saturam non scribere; nam quis est tam patiens malae urbis ut se teneat? (Juvenal)

   satura,-ae = f., satire   *patiens,-ntis* = tolerant of

6. Ita praeclara est recuperatio libertatis ut ne mors quidem in hāc re sit fugienda. (Cicero)

   praeclarus,-a,-um = noteworthy   *recuperatio,-onis* = f., recovery

7. Dictum est nihil esse tam difficile ut labore duro geri non possit.

8. Semper quidem magno cum metu incipio dicere. Mihi videor in iudicium venire non solum ingenii sed etiam virtutis atque officii. Tum ita perturbor ut omnia timeam. Sed tandem me collego et sic pugno, et sic omni ratione contendo ut nemo me neglexisse hanc causam putaverit. (Cicero)

   collego,-legere,-legi,-lectum = to collect

   contendo,-tendere,-tendi,-tentum = to contend

   ingenium,-i = n., ability

   perturbo (1) = to perturb/disturb

   pugno (1) = to fight

Text Translation

In making his invasion of Britain, Caesar found out the <u>hard</u> <u>way</u> not only about the weather in and around the English Channel, but also about tides, which essentially do not occur in the Mediterranean Sea.

Eādem nocte accidit ut esset luna[1] plena,[2] qui dies maximos aestus[3] in

Oceano[4] efficit; nostrisque id erat incognitum.[5] Ita uno tempore et longas

naves, quibus Caesar exercitum transportaverat,[6] quasque in litore

traxerant, aestus complebat,[7] et onerarias,[8] quae ad ancoras[9] deligatae[10]

erant, tempestas iactabat.[11] Complures[12] naves deletae sunt; reliquae[13] tam

frangebantur[14] ut non possent navigari. Cum Britanni intellegebant Romanos

carere equitibus[15] et frumentis[16] et nunc navibus, constituerunt rebellare[17] ut

nostros frumento prohiberent[18] et rem in hiemem[19] producerent.[20] Caesar

nondum[21] eorum consilia cognovit sed quod accidit fore[22] id exspectabat.

Itaque effecit ut materiā[23] atque aere[24] navium fractarum navigare posset,

solis duodecim[25] navibus amissis.

(*The Gallic War* Bk. IV, xxix–xxxi)

1. **luna,-ae** f., moon
2. **plenus,-a,-um** full
3. **aestus,-us** m., tide
4. **Oceanus,-i** m., ocean/sea that encompasses the earth
5. **incognitus,-a,-um** unknown
6. **transporto (1)** to transport
7. **compleo,-plere,-plevi,-pletum** to fill up
8. **onerarius,-a,-um** of burden; *oneraria navis* transport ship
9. **ancora,-ae** f., anchor
10. **deligo (1)** to tie down
11. **iacto (1)** to hurl about
12. **complures,-ium** several
13. **reliquus,-a,-um** remaining
14. **frango, frangere, fregi, fractum** to break/shatter
15. **eques, equitis** m., horseman; pl., cavalry
16. **frumentum,-i** n., grain
17. **rebello, rebellare** to revolt
18. **prohibeo,-hibere,-hibui,-hibitum** to prohibit
19. **hiems, hiemis** f., winter
20. **produco,-ducere,-duxi,-ductum** to draw out
21. **nondum** not yet
22. **fore** alternate form for *futurus,-a,- um esse*
23. **materia,-ae** f., wood/timber
24. **aes, aeris** n., bronze
25. **duodecim** twelve

Vocabulary: Chapters XXV–XXVIII

accidō, accidere, accidī to happen
āmittō, āmittere, āmīsī, amissum to lose
appellō (1) to call/name

beneficium,-ī neut., favor/kindness/benefit

cēdō, cēdere, cessī, cessum to yield/withdraw
constituō, constituere, constituī, constitutum to decide/draw up
creō (1) to beget/make

discēdō, discēdere, discessī, discessum to go away/depart
dissimilis,-e unlike/different/dissimilar

efficiō, efficere, effēcī, effectum to effect/bring about
ēveniō, ēvenīre, ēvēnī, eventum to turn out/result

facilis,-e easy/agreeable

gracilis,-e slender

humilis,-e humble/lowly

insula,-ae f., island
interficiō, interficere, interfēcī, interfectum to kill
ita adv., so/thus

levis,-e light/slight
lītus, lītoris neut., shore

maiorēs, maiōrum m., ancestors
mereō, merēre, meruī, meritum to deserve/earn

mīles, mīlitis m., soldier
mortuus,-a,-um dead

nāvigō (1) to sail
nē + subjunctive verb negative conjunction
nē . . . quidem not . . . even
nisi except/unless
nōndum adv., not yet

ob + acc. on account of
occāsiō, occāsiōnis f., opportunity/occasion

praestō, praestāre, praestitī, praestitum to excel/exhibit/supply

quidem adv., indeed/certainly

requiescō, requiescere, requiēvī, requiētum to rest/repose

sapiēns, sapientis adj./noun, wise/wise man/philosopher
sīc adv., so/thus
similis,-e similar
sōl, sōlis m., sun
stēlla,-ae f., star
stō, stāre, stetī, statum to stand/stand firm
superus,-a,-um above/higher

tam adv., so/to such a degree
tantus,-a,-um so great/so much

-ve enclitic, or/nor

Cum Clauses
Positive, Comparative, and
Superlative Adverbs
Irregular Adjectives and Adverbs

XXIX

Objectives

To enable you to:

1. recognize and translate Subjunctive ***Cum*** Clauses;
2. recognize and form Regular Positive, Comparative, and Superlative Adverbs;
3. recognize and form Irregular Positive, Comparative, and Superlative Adverbs.

Cum *Clauses*

You are already familiar with *cum* ("with") in Ablative Prepositional Phrases. *Cum* can also be used as a Conjunction to introduce a clause relaying the circumstances under which something occurs. ***Cum*** followed by a clause containing a **Subjunctive Verb** is translated ***when, since, although*** according to context. When the Romans wanted to emphasize the time or date of an event rather than the circumstances surrounding it, they used ***cum*** followed by an **Indicative Verb**. In this instance *cum* is always translated ***when***.

1. When they understood this, the students were happier.
    Cum scirent hoc, discipuli erant feliciores.
2. Since the sphinx had been conquered, Thebes was free from fear.
    Cum sphinx victa esset, Thebae liberabantur e timore.
    sphinx, sphingis = f., mythical monster   *Thebae,-arum* = f., Thebes
3. Although he had seen the signal, nevertheless he did not come.
    *Cum signum vidisset, **tamen*** non venit.*
    *When ***tamen*** (nevertheless) appears in the main clause, ***cum*** is always translated "**although**."
4. When Romulus gave the signal, the Sabine women were seized.
    Cum Romulus signum dedit,** mulieres Sabinorum rapiebantur.
    ** Indicative Verb.

223

Positive, Comparative, and Superlative Adverbs

Positive Adverbs are formed from the stems of Positive Adjectives. The form of a Positive Adverb depends on the Declension of the Adjective.

    1. For 1st–2nd Declension Adjectives, add *-ē* to the Genitive Singular Stem.

longus,-a,-um long   *pulcher,-chra,-chrum* beautiful
   longē adv., far   **pulchre** adv., beautifully
                liber, libera, liberum free
                libere adv., freely

    2. For 3rd Declension Adjectives, add *-iter* to the Genitive Singular Stem.

fortis,-e → **fortiter**
brave   adv., bravely

Comparative Adverbs have the same form as the Nominative Neuter Singular Comparative Adjective.

longius farther   *pulchrius* more beautifully   *fortius* more bravely

To form **Superlative Adverbs**, add *-ē* to the Genitive Singular Stem of the Superlative Adjective.

longissimus,-a,-um	→	**longissime**
longest		farthest
pulcherrimus,-a,-um	→	**pulcherrime**
most beautiful		most/very beautifully
fortissimus,-a,-um	→	**fortissime**
bravest		most/very bravely
facillimus,-a,-um	→	**facillime**
easiest		most/very easily

It is easier to remember the above rules if you form the Comparative and Superlative Adjectives first and then form the corresponding Adverbs.

Positive	Comparative	Superlative
longus,-a,-um long *longē* far	*longior, longius* longer *longius* farther	*longissimus,-a,-um* longest *longissimē* farthest
fortis,-e brave *fortiter* bravely	*fortior, fortius* braver *fortius* more bravely	*fortissimus,-a,-um* bravest *fortissimē* most bravely
līber,-a,-um free *līberē* freely	*līberior, līberius* freer *līberius* rather freely	*līberrimus,-a,-um* freest *līberrimē* very freely
similis,-e similar *similiter* similarly	*similior, similius* more similar *similius* rather similarly	*simillimus,-a,um* most similar *simillimē* very similarly

Irregular Adjectives and Adverbs

In Chapter XXV, you were introduced to Irregular Comparative and Superlative Adjectives. These irregularities are generally retained in the formation of Adverbs and, again, are easier to remember if you recall the Adjectives first.

Positive	Comparative	Superlative
bonus,-a,-um good	*melior, melius* better	*optimus,-a,-um* best
bene well	*melius* better	*optime* best
magnus,-a,-um great	*maior, maius* greater	*maximus,-a,-um* greatest
magnopere greatly	*magis* more, i.e., quality	*maxime* especially
malus,-a,-um bad	*peior, peius* worse	*pessimus,-a,-um* worst
male badly	*peius* worse	*pessime* worst
parvus,-a,-um small	*minor, minus* smaller	*minimus,-a,-um* smallest
parum little	*minus* less	*minime* least
multus,-a,-um much	*plures, plura* more, i.e., numerous	*plurimus,-a,-um* most
multum much	*plus* more, i.e., quantity	*plurimum* most
diu a long time	*diutius* longer time	*diutissime* longest time
saepe often	*saepius* more often	*saepissime* very often
facilis,-e easy	*facilior, facilius* easier	*facillimus,-a,-um* easiest
facile easily	*facilius* more easily	*facillime* most easily

Summary of New Terminology

1. Indicative *Cum* Clause: A subordinate clause introduced by the conjunction **cum** followed by a verb in the Indicative Mood.
2. Subjunctive *Cum* Clause: A subordinate clause introduced by the conjunction **cum** followed by a verb in the Subjunctive Mood.

Vocabulary

comprehendō,-hendere,-hendī,-hēnsum to arrest/comprehend/understand
incolō, incolere, incoluī to inhabit
pōnō, pōnere, posuī, pōsitum to put/place
pugnō (1) to fight

cēterī,-ae,-a the rest/the other
ōra,-ae f., shore

iniustus,-a,-um unjust
iustus,-a,-um just

subitō adv., immediately
tamen nevertheless/yet

Exercises

A. Form a synopsis in 3rd Singular Neuter of the Indicative and Subjunctive of *pono, ponere, posui, positum*. Give the English translation of the Indicative.

B. Using a paradigm format labeling Tense and Voices, form the Participles (Nom. Sing. Forms) and then the Infinitives of *pono, ponere, posui, positum*.

C. Translate the Indicative Verbs; identify the Subjunctives and Infinitives by tense and voice.

   1. posuisse
   2. pugnavisset
   3. comprehenduntur
   4. incolant
   5. appellatus est
   6. discedant
   7. discedite
   8. efficiat
   9. accideret
   10. eventum esset

D. Form the Comparative and Superlative Adjectives (Nominative Forms only) and then the Positive, Comparative, and Superlative Adverbs of:

   1. facilis,-e
   2. pulcher,-chra,-chrum
   3. iustus,-a,-um
   4. brevis,-e
   5. bonus,-a,-um
   6. magnus,-a,-um

E. Translate the following adverbs.

   1. facillime
   2. parum
   3. celeriter
   4. liberrime
   5. plus
   6. optime
   7. facilius
   8. maxime
   9. diutius
   10. facile
   11. magnopere
   12. magis

F. **Parse** (identify the grammatical construction of) the underlined phrases and/or clauses in the space above it, then **Translate** the sentence.

   1. Homines libenter id credunt <u>quod cupiunt credere.</u> (Caesar)

      libenter = gladly
   2. <u>Maxime eum laudemus</u> qui pecuniā non movetur.
   3. Nemo quidem tam ferus est <u>ut non mitescere possit,</u>[a] <u>culturā datā.</u>[b] (Horace)

      ferus,-a,-um = uncultivated/wild

      mitesco, mitescere = to become tame

      cultura,-ae = culture
   4. Pares <u>cum paribus</u> facillime congregantur. (Cicero)

      par, paris = f., equal

      congrego (1) = to collect together

5. <u>Cum Caesar videret</u>[a] <u>suos milites premi</u>,[b] subito auxilium misit.

6. Multum <u>de magistris meis</u>[a] plus <u>de conlegis meis</u>[b] sed plurimum <u>de discipulis meis</u>[c] didici. (Ethics of the Fathers)

    conlega,-ae = m., colleague

7. "Magna spes," inquit, "me tenet, iudices, bene mihi evenire <u>quod mittar ad mortem</u>.[a] Si vera sunt quae dicuntur <u>mortem esse migrationem ad eas oras</u>[b] quas ei <u>qui e vita discesserunt</u>[c] incolunt, di boni, id multō iam beatius est." (Socrates)

    iudex, iudicis = m., judge

    migratio, migrationis = f., migration

    multo = translate "by much" (abl. of degree of difference)

8. Amicus Plato, sed <u>magis</u> amica veritas. (Aristotle)

9. <u>In bello</u> semper victima prima est veritas. (Herodotus)

    victima,-ae = victim

    primus,-a,-um = first

Text Translation

In this first excerpt Cicero gives the following example of Roman humor. It is an old story about the poet Ennius and his friend, Nasica. **Parse the underlined portions** before attempting a translation.

Nasica ad poetam Ennium venerat. <u>Cum ab ostio Ennium quaesivisset,</u>

serva dixit <u>eum non esse ibi</u>. Nasica autem sensit <u>servam hoc dixisse iussū</u>

<u>domini et Ennium esse intus.</u> <u>Paucis diebus</u> Ennius ad Nasicam venit et

<u>cum ab ostio eum quaesivisset</u>, Nasica ipse exclamavit <u>se non esse hīc.</u>

Tum Ennius "Quid?!" inquit "Ego non cognosco vocem tuam?!" Nasica

respondit "Homo es impudens. Cum te quaererem, servae tuae credidi* <u>te</u>

<u>non esse ibi</u>; tu mihi ipsi non credes?!"

(De Oratore II, lxviii)

dominus,-i m., master
Ennius,-i m., Proper Noun
exclamo, exclamare to exclaim
impudens, impudentis impudent
intus adv., inside

iussu at the command of
Nasica,-ae m., Proper Noun
ostium,-i n., door
vox, vocis f., voice

* *credo, credere, credidi, creditum*
    + dat = to (give) trust (to)/believe
    + acc (Indirect Statement) = to believe

Text Translation

Dionysius the tyrant of Syracuse (405–367 BC) had a poor reputation during his lifetime. His reputation only became worse after his death, because Roman orators of the Republic often incorporated him into their speeches as the epitome of tyrannical behavior. This is why Cicero (106–43 BC) included Dionysius in his *Disputationes Tusculanae*. Parse the underlined portions before beginning your translation.

<u>Multos annos</u>[a] tyrannus Syracusarum fuit Dionysius et pulcherrimam

urbem servitute oppressam tenuit. At <u>a bonis auctoribus</u>[b] accepimus <u>eum</u>

<u>fuisse hominem in victu summae temperantiae et acrem et industrium,</u>

<u>eundem tamen maleficium naturā et iniustum et miserrimum</u> nam nemini

credere audebat. Itaque propter iniustam cupiditatem dominatus in carcerem

quodam modo ipse se incluserat. Autem <u>ne tonsori collum committeret,</u>[d]

filias suas artem tonsoriam docuit. Ita hae regiae virgines tondebant

barbam et capillum patris. Sed tamen <u>cum essent adultae,</u>[e] ferrum removit

iussitque ut candentibus iuglandium putaminibus barbam sibi et capillum

adurerent.

(*Disputationes Tusculanae* V, xx, 57–58

adultus,-a,-um adult/grown-up
aduro,-urere,-ussi,-ustum to singe
at but
barba,-ae f., beard
candens, candenti glowing with heat
capillus,-i m., hair
carcer, carceris m., prison
collum,-i n., neck
Dionysius,-i m., Proper Noun
dominatus,-us m., absolute power
ferrum,-i n., scissors for haircutting
includo, includere, inclusi, inclusum to
   enclose/shut in
industrius,-a,-um industrious

iuglans, iuglandis f., a walnut
maleficius,-a,-um unscrupulous
opprimo,-primere,-pressi,-pressum to oppress
putamen,-inis n., shell
regius,-a,-um royal
servitus, servitutis f., slavery
Syracusae,-arum f., Syracuse, city in Sicily
temperantia,-ae f., temperance/self-control
tondeo, tondere, totondi, tonsum to
   shave/clip/shear
tonsor, tonsoris m., barber
tonsorius,-a,-um of clipping/barbering
victus,-us m., mode of livng

229

Review Work Sheet: Chapters XXVI–XXIX

I. Give a Synopsis in the Indicative and Subjunctive of **amitto, amittere, amisi, amissum** in 3rd Pl. N. Give the English translations of each Indicative form.

II. Using paradigm formats, form the Imperatives, Participles (Nom. Sing. forms), and Infinitives of **amitto, amittere, amisi, amissum.**

III. Give the Latin adverbs for the following English forms.

1. far
2. worst
3. seriously
4. more freely
5. better

6. little
7. more (quality)
8. especially
9. farther
10. very keenly

IV. **Parse** the underlined phrases/clauses, then **render the sentences into Latin.**

1. <u>May we always be very good friends</u>.
2. <u>Although I knew him</u>, nevertheless we came.
3. <u>Let us not do this</u> <u>in order that there not be a war</u>.
4. They knew <u>that we would not understand</u>.
5. So great were his faults <u>that he could not be helped</u>.
6. We esteem those <u>who do not do evil</u>.
7. <u>Departing from the war</u>, the soldiers exhibited no fear.
8. <u>Since the remedies were known</u>, the cure was most easy.
9. <u>After the leader was expelled</u>, the soldiers went away.

Subjunctive Indirect Questions
Irregular Verb *eo, ire, ii, itum*

Objectives

To enable you to:

    1. recognize and translate Subjunctive Indirect Questions;

    2. understand that ***miror, mirari, miratus sum*** has only Passive Forms;

    3. recognize, conjugate, and translate the irregular verb ***eo, ire, ii, itum.***

Subjunctive Indirect Questions

Direct Questions

1. Where is the dog?	*Ubi est canis?*	(*canis,-is* = c, dog)
2. What is he doing?	*Quid facit?*	
3. Is he destroying the house?	*Domumne delet?*	(*domus, -us* = f., house)

Indirect Questions

By employing Introductory Verbs of "asking, saying, knowing," and "perceiving," these questions can be rendered indirectly. In Latin the verbs in Indirect Questions are in the Subjunctive.

1. Do you know where the dog is?	*Scisne ubi sit canis?*
2. I wonder what the dog is doing.	*Miror quid canis faciat.**

    **miror, mirari, miratus sum* (to wonder) is a Deponent Verb, i.e., it has only Passive Endings.

3. You do not wish to know what the dog has done.	*Non cupis scire quid canis fecerit!*
4. The undertaker asked what the dog had done.	*Vespillo rogavit quid canis fecisset.* (*vespillo,-onis* = m., undertaker)

231

Subjunctive Indirect Questions follow verbs of **"asking, knowing, thinking, perceiving"** and are **introduced** by **Interrogative Pronouns, Adverbs,** or **Adjectives** such as:

quis? quid?	who? what?
qui? quae? quod?	which?
cur?	why?
ubi?	when? where?
quomodo?	how?
quam?	how?
uter, utra, utrum?	which *of two?*
utrum . . . an?	whether . . . or
an?	whether

Irregular Verb eo, ire, ii, itum

The irregular verb *eō, īre, iī, ītum** (to go) has **irregular forms,** particularly in the **Present Indicative** and the **Present Subjunctive.** The Future Tense is formed the same as for 1st and 2nd Conjugation Verbs. All other tenses follow Regular Verb conjugation patterns.

* Passive forms are rarely seen and these only in 3rd Person Impersonal.

Indicative Tenses

Pres.	Imp.	Fut.	Perf.	PluP.	FutP.
eō	ībam	ībō	iī	ieram	ierō
is	ībās	ībis	*istī	ierās	ieris
it	ībat	ībit	iit	ierat	ierit
īmus	ībamus	ībimus	iīmus	ierāmus	ierimus
itis	ībatis	ibitis	īstis*	ierātis	ieritis
eunt	ībant	ībunt	iērunt	ierant	ierint

Subjunctive Tenses

Pres.	Imp.	Perf.	Plup.
eam	īrem	ierim	īssem*
eās	īrēs	ierīs	issēs*
eat	īret	ierit	īsset*
eāmus	īrēmus	ierīmus	īssēmus*
eātis	īrētis	ierītis	īssētis*
eant	irent	ierint	īssent*

Common Participles

Pres.	**iens, <u>euntis</u>**
Fut.	**itūrus,-a,-um**

Infinitives

Pres.	**ire**
Perf.	**isse**
Fut.	**itūrus esse**
Imperatives	**i, īte**

* *ii* before an *s* contracts to a single *i*.

While *eō, īre, iī, itum* generally has no Passive Voice, compounds of this verb such as *praetereō,-īre,-iī,-itum* (to pass by) occur and have a Passive Voice.

> *Vir qui dixit id non posse faci praeteritus est ab eā faciente id.* (Wisdom from a
>   Fortune Cookie)
> The man who said it was not able to be done was passed by her doing it.

Vocabulary

abeō, abīre, abiī, abitum to go away/depart
eō, īre, iī, itum to go (no Passive Voice)
miror, mirārī, mirātus sum deponent; to wonder/be astonished
pereō, perīre, periī, peritum to pass away/perish
redeō, redīre, rediī, reditum to go back/return
rogō (1) to ask

domus,-us f., house/home (2nd Declension endings: locative *domi*, ablative *domo*,
    accusative *domum/domos*)
aequus,-a,-um level/even/equal/just
mediocris,-e ordinary/moderate/mediocre
quantus,-a,-um how large/howgreat/how much
uter, utra, utrum which (of two)
        genitive: utrius dative: utri

an whether
utrum . . . an correlative, whether . . . or
apud + acc among/in the presence of/at the house of/in front of
quōmodo adv., how

Exercises

A. Give a Synopsis in 3rd Sing. M. in the Indicative and Subjunctive of the following verbs. Give the English translation of the Indicative forms.

    1. *eo, ire ,ii, itum* (Active Forms Only)
    2. *miror, mirari, miratus sum* (Passive Forms Only)

B. Translate the Indicative and Imperative forms; parse the other forms.

1. redeunt	6. i
2. perierat	7. peribimus
3. abite	8. mirabantur
4. issetis	9. redisse
5. erint	10. abiit

C. Give the declined meaning of the following.

1. melioribus consiliis	6. ponentes
2. cum abeuntibus	7. summum mortale factum
3. iniustius bellum	8. rediens
4. culpa ponenda	9. hoc comprehenso
5. viris pugnaturis bellum	10. pessimae rationi

D. Translate the following sentences.

1. Me rogavit uter fidelior esset.	6. Rogabit ubi fueris.
2. Eum rogavit cur non fugisset.	7. Scit quis sis; scio cur veneris.
3. Miratur ubi donum sit.	8. Rogaverunt ubi abissemus.
4. Miramur cur donum datum sit.	9. Quaesivit cuius amicus perisset.
5. Viderunt quomodo comprehensus esset.	10. Scisne ubi sis et quid facias?

E. Sentence translations.

    1. Mortalia facta peribunt.   (Horace)
    2. Nemo est tam senex ut non putet se unum annum posse vivere. (Cicero)
    3. Nescire quid acciderit antequam natus sis, est semper esse puer. (Cicero)
        antequam = before
        nascor, nasci, natus sum = deponent, to be born
    4. Dulce est videre quibus malis ipse careas. (Lucretius)
    5. Cum essem parvulus loquebar ut parvulus sapiebam ut parvulus cogitabam ut parvulus quando factus sum vir evacuavi quae erant parvuli. (Corinthians I 13:11)

        evacuo (1) = to give up/put away   *quando* = adv., when
        loquor, loqui, loctutus sum = to speak   *sapio, sapire, sapivi* = to reason
        parvulus,-a,-um = small (child)

6. Auctorem Troiani belli relegi, qui dicit quid sit pulchrum, quid turpe, quid utile, quid non. (Horace)

> *relego,-legere,-legi,-lectum* = to read again
> *utilis,-e* = useful

7. Multi dubitant quid optimum sit. (Cicero)

> *dubito* (1) = to be uncertain

8. Doctos rogabis quā ratione bene agere vitam possis, utrum virtutem disciplina paret an natura det, quid minuat curas, quid te amicum tibi faciat. (Horace)

> *disciplina,-ae* = f., teaching
> *doctus,-a,-um* = learned/educated
> *minuo, minuere* = to lessen

9. Consilio melius vincere possumus quam irā. (Publilius Syrus)

10. Sed tempus est iam me discedere ut cicutam bibam, et vos discedere ut vitam agatis. Utrum autem sit melius, di immortales sciunt: hominem quidem nullum scire credo. (Socrates' parting words to his judges)

> *bibo, bibere, bibi, bibitum* = to drink
> *cicuta,-ae* = f., hemlock

Text Translation

Lucius Annaeus Seneca (died AD 65) was a Stoic philosopher of some note in addition to having been the tutor of Nero. Even a random reading of his letters and moral essays will explain why early Christian writers liked to think him Christian and, in one case at least, went so far as to make him an acquaintance of Paul of Tarsus.

Nos ne cognoscimus quidem nos; igitur cur iudicamus vicinum? Quis scit

qui dolor sit post virtutem aut qui metus (sit) post vitium? Nemo denique

scit quid faciat virum; et Deus solus scit sententias eius, gaudia eius,

acerbitates eius, aegritudines eius, iniusta commissa adversum eum, iniusta

quae committit. . . . Deus obscurior est nostris parvis mentibus. Mihi venit

omnes nostras vitas, utrum bonas an in errore, tristes an laetas, obscuras an

claras, graves an beatas esse prologum ad amorem praeter tumulum ubi

omnia intellegantur et paene omnia ignota sint.

(Adapted from Seneca)

acerbitas,-tatis f., bitterness
adversum + acc. against
aegritudo,-tudinis f., agony
dolor, doloris m., pain
error, erroris m., error
gaudium,-i n., joy
ignosco, ignoscere, ignovi, ignotum to forgive
iudico (1) to judge
laetus,-a,-um joyous

obscurus,-a,-um obscure
paene adv., almost
post adv., behind
praeter adv., beyond
prologus,-i m., prologue
tristis,-e mournful
tumulus,-i m., tomb
vicinus,-i m., neighbor

Text Translation

The following excerpt is from a letter written by Seneca to his nephew, Lucilius. Seneca recommended mercy, tolerance, kindness, and generosity to all. His *humanitas* is further illustrated by his attitude toward slavery. In this letter Seneca presents the two sides of the issue by quoting the *vox populi* (*vox, vocis* = f., voice), the common opinion.

Seneca Lucilio Suo (Dicit) Salutem

Libenter ex iis qui a te venerunt cognovi familiariter te cum servis tuis

vivere: hoc prudentiam tuam, hoc eruditionem tuam decet. "Servi sunt!"

Immo homines. "Servi sunt!" Immo contubernales. "Servi sunt!" Immo humiles amici. "Servi sunt!" Immo conservi, si cogitaveris quantum fortunae in utrosque licere.

(Adapted from *Moral Epistles,* xlvii)

cognosco, cognoscere, cognovi, cognitum to find out
conservus,-i m., fellow slave
contubernalis,-is comrade
dicit salutem says greetings
decet, decere, decuit to fit; usually 3rd Impersonal
eruditio,-ditionis f., education
familiaris,-e familiar
iis alternate form of *eis*

immo on the contrary
libenter adv., gladly
licet, licere, licuit to be allowed/permitted
Lucilius,-i m., Proper Noun
prudentia,-ae f., prudence/discretion
quantus,-a,-um how much
uterque, utraque, utrumque both

Review Work Sheet: Chapter XXX

I.   Give a synopsis in 2nd Pers. Sing., Indicative and Subjunctive, of *eo, ire, ii, itum*.

II.   Translate the following Participles, Imperatives, and Indicatives; parse the Subjunctive and Infinitive Forms.

    1. iens   6. abiit

    2. isse   7. rediremus

    3. eunt   8. peribitis

    4. ierint   9. ire

    5. redite   10. reditum esset

III.   Render the following into Latin.

    1. we will go   6. Let's go

    2. we will go back   7. May he return!

    3. he went   8. Are you (pl.) going?

    4. he had passed away   9. to perish

    5. you (sing.) used to go   10. Which (of the two) is returning?

IV.   Translate the following into English.

    1. Scio   eum facere hoc.

                    eum fecisse hoc.

                    eum facturum esse hoc.

                    id faci ab eo.

                    id factum esse ab eo.

    2. Scivi   eum facere hoc.

                    eum fecisse hoc.

                    eum facturum esse hoc.

                    id faci ab eo.

                    id factum esse ab eo.

    3. Scio   quis faciat hoc.

                    quis fecerit hoc.

                    cur id faciatur ab eo.

                    cur id factum sit ab eo.

    4. Scivi   quis faceret hoc.

                    quis fecisset hoc.

                    cur id faceretur ab eo.

                    cur id factum esset ab eo.

Irregular Verb *fero, ferre, tuli, latum*
Subjunctive Jussive Noun Clauses

Objectives

To enable you to:

1. recognize, conjugate, and translate the irregular verb *fero, ferre, tuli, latum*
2. recognize and translate Subjunctive Jussive Noun Clauses.

Irregular Verb fero, ferre, tuli, latum

Ferō, ferre, tulī, lātum (to carry, bear, endure) is a 3rd Conjugation Verb that lacks the connecting vowel in the Present Infinitive; instead of *ferere*, it is *ferre*. *Ferō* is **irregular** in the **Present Indicative** and its **Imperatives**; otherwise, it is conjugated exactly as all other 3rd Conjugation verbs.

Indicative

Present Active	Present Passive	Imperfect Active	Imperfect Passive	Future Active	Future Passive
ferō	feror	ferēbam	ferēbar	feram	ferar
fers	ferris	ferēbās	ferēbāris	ferēs	fereris
fert	fertur	ferēbat	ferēbātur	feret	feretur
ferimus	ferimur	ferēbāmus	ferēbāmur	ferēmus	ferēmur
fertis	feriminī	ferēbātis	ferēbāminī	ferētis	ferēminī
ferunt	feruntur	ferēbant	ferēbantur	ferent	ferentur

Perfect Active	Perfect Passive	Pluperfect Active	Pluperfect Passive	Future Perfect Active	Future Perfect Passive
tulī	lātus sum	tuleram	lātus eram	tulerō	lātus erō
tulistī	lātus es	tulerās	lātus eras	tuleris	lātus eris
tulit	lātus est	tulerat	lātus erat	tulerit	lātus erit
tulimus	lātī sumus	tulerāmus	lātī eramus	tulerimus	lati erimus
tulistis	lātī estis	tulerātis	lātī erātis	tuleritis	lātī eritis
tulērunt	lātī sunt	tulerant	lātī erant	tulerint	lātī erunt

Subjunctive

Present		Imperfect	
Active	Passive	Active	Passive
feram	**ferar**	**ferrem**	**ferrer**
ferās	**ferāris**	**ferrēs**	**ferrēris**
ferat	**ferātur**	**ferret**	**ferrētur**
ferāmus	**ferāmur**	**ferrēmus**	**ferrēmur**
ferātis	**ferāminī**	**ferrētis**	**ferrēminī**
ferant	**ferantur**	**ferrent**	**ferrentur**

Perfect		Pluperfect	
Active	Passive	Active	Passive
tulerim	**lātus sim**	**tulissem**	**lātus essem**
tulerīs	**lātus sīs**	**tulissēs**	**lātus essēs**
tulerit	**lātus sit**	**tulisset**	**lātus esset**
tulerīmus	**lātī sīmus**	**tulissēmus**	**lātī essēmus**
tulerītis	**lātī sītis**	**tulissētis**	**lātī essētis**
tulerint	**lātī sint**	**tulissent**	**lātī essent**

Infinitives

	Active	Passive
Pres.	**ferre**	**ferrī**
Perf.	**tulisse**	**lātus,-a,-um esse**
Fut.	**lātûrus esse**	

Participles

	Active	Passive
Pres.	**ferēns,-ntis**	
Perf.		**lātus,-a,-um**
Fut.	**lātūrus,-a,-um**	**ferendus,-a,-um**

Imperatives

fer   **ferte**

Subjunctive Jussive Noun Clauses

Noun Clauses are clauses that act as nouns in that Noun Clauses can be the Direct Objects of Independent Verbs, a function normally reserved for nouns. Functioning as Direct Objects, Noun Clauses answer the question "what?" By this definition all Indirect Statements, many Subjunctive Clauses, and some Relative Clauses are Noun Clauses.

A Jussive Noun Clause is a particular type of Subjunctive Clause that follows an Introductory Verb of **"urging, admonishing, commanding, persuading, requesting"** such as *moneo, curo, hortor, persuadeo, peto, oro, rogo, impero*. Jussive Noun Clauses are introduced by the conjunctions *ut* (positive) or *nē* (negative), are always in the Subjunctive Mood, and are always the Direct Objects of Jussive ("commandlike") Introductory Verbs.

1. *Monet ut veniamus soli.*
   He advises that we come alone/us to come alone.
2. *Cura ut hoc faciatur.*
   Take care that this is done/to do this.
3. *Hortor te ne hoc facias.*
   I urge you that you not do this/you not to do this.
4. *Persuasit nobis ut hoc esset optimum consilium.*
   He persuaded us that this was the best plan.
5. *Petit/orat/rogat ne abeatis.*
   He begs/pleads/asks that you not go away/you not to go away.
6. *Imperavit ei ut faceret hoc.*
   He ordered (to) him that he do this/him to do this.

Vocabulary

antepōnō,-pōnere,-posuī,-positum* to prefer/put before
cēnō (1) to dine
cōnferō, cōnferre, cōntulī, collātum to bring together/compare;
   sē cōnferre to betake oneself
cūrō (1) to take care
ferō, ferre, tulī, lātum to carry/bear/endure/bring
hortor, hortārī, hortātus sum deponent, to urge/implore
imperō (1) + dat to give orders to/command
offerō, offerre, obtulī, oblātum to offer
ōrō (1) to beg/entreat/beseech
persuādeō, persuādēre, pērsuasī, persuāsum + dat to make sweet to/to persuade

cēna,-ae f., dinner
vīnum,-ī n., wine

* Like many compounded transitive verbs, *antepono* is capable of taking an Indirect
   Object as well as a Direct Object, i.e.,
   Anteponit veritatem famae.   He puts truth before/prefers truth to rumor.

Exercises

A. Give a Synopsis in 3rd Pl. M. in the Indicative and Subjunctive of *offero, offerre, obtuli, oblatum*.

B. Form the Imperatives, Participles (Nom. and Gen. Sing. of the Pres. Act.; Nom. Sing. forms of the rest), and Infinitives of Indirect Statement of *offero, offerre, obtuli, oblatum*.

C. Translate the following Indicative and Imperatives; identify the other forms.

<table>
<tr><td>1. tulissemus</td><td>6. offerant</td></tr>
<tr><td>2. laturus esse</td><td>7. ferri</td></tr>
<tr><td>3. confer te</td><td>8. collatus esse</td></tr>
<tr><td>4. obtulerunt</td><td>9. offeremus</td></tr>
<tr><td>5. ferenda sunt</td><td>10. latus est</td></tr>
</table>

D. Provide the Latin forms for the following:

1. He persuades us
2. She betook herself
3. He puts wisdom before money
4. The gifts had been compared
5. With the gifts having been compared
6. You (pl.) endured
7. With (the men) enduring the storm
8. It will have been lost
9. We urge you (sing.)
10. I command them

E. Parse the underlined words, clauses or phrases and then translate the sentence.

1. Et quid a te rogat Deus sed <u>ut facias iustitiam, diligas misericordiam, et ambules humiliter cum Deo tuo</u>. (Micah 6:8)

   ambulo (1) = to walk   *iustitia,-ae* = f., justice

   humilis,-e = humble   *misericordia,-ae* = f., mercy

2. <u>Discamus</u> ferre difficiles res <u>quas vita fert</u>.

3. Occasio non <u>facile</u> offertur sed facile amittitur. (Publilius Syrus)

4. Ego vos hortor ut amicitiam omnibus rebus humanis anteponatis. (Cicero)

5. Hoc unum scio; <u>quod fortuna fert</u>, id feremus aequo animo. (Terence)

   aequus,-a,-um = equal/even/calm

6. <u>Quid vesper ferat</u>, incertum est. (Virgil)

   vesper, vesperis = m., evening

7. Virtuti melius quam Fortunae credamus; virtus non (cog)noscit <u>calamitati</u> cedere. (Publilius Syrus)

   calamitas, calamitatis = f., calamity/disaster

8. Cenabis bene, mi Fabulle, apud me <u>paucis diebus</u> si <u>tecum</u> tuleris bonam atque magnam cenam non sine bellā puellā et vino et sale. Haec si, tuleris, inquam, cenabis bene, nam sacculus tui Catulli plenus est <u>aranearum</u>. (Catullus)

aranea,-ae = f., spiderweb	*plenus,-a,-um* = full
Fabullus,-i = Proper Noun	*sacculus,-i* = m., purse
inquam = I say	*sal, salis* = m., salt/wit

9. Ignaviā nemo immortalis factus est; neque quisquam parens liberis <u>ut aeterni essent</u>, optavit; magis <u>ut boni honestique vitam exigerent</u>. (Sallust)

aeternus,-a,-um = forever/eternal	*liberi,-orum* = m., children
exigo,-ere,-egi,-actum = to complete/finish	*opto* (1) = to choose
honestus,-a,-um = honest	*parens,-ntis* = c., parent
ignavia,-ae = f., idleness	*quisquam, quaequam, quidquam* = any

F. **Election Graffiti** *Nihil novum sub sole!*

In 79 AD the eruption of Vesuvius buried the Roman city of Pompeii under twenty feet of ash. Excavation of Pompeii in modern times has resulted in a vivid and detailed picture of the people and the lives of that time. Of particular interest are the more than one thousand five hundred election graffiti. Pompeii had four major officials who were elected on an annual basis: *duo viri (IIv)*, two men who acted as judges; and *aediles*, two men responsible for the maintenance of public buildings and order. Since campaigning was fierce and space limited, a shorthand for economically and succinctly rendering campaign slogans evolved, demonstrated by some of the actual excavated graffiti that follow. I have translated the first one for you. See if you can translate the others.

P.Carpin. IIv v.b.o.v.f.
P. Carpinium IIv virum bonum oro vos (ut) faciatis
I urge you that you make Publilius Carpinius, a good man a judge.

1. ***C. Iulium Polybium aedilem o.v.f.***
   Panem bonum fert.

C. Iulius Polybius	m., Proper Noun
aedilis,-is	m., aedile
o.v.f.	*oro vos (ut) faciatis*
panis,-is	m., bread

2. ***M. Holconium Priscum, C. Gavium Rufum IIvir***
   Phoebus cum emptoribus suis rogat.

M.Holconius Priscus	m., Proper Noun
C. Gavius Rufus	m., Proper Noun
Phoebus,-i	m., Proper noun
emptor, emptoris	m., customer

"Mud-slinging" guilt-by-association slogans as well as slams seem to have been as common in Pompeii as they are today.

3. ***M. Cerrinium Vatiam aed. o.v.f. seribibi universi.***
   Scripsit Florus cum Fructo.

M. Cerrinius Vatia	m., Proper Noun
aed.	*aedilis,-is* m., aedile
seribibus,-i	m., alcoholic
universus,-a,-um	all
Florus,-i	m, Proper Noun
Fructus,-i	m, Proper Noun

4. ***Vatiam aed. furunculi rogant.***

Vatia,-ae	m., Proper Noun
furunculus,-i	m., pickpocket/thief

5. ***Claudium IIvir. animula faciet.***

animula,-ae	f., a small mind

ASSIGNMENT: Render your own election graffiti **in Latin** in the space below.

Text Translation

In this excerpt from Cicero's *Tusculanae Disputationes,* he discusses, among other things, the problems of tyranny as a form of government. Cicero uses an anecdote about Dionysius the tyrant of Syracuse to point out that the life of a tyrant is a life of constant fear. Parse the underlined portions before translating.

Dionysius tyrannus constituit <u>se demonstraturum esse</u>[a] <u>quam "beatus"</u> <u>esset</u>.[b] <u>Cum quidam Damocles, unus ex eius adsentatoribus, commemoraret</u> <u>copias eius, maiestatem dominatus, abundantiam eius rerum negaret</u>[c]que <u>quemquem umquam beatiorem fuisse</u>,[d] "O Damocle," Dionysius inquit, "quoniam te haec vita delectat, cupisne degustare eandem vitam et experiri meam fortunam?" <u>Cum ille se cupere dixisset</u>,[e] Dionysius hunc hominem <u>in</u> <u>aureo lecto</u>[f] locari iussit et mensas argento auroque ornari. Tum iussit <u>cenam exquisitissimam inferri</u>.[g] Fortunatus sibi Damocles videbatur. In cenae medio, Dionysius gladium saet, equin, demitti iussit <u>ut impenderet</u> <u>illius "beati" cervicem</u>.[h] Damocles, <u>cum gladium vidisset</u>,[i] non longius cupivit "beatus" esse et oravit tyrannum <u>ut abire liceret</u>.[j] Satisne Dionysius videtur demonstravisse <u>nihil esse ei beatum</u>[k] <u>cui semper aliqui terror</u> <u>impendeat</u>?*[l]

(*Disputationes Tusculanae* V, xx, 61–62)

---

* A relative clause within an Indirect Statement requires a subjunctive verb.

---

abundantia,-ae f., abundance
adsentator,-oris m., a flatterer
aliqui, aliquae, aliquod indef. adj., some
argentum,-i n., silver
aureus,-a,-um golden
aurum,-i n., gold
cervix, cervicis f., neck
commemoro (1) to remind (another person of something)/recount
Damocles,-is m., a courtier of Dionysius, the tyrant of Syracuse
degusto,-gustare to taste/try
delecto, delectare to delight/attract
deligo, deligere, delexi, delectum to choose/select carefully
demitto,-mittere,-misi,-missum to let down
dominatus,-us m., rule
demonstro (1) to demonstrate

experior, experiri, expertus sum to experience
exquisitus,-a,-um exquisite
fortunatus,-a,-um fortunate
gladius,-i m., sword
impendo,-pendere,-pendi,-pensum to be suspended above/hang over/threaten
infero,-ferre,-tuli,-latum to carry in/bring in
licet, licere + dat 3rd Pers. Impersonal, to be permitted
lectus,-i m., couch
loco (1) to place/locate
medium,-i n., midst/middle
maiestas, maiestatis f., majesty/greatness
mensa,-ae f., table
orno (1) to adorn
quisquis, quaequae, quidquid anyone/anything
saeta equina, saetae equinae f, a horse hair
terror, terroris m., fear/terror

Conditional Statements
Irregular Verbs *volo, malo, nolo*

Objectives

To enable you to:
1. recognize and translate Subjunctive Conditional Statements;
2. recognize and conjugate the Irregular Verbs *volo, nolo, malo*.

Conditional Statements

A Conditional Statement is composed of two parts: a Conditional Clause and a Conclusion. In Latin, Positive Conditional Statements are introduced by the conjunction *sī* (if); Negative Conditional Statements are introduced by *nisi* (if . . . not/unless/except). If the Condition states a **fact, Indicative Verbs** are used.

Present Tense: ***Si studet, facit A.***
                     If he is studying, he is making an A.
Future Tense: ***Si studebit, faciet A.***
                     If he will study, he will make an A.
Past Tense: ***Si studebat/studuit, fecit A.***
                     If he studied, he made an A.

Subjunctive Conditional Statements

If the Conditional Clause is **not** stating **a fact**, **Subjunctive Verbs** are used in the Condition and in the Conclusion. In Latin there are three types of Conditional Subjunctive Statements, each of which is formed by employing a specific tense of the Subjunctive.

1. In **Future Less Likely** (**should/would clauses**) Conditional Statements, **Present Subjunctive** Verbs appear in the Condition and in the Conclusion.
    Si studeat, faciat A.   If he should/should he study, he would make an A.
    Nisi studeas, hoc sit difficile.   Should you not study, this would be difficult.

2. In **Contrary to Fact in the Present** Conditional Statements, **Imperfect Subjunctive** Verbs appear in the Condition and in the Conclusion.

Si studeret, faceret A.	If he were/were he studying, he would make an A.
Nisi studeret, non intellegeret.	Were he not studying, he would not understand.

3. In **Contrary to Fact in the Past** Conditional Statements, **Pluperfect Subjunctive** Verbs appear in the Condition and in the Conclusion.

Si studisset, fecisset A.	If he had/had he studied, he would have made an A.
Nisi studisset, non fecisset A.	Had he not studied, he would not have made an A.

Irregular Verbs volo, nolo, malo

The Irregular Verbs *volō, nōlō, mālō* have no Passive Voice and are **irregular** only in the **Present Indicative** and the **Present Subjunctive**. Notice that the Future Tense of these verbs follows a 3rd Conjugation pattern. Also, all forms of these verbs are generally followed by a Complementary Infinitive.

volō, velle, voluī	*nōlō ,nōlle ,nōluī*	*mālō, mālle, māluī*
(to wish/be willing)	(to refuse/be unwilling)	(to prefer)

Present Indicative

volō	**nōlō**	**mālō**
vīs	**nōn vīs**	**māvīs**
vult	**nōn vult**	**māvult**
volumus	**nōlumus**	**mālumus**
vultis	**nōn vultis**	**māvultis**
volunt	**nōlunt**	**mālunt**

Imperfect Indicative

volēbam	**nōlēbam**	**mālēbam**
volēbās	**nōlēbās**	**mālēbās**
volēbat	**nōlēbat**	**mālēbat**
volēbāmus	**nōlēbāmus**	**mālēbāmus**
volēbātis	**nōlēbātis**	**malebatis**
volēbant	**nōlēbant**	**mālēbant**

247

Future Indicative

volam	nōlam	mālam
volēs	nōlēs	mālēs
volet	nōlet	mālet
volēmus	nōlēmus	mālēmus
volētis	nōlētis	mālētis
volent	nōlent	mālent

The **Perfect, Pluperfect and Future Perfect Indicative** are **Regular**. (Conjugated completely on page 305.)

Present Subjunctive

velim	nōlim	mālim
velīs	nōlīs	mālīs
velit	nōlit	mālit
velīmus	nōlīmus	mālīmus
velītis	nōlītis	mālītis
velint	nōlint	mālint

The **Imperfect, Perfect**, and **Pluperfect Subjunctive** are **Regular**. (Conjugated completely on page 305.)

	Infinitives				Participles		
Pres.	**velle**	**nōlle**	**mālle**	Pres.	**volēns,**	**nōlēns,**	—
Perf.	**voluisse**	**nōluisse**	**māluisse**		**volentis**	**nōlentis**	—

Imperatives   **nōlī**   **nōlīte**

The Imperatives of *nolo* followed by an Infinitive are commonly used for negative commands.

Noli facere hoc.	Refuse to do this!/Don't do this!
Nolite ire.	Refuse to go!/Don't go!

Vocabulary

mālō, mālle, māluī to prefer
nōlō, nōlle, nōluī to wish not/be unwilling/to refuse
studeo, studēre, studuī + dat. to be eager for/study
suscipiō, suscipere, suscēpī, susceptum to undertake
trādō, trādere, trādidī, trāditum to hand down/transmit/give over
volō, velle, voluī to wish/be willing

sī quis, sī quid/ nisi quis, nisi quid/ ne quis, ne quid* = Indefinite Pronouns, if
 any_____ *or* if anyone/anything

dīves, dīvitis = adj., wealthy
pār, paris = adj., equal/like
pauper, pauperis = adj./noun, poor/poor man/pauper

*Indefinite Pronouns (such as *any, anyone, anything*) are pronouns that do not refer to specific persons or things. In combination with the conjunctions *si, nisi,* and *ne,* the Interrogative Pronouns *quis* and *quid* become Indefinite Pronouns and take on new meanings.

> *Si quis putat* = If any _____/anyone thinks
> *Nisi quis est* = If any _____/anyone is not
> *Ne quis* = Lest any _____/anyone

Exercises

A. Translate the following Indicative Verbs; parse the others.

1. noluerat		11. non vis	
2. voluisses		12. mallet	
3. vultis		13. volebat	
4. mavult		14. vult	
5. velim		15. noles	
6. mavis		16. voluerit	
7. nolam		17. malle	
8. nolo		18. vis	
9. velint		19. noluisse	
10. malo		20. velle	

B Translate the following statements.

1. Si petivisset veritatem, invenisset scientiam.
2. Si peteres veritatem, invenires scientiam.
3. Invenias scientiam, si petas veritatem.
4. Nisi iram vitabitis, multos amicos amittetis.
5. Nisi iram vitetis, multos amicos amittatis.
6. Multos amicos amisisset nisi iram vitavisset.
7. Si meliores libros legeremus, magis disceremus.
8. Magis discamus, si meliores libros legamus.
9. Si meliores libros legissemus, magis didicissemus.
10. Proxima inquisitio erit facilior, si haec memoriā tenebis.
    proximus,-a,-um = next   *inquisitio,-onis* = f., exam

C. Render the following Conditional Statements into Latin.

1. Should he refuse, I would understand.
2. Had he been willing, I would have helped.
3. You would help, were you a friend.
4. If he prefers poverty, he will find it.
   paupertas, paupertatis = f., poverty
5. If they did these things, they had reasons.
6. I will help you if you will undertake this task.
7. Had his wealth not been great, he would not have come.
8. If anyone should seek wisdom, he would also seek virtue.
9. Unless there are arms, there cannot be a war.
10. Were I not eager for wisdom, these sentences would be too difficult.
    sententia,-ae = f., sentence

D. Parse the underlined words and then translate the sentences.

1. Si vis scire <u>quam nihil mali in paupertate sit,</u> <u>confer</u> pauperem et divitem: pauper saepius et fidelius ridet. (Seneca)

    paupertas,-tatis = f., poverty

2. Multa eveniunt homini <u>quae vult</u> et quae non vult. (Plautus)

3. Minus saepe erres si scias <u>quid nescias</u>. (Publilius Syrus)

4. Arma sunt parvi pretii nisi consilium est <u>in patriā</u>. (Cicero)

    pretium,-ii = n., value

5. Laudas fortunam et mores antiquae plebis; sed <u>si quis ad illa subito te agat,</u> <u>illum modum vitae recuses</u>. (Horace)

    plebs, plebis = f., common people

    recuso (1) = to refuse

6. Fere libenter homines id <u>quod volunt</u> credunt. (Caesar)

    fere = adv., generally   *libenter* = adv., willingly

7. Putatis <u>hominem ire dis</u>. Immo Deus hominibus venit; quid est verius, in homines venit; nullum bonum sine Deo potest esse. (Seneca)

    dis = Irregular Dat. Pl. of *deus*

8. An Philippus rex Macedonum <u>voluisset</u> Alexandro filio suo prima elementa litterarum tradi ab Aristotele, summo eius aetatis philosopho, aut hic <u>suscepisset</u> hoc officium, nisi <u>initia studiorum pertinere ad summam partem</u> credidisset? (Quintillian)

    Aristoteles,-is = m., Aristotle   *Macedones,-um* = Macedonians

    elementum,-i = n., element   *pertineo,-tinere,-tinui* = to pertain

    initium,-i = n., beginning   *philosophus,-i* = m., philosopher

9. <u>Quisque inveniat</u> quod velit; non omnibus unum est quod placet; hic spinas colligit; ille rosas. (Petronius)

    colligo,-ligere,-legi,-lectum = to collect

    placeo, placere, placui = to be pleasing

    rosa,-ae = f., rose

    spina,-ae = f., thorn

10. Si quoties homines peccant, sua fulmina mittat Juppiter, <u>exiguo tempore</u> inermis sit. (Ovid)

    exiguus,-a,-um = short

    fulmen,-inis = n., thunderbolt/strike of lightning

    inermis,-e = unarmed

    pecco (1) = to sin

    quoties = adv., as often as

Text Translation

Parse the underlined portions and then translate the selections below.

Martial (AD 40–103) was a contemporary of Seneca and Juvenal, and, like them, a master of satire. His epigrams (short, witty poems or sayings) are famous.

<u>Quid mihi reddat ager</u> quaeris, Line, Nomentanus?

<u>Hoc mihi reddit ager</u>: te Line, non video.

(*Epigrams* Bk. II, xxxviii)

Linus,-i m., Proper Noun
Nomentanus,-a,-um of Nomentum, a town
    northeast of Rome

reddo, reddere, reddidi, redditum to return/give
    back

Martial was disgusted by legacy hunters who sought out widows in ill health for marriage. In this poem, Gemellus is seeking marriage with Maronilla because she has tuberculosis.

Petit Gemellus nuptias Maronillae

et cupit et instat et <u>precatur</u> et donat.

adeone pulchra est? immo <u>foedius</u> nil est.

quid ergo in illā petitur et placet? Tussit.

(*Epigrams* Bk. I, x)

adeo adv., so
Maronilla,-ae f., Proper Noun
dono (1) to give
nuptia,-ae f., marriage
foedus,-a,-um ugly/loathsome
placeo, placere, placui, placitum pleasing to; to be
    pleasing to

Gemellus,-i m., Proper Noun
immo on the contrary
precor (1) deponent, to beg
insto (1) to insist
tussio, tussire to cough

CHAPTER XXXII

Text Translation

Quintus Horatius Flaccus (65–9 BC), better known as Horace, was in effect the poet laureate of the empire under Augustus. Horace was a native of Venusia and the son of a freedman, at whose sacrifice and expense he received an excellent education. Despite the entreaties of his father, Horace became involved in politics while at the university in Athens, and found himself on the losing side of the Republicans at Philippi. He returned home to find his father dead and himself stripped of his property. Horace never forgot the sacrifices his father had made on his behalf nor the bitter experiences of his early manhood. He learned well from his personal mistakes and developed a deep compassion for his fellow man, reflected in his soft satire and gentle chiding.

Atque si mea natura est mendosa vitiis mediocribus ac paucis sed alioqui recta, si vivo carus amicis, causa fuit pater meus. Qui cum pauper in macro agello esset, tamen noluit in ludum Flavii me mittere sed puerum <u>ausus est</u> portare me <u>Romam</u> docendum artes quas senatores suos filios docent.

(*Satires* I, vi, 65–75)

agellus,-i m., small farm
alioqui adv., otherwise
audeo, audere, ausus sum semi-depon, translate
   Perfect System actively
Flavius,-ii m., Proper Noun
ludus,-i m., school
porto (1) to carry

macer,-cra,-crum poor/scrawny
mendosus,-a,-um faulty
rectus,-a,-um right/straight
<u>Romam</u> Accusative of Place to Which, translate "to
   Rome"
senator, senatoris m., senator

Horace became a government employee in Rome, but continued to write poetry, and ultimately became a good friend of Augustus and poet laureate of Rome. Augustus gave Horace a small farm which Horace loved and where he spent the majority of his time. However, he occasionally was compelled to come to the palace court in Rome and present readings. When he was in Rome, he always missed his farm and the unaffected rural people who were quite often his dinner guests. In this excerpt he is longing to be back home.

O rus, quando te aspiciam? Quandoque mihi licebit uti nunc libris veterum auctorum, nunc somno et inertibus horis sine curis sollicitae vitae? O noctes cenaeque deorum! Sermo oritur non de villis et domis alienis; sed quaerimus et agitamus quod magis ad nos pertinet et nescire malum est: utrumne divitiis an virtute homines sint beati; quidve ad amicitiam trahat nos, usus an rectum, et quae sit natura boni et quid sit summum bonum.

253

Cervius vicinus de re fabulam dicit olim rusticus mus urbanum murem accepit paupere cavo. Neque ille sepositi ciceris nec avenae invidit, et ferens ore acinum aridum semesaque lardi frusta dedit, cupiens variā cenā vincere fastidia amici dente superbo. Tandem urbanus as hunc "Amice bone," inquit, "homines urbsque feris silvisque anteponuntur. Carpe viam, dum licet, vive beatus in rebus iucundis, memoriā tene quam brevis sit vita." Haec verba rustico persuadebant ut abeat domo et ambo profecti sunt ad urbem. Iam erat nox, cum ponerent in divite domo vestigia, invenientes eburnos lectos multaque fercula relicta de magnā cenā. Ergo ubi in purpureā veste rusticum porrectum locavit, quasi hospes cursitat continuatque magnam cenam verniliter praelambens omne quod offert. Rusticus cubans gaudet mutatā fortunā bonisque rebus, cum subito ingens strepitus valvarum de lectis utrum iecit. Pavidi currunt, timentes magis cum latratus Molossorum audiant. Tum rusticus: "Non mihi est hac vita," ait "valeas: silva, tenue ervum, cavus tutus de insidiis mihi placent."'

(Horace *Satires* II, vi)

acinum,-i n., a berry
agito (1) to discuss
alienus,-a,-um belonging to another
ambo together
aridus,-a,-um dry
aspicio, aspicere, aspexi to see
avena,-ae f., wild oats
cavus,-i m., hole
Cervius, -ii m., Proper noun
cicer, ciceris n., a chickpea
continuo, continuare to continue
cubo, cubare, cubui, cubitum to recline
cursito (1) to run up and down
dens, dentis m., tooth
do, dare, dedi, datum to serve
domus,-us f., home/house
dum while
eburnus,-a,-um ivory/made of ivory
ervum,-i n., vetch
fastidium,-i n., loathing/disgust
fera,-ae f., wild beast
ferculum,-i n., a course/dish (for serving food)
frustum,-i n., morsel
gaudeo, gaudere, gavisus sum to take delight in

hospes, hospitis m., host
iners, inertis idle
ingens, ingentis huge
invideo,-videre,-vidi,-visum + gen. to begrudge
lardum,-i n., bacon
latratus,-us m., a barking
lectus,-i m., couch (for dining)
licet, licere, licuit + dat. and inf. to be permitted, usually in 3rd Sing. Impersonal
loco (1) to locate
olim adv., once
Molossus,-i m., molossian hound
mus, muris c., mouse
orior, oriri, ortus sum Deponent, to arise
os, oris n., mouth
pavidus,-a,-um panic-stricken
pertineo, pertinere, pertinui to pertain
porrectus,-a,-um stretched out
praelambens,-ntis tasting beforehand
proficiscor, proficisci, profectus sum Deponent, to set out
purpureus,-a,-um purple colored
quando when?
rectus,-a,-um right

rus, ruris n., farm/country (as opposed to the city)
rusticus,-a,-um country (of the country)
semesus,-a,-um half eaten
sepono,-ponere,-posui,-positum to reserve/put away
sermo, sermonis m., conversation
silva,-ae f., forest
sollicitus,-a,-um troubled/anxious
somnus,-i m., sleep
strepitus,-us m., loud noise/crashing
superbus,-a,-um haughty/arrogant
tenuis,-e meager/low/common
urbanus,-a,-um city (of the city)

usus,-us m., advantage
utor, uti, usus sum + Abl. of Means Deponent, to enjoy
valvae,-arum f., folding doors
varius,-a,-um diverse/varied
verniliter adv., like a slave
vestigium,-i n., track/footprint
vestis,-is f., covering/slipcover
vetus, veteris ancient
vicinus,-i m., neighbor
villa,-ae f., villa/house

Vocabulary: Chapters XXIX–XXXII

abeō, abīre, abiī, abitum to go away/depart
aequus,-a,-um level/even/equal/just
antepōnō,-pōnere,-posuī,-positum to prefer/put before
apud + acc. among/in the presence of/at the house of/in front of

cēna,-ae f., dinner
cēnō (1) to dine
cēterī,-ae,-a the other/the rest
comprehendō,-prehendere,-prehendī, -prehēnsum to comprehend
cōnferō, cōnferre, cōntulī, collātum to bring together/compare
cūrō (1) to take care

dīves, dīvitis adj., wealthy
domus,-us f., house/home

eō, īre, iī, itum to go

ferō, ferre, tulī, lātum to carry/bear/endure/bring

hortor, hortārī, hortātus sum deponent, to urge/implore

imperō (1) + dat to give orders to/command
incolō, incolere, incoluī to inhabit
iniustus,-a,-um unjust
iustus,-a-um just

mālō, mālle, māluī to prefer
mediocris,-e ordinary/moderate/mediocre
miror, mirārī, mirātus sum deponent, to wonder/be astonished
mortalis,-e mortal

nōlō, nōlle, nōluī to wish not/be unwilling
offerō, offerre, obtulī, oblātum to offer
ōra,-ae f., shore
ōrō (1) to beg/entreat/beseech

pār, paris f., equal
pauper, pauperis adj./m., poor/poor man/pauper
pereō, perīre, periī, peritum to pass away/perish
persuādeō,-suādēre,-suāsī,-suāsum + dat. to persuade/make sweet to
pōnō, pōnere, posuī, positum to put/place
pugnō (1) to fight

quantus,-a,-um how large/how great/how much
quōmodo adv., how

redeō, redīre, rediī, reditum to go back/return
rogō (1) to ask

sī quis, sī quid/ nisi quis, nisi quid indefinite pronoun, if/unless anyone, anything
studeō, studēre, studuī + dat. to be eager for/study
subitō adv., immediately
suscipiō, suscipere, suscēpī, susceptum to undertake

tamen nevertheless
trādō, trādere, trādidī, trāditum to hand down/transmit/give over

unde adv., whence/from which
uter . . . an whether . . . or
uter, utra, utrum which (of two)

vīnum,-i neut., wine
volō, velle, voluī to wish/be willing

Review Work Sheet: Chapter XXXII

I. Provide the Latin verb forms for the following.

       1. they had gone   6. I returned
       2. they preferred   7. you were returning
       3. they refused   8. It has been handed down
       4. they will endure   9. Will he perish?
       5. we wish   10. it will have been placed

II. Render the following sentences into Latin, being sure to keep in mind specific Subjunctive usages.

    1. Let us undertake a plan for/of peace in order to avoid a war.
    2. I urge you that you remember who you are.
    3. He offered so much help that we were able to endure for many days without our friends.
    4. Should you (pl.) ask him, he would return.
    5. Had they understood the injustice, they would have refused to do this.
        (*iniustitia,-ae* = f., injustice)
    6. They knew that we were not wealthy.
    7. We wish to know who is sending help.
    8. Although we had sought their help for many years, nevertheless they never came.
    9. May the gods persuade you not to go.
   10. Were the man whom you seek living here, I would be able to tell you the thing that you wish to know.

Pre-Chapter Review Work Sheet: Chapter XXXIII

I.   Relative Pronouns and Interrogative Adjectives are identical in declension. Using a paradigm format indicating cases, decline *qui, quae, quod*.

II. Using a paradigm format, decline the Interrogative Pronouns *quis, quid*.

III. Fill in the blank with the correct form of the Relative Pronoun, Interrogative Adjective, or Interrogative Pronoun then translate the sentence.

1. Abiit cum viro _____ vidisti.
    whom

2. _____ labores suscipiebantur?
    Which

3. _____ auxilium oblatum erat?
    To whom

4. Cetera _____ tradita sunt non sunt vera.
    which

5. Viri de _____ dicebas tulerant mala multa.
    whom

6. Vita _____ mortalis cur, caret?
    of which

7. _____ miratur ista accidere?
    Who

8. _____ eā nocte cenaverunt?
    With whom

9. Volunt cognoscere _____ viri hoc fecerint.
    which

10. Me rogaverunt _____ hoc officium suscepisset.
    who

Subjunctive Relative Clauses of Characteristic
Deponent Verbs
Participles of Deponent Verbs
Infinitives of Deponent Verbs
Imperatives of Deponent Verbs

XXXIII

Objectives

To enable you to:

    1. recognize and translate Subjunctive Relative Clauses of Characteristic;

    2. recognize and conjugate Deponent Verbs.

Subjunctive Relative Clauses of Characteristic

We have now arrived at the last major use of the Subjunctive covered in this book, Subjunctive Relative Clauses of Characteristic, really not that difficult to understand if you have a firm grasp of Indicative Relative Clauses (chapter XII).

An **Indicative Relative Clause states a fact** about a particular antecedent. A **Subjunctive Relative Clause of Characteristic implies an opinion** about a general antecedent. The following example sentences should illustrate the translation differences of a Subjunctive Relative Clause of Characteristic (an opinion) as opposed to an Indicative Relative Clause (a fact).

Indicative Relative Clause

Cicero est vir qui <u>credit</u> huic.
Cicero is the man who believes this.

Hoc est factum quod <u>cognoscitur</u> omnibus.
This is a fact which is known to all.

Relative Clause of Characteristic

Quis est qui <u>credat</u> huic?
Who is there who would believe this?

Sunt quae <u>cognoscantur</u> omnibus.
There are things which would be known to all.

Subjunctive Relative Clauses of Characteristic are, therefore, Dependent Subjunctive Clauses. **Subjunctive Relative Clauses of Characteristic express a quality or characteristic of a general or indefinite antecedent and are used especially after such expressions as:**

1.	*est quī/quae*	he/she is someone who
2.	*est quod*	it is something which
3.	*sunt quī*	there are those who
4.	*sunt quae*	there are things which
5.	*nēmo/nūllus est quī*	there is no one who
6.	*nihil est quod*	there is nothing which
7.	*ūnus/sōlus est quī*	he is the only one who
8.	*quis est quī?*	who is there who?

If you **commit the above expressions and standard translations to memory**, you will never have trouble recognizing or translating Subjunctive Relative Clauses of Characteristic.

Deponent Verbs

Deponent Verbs differ from Regular Verbs in two distinct ways:

1. they have **only Passive Forms;**
2. these Passive Forms are **translated actively**.

The Principal Parts of Deponent Verbs are easily recognized by their Passive Forms.

1st	**hortor, hortārī, hortātus sum**	to urge/encourage
2nd	**fateor, fatērī, fassus sum**	to confess
3rd	**sequor, sequī, secutus sum**	to follow
3rd-*io*	**morior, morī, mortuus sum**	to die
4th	**orior, orīrī, ortus sum**	to arise

Notice in the examples below that Deponent Verbs are conjugated in exactly the same way as Regular Verbs but have only Passive Endings. (**See the tables on pages 307–309 for the complete conjugations of Deponent Verbs.**)

1.	*Ei bella saepe hortantur.*	Often they encourage wars.
2.	*Fassus est se vidisse eam.*	He confessed that he had seen her.
3.	*Longum tempus eos secuti sumus.*	We followed them for a long time.
4.	*Multi viri in bello mortui sunt.*	Many men died in the war.
5.	*Sol ortus est.*	The sun has arisen.

Participles of Deponent Verbs

The Participles of Deponent Verbs are formed in the same way as those of Regular Verbs, but notice that the Perfect Passive Participle is translated actively.

	Active		Passive	
Pres.	**hortāns,-ntis**	urging	—	
Perf.	**hortātus,-a,-um**	(having) urged	—	
Fut.	**hortātūrus,-a,-um**	about to urge	**hortandus,-a,-um**	fit to be urged

	1st Conj.	2nd Conj.	3rd Conj.	3rd-*io* Conj.	4th Conj.
			Active		
Pres.	**hortāns,-ntis**	**fatēns,-ntis**	**sequēns,-ntis**	**moriēns,-ntis**	**oriēns,-ntis**
Perf.	**hortātus**	**fassus**	**secūtus**	**mortuus**	**ortus**
Fut.	**hortātūrus**	**fassūrus**	**secūtūrus**	**moritūrus***	**ortūrus**
			Passive		
Fut.	**hortandus**	**fatendus**	**sequendus**	**moriendus**	**oriendus**

Infinitives of Deponent Verbs
Active

	1st Conj.	2nd Conj.	3rd Conj.	3rd-*io* Conj.	4th Conj.
Pres.	**hortārī**	**fatērī**	**sequī**	**morī**	**orīrī**
Perf.	**hortātus esse**	**fassus esse**	**secūtus esse**	**mortuus esse**	**ortus esse**
Fut.	**hortātūrus esse**	**fassūrus esse**	**secūtūrus esse**	**moritūrus* esse**	**ortūrus esse**

* The Future Participle of *morior* is irregular, accounting for the *i*.

Imperatives of Deponent Verbs

Deponent Verb Imperatives differ from the Imperatives of regular verbs in that:

1. the **Singular Imperative is in the form of an Active Infinitive;**
2. the **Plural Imperative is the same form as the 2nd Person Plural Indicative.**

	Singular	Plural
hortor, hortārī, hortātus sum	**hortāre**	**hortāminī**
fateor, fatērī, fassus sum	**fatēre**	**fatēminī**
sequor, sequī, secutus sum	**sequere**	**sequiminī**
morior, morī, mortuus sum	**morere**	**moriminī**
orior, orīrī, ortus sum	**orīre**	**orīminī**

Vocabulary

arbitror, arbitrarī, arbitrātus sum to judge/think
experior, experīrī, expertus sum to experience/try/test
fateor, fatērī, fassus sum to confess
irāscor, irāscī, irātus sum to be angry
loquor, loquī, locūtus sum to say/speak/tell
morior, morī, mortuus sum to die
nāscor, nāsci, nātus sum to be born
orior, orīrī, ortus sum to arise
patior, patī, passus sum to endure
proficiscor, proficiscī, profectus sum to set out
sequor, sequī, secūtus sum to follow
ūtor, ūtī, ūsus sum + abl. of means to benefit oneself by means of/use/enjoy
placeō, placēre, placuī, placitum + dat. to be pleasing to
licet,* licēre, licuit + dat. and inf. impersonal, it is allowed/permitted

* The verb *licet* only appears in 3rd Singular and is usually translated impersonally ("it"), with the person granted permission appearing in the Dative Case and the action permitted as an Infinitive.

    Licuit ei abire.   He was allowed to leave. (It was permitted to him that he leave.)

Exercises

A. Identify the conjugation of the following verbs:

1. pono, ponere
2. loquor, loqui
3. audio, audire
4. experior, experiri
5. suscipio, suscipere

6. patior, pati
7. placeo, placere
8. fateor, fateri
9. oro, orare
10. arbitror, arbitrari

B. Form the Singular and Plural Imperatives of the above verbs.

C. Give a synopsis in 1st Pl. M. in the Indicative and Subjunctive, with English translations of the Indicative of *sequor, sequi, secutus sum*.

D. Form the Participles (Nom. Sing. forms) with English translations and then the Infinitives of *loquor, loqui, locutus sum*.

E. **Translate** the following Indicative, Imperative, and Participle forms; **parse** the other forms.

1. usurus
2. patiantur
3. sequere
4. moriemur
5. usus est

6. proficiscitur
7. ortus
8. passi
9. profectus esset
10. arbitrati erant

F. Supply the correctly <u>declined</u> form of *is* or *id* and then translate the sentence.

1. Persuasi   _____.
2. Usus es   _____.
3. Sequuntur   _____.
4. Hortati sunt   _____.
5. Offeramus auxilium _____.

6. Amisimus   _____.
7. Imperavistis   _____.
8. Cenabimus cum   _____.
9. Se contulit ad   _____.
10. Anteponis eam   _____.

G. Parse the underlined portions and then translate the sentences into English.

1. Hic vir <u>quem comprehendisti</u> expertus est multa.
2. Sunt multi <u>qui laudent eum</u>.
3. Sunt soli <u>qui credant huic</u>.
4. Nemo est <u>cui iniustitiae placeant</u>.
5. Unus est <u>qui civitatem possit servare</u>.
6. Arbitratus est <u>nos hāc scientiā usuros esse</u>.
7. Peto a te <u>ne facias</u> hoc.
8. Quis est <u>qui credat</u> eum esse meum amicum?

H. Identify the required Latin form for the underlined English words and then render the sentence into Latin.

    1. I encouraged him <u>to study</u>.
    2. <u>Although we were enemies</u>, nevertheless I thought that he would help.
    3. They were wondering <u>when we had set out</u>.
    4. <u>Let us confess</u> that we were there.
    5. There is no one <u>who would believe</u> <u>what has happened</u>.

I. Sentence translations.

    1. Nam nemo sine vitiis nascitur; optimus ille est qui minima habet. (Horace)
    2. Tarde sed graviter vir sapiens irascitur. (Publilius Syrus)
       tardus,-a,-um = slow
    3. Cura pecuniam crescentem sequitur. (Horace)
       cresco, crescere, crevi, cretum = to increase
    4. Horae quidem et dies et anni discedunt; nec praeteritum tempus umquam revertitur, nec quid sequatur potest sciri. (Cicero)
       revertor,-verti,-versus sum = to return
    5. Nisi laus nova oritur, etiam antiqua laus amittetur. (Publilius Syrus)
    6. Mundus est communis urbs deorum atque hominum; hi enim soli ratione utentes, iure ac lege vivunt. (Cicero)
       ac = *atque*
    7. Frustra adulescentes aut pecuniae aut imperiis aut divitiis aut gloriae student; potius studeant virtuti et dignitati et scientiae et alicui arti. (Cicero)
       aliqui, aliquae, aliquod = some other
       dignitas,-atis = f., honor/official rank
       frustra = adv., in vain
       potius = rather
    8. Si quis petit magnitudinem, obliviscatur magnitudinem et quaerat veritatem et inveniet utrasque. (Thomas Mann)
       magnitudo, magnitudinis = f., greatness
       obliviscor, oblivisci, oblitus sum = to forget
       uterque, utraque, utrumque = both
    9. Si cui libri Ciceronis placent, ille sciat se profecisse. (Quintillian)
       proficio,-ficere,-feci,-fectum = to progress
    10. Cum tu omnibus pecuniam anteponas, miraris si nemo tibi amorem praestat? (Horace)
    11. Ars prima ducis te posse invidiam pati.
       primus,-a,-um = first   *invidia,-ae* = f., unpopularity/hatred
    12. Quis est qui enim aut eum diligat quem metuat aut eum a quo se metui putet? (Cicero)
       metuo, metuere, metui, metutum = to fear

Text Translation

In this excerpt from *De Amicitiā*, Cicero discusses the nature and value of friendship, which he ranks second only to wisdom in the gifts/benefits given to man by the gods. Parse the underlined portions and then translate the reading.

Ego vos hortor <u>ut amicitiam omnibus rebus humanis anteponatis</u>;[a] nihil est tam aptum naturae, tam conveniens ad res vel secundas vel adversas. Haud scio an, <u>exceptā sapientiā</u>,[b] quidquam melius homini <u>a deis immortalibus</u>[c] datum sit. Alii anteponunt divitias; alii, bonam valetudinem; alii, potentiam; alii, honores; multi, etiam voluptates. Illa autem caduca et incerta, <u>posita</u>[d] non tam <u>in consiliis nostris</u>[e] quam in fortunae temeritate. Sunt <u>qui in virtute summum bonum ponunt</u>,[f] hoc est praeclarum quidem, sed ipsa virtus amicitiam continet; nec sine virtute amicitia <u>esse</u>[g] potest. Denique ceterae res, <u>quae petuntur</u>,[h] opportunae sunt rebus singulis: divitiae, <u>ut eis utaris</u>;[i] opes, ut colaris; honores, ut lauderis; voluptas, ut vitam gaudeas; valetudo, ut <u>dolore</u>[j] careas et <u>rebus</u>[k] corporis utaris. Amicitia res plurimas continet; <u>nullo loco</u>[l] excluditur; numquam intempestiva est, numquam molesta est. Itaque <u>neque aquā neque igne</u>,[m] ut aiunt, in locis pluribus utimur quam amicitiā. Nam amicitia secundas res <u>splendidiores</u>[n] facit et adversas res leviores. Quis est qui <u>velit se circumfluere copiis atque in abundantiā omnium rerum ita vivere</u>[o] <u>ut neque diligat quemquam neque ipse ab ullo diligatur</u>?[p] Haec enim est tyrannorum vita, in quā nulla fides, nulla caritas, nulla benevolentia potest esse; omnia semper suspecta atque sollicita, nullus locus est amicitiae. Quis est qui enim aut <u>eum diligat quem metuat aut eum a quo se metui putet</u>?[q] Et si forte ceciderunt, ut saepe evenit, tum intellegunt <u>quam inopes amicorum fuerint</u>.[r] Quid autem <u>stultius</u>[s] quam cetera parare <u>quae parantur pecuniis</u>[t] sed amicos non parare, quasi optimam et pulcherrimam supellectilem vitae?

(De Amicitiā IV, VI, XV)

alii . . . alii some . . . others
aptus,-a,-um apt/suitable
aqua,-ae f., water
benevolentia,-ae f., kindness
cado, cadere, cecidi to fall on hard times

caducus,-a,-um transitory/fleeting
caritas, caritatis f., affection
circumfluo,-fluere,-flui,-fluxum to encompass/surround
colo, colere, colui, cultum to promote/cultivate

conveniens,-entis agreeable
dolor, doloris m., pain
excipio,-cipere,-cepi,-ceptum to except
excludo,-cludere,-clusi,-clusum to exclude
forte by chance
gaudeo, gaudere, gavisus sum to delight in/take
    pleasure in
haud adv., hardly
inops, inopis bereft
intempestivus,-a,-um untimely
metuo, metuere, metui, metutum to fear
molestus,-a,-um bothersome
nobilis,-e noble
opes,-um f. pl., power/influence
opportunus,-a,-um suitable

potentia,-ae f., power
praeclarus,-a,-um noteworthy
quasi as if
quisquam, quaequam, quidquam
    anyone/anything
secundus,-a,-um favorable
singulus,-a,-um singular/individual
sollicitus,-a,-um disquieting
splendidus,-a,-um splendid
supellex, supellectilis f., furniture
suspectus,-a,-um suspect
temeritas,-atis f., accident/chance/fickleness
valetudo,-inis f., health
vel . . . vel whether . . . or
voluptas, voluptatis f., pleasure

Review Work Sheet: Chapter XXXIII

Translate the following Imperatives, Indicative Verbs, and Participles; identify the tense and voice of the Subjunctive Verbs and Infinitives.

1. utentur

2. profecturus esse

3. oriens

4. arbitratus est

5. secuti erant

6. mori

7. hortari

8. loquere

9. iratus sit

10. placebunt

11. licuerat

12. patimini

13. nascebatur

14. patientes

15. fassi essent

16. oritur

17. fateamur

18. usus esse

19. mortuus

20. proficiscere

Gerunds
Gerundives
Two New Ways of Expressing Purpose

XXXIV

Objectives

To enable you to:
1. recognize and form Gerunds;
2. understand the difference between a Gerund and a Gerundive;
3. recognize two new methods of expressing "purpose."

Gerunds

A Gerund is a Verbal Noun; in English a Gerund is formed by adding *-ing* to a verb: *Reading is fun*. In Latin there are only four declined forms of the Gerund, which are identical in form to the corresponding cases of the Neuter Singular Future Passive Participle. There is no nominative form of the Gerund, this use being accomplished by the Active Infinitive as you will see in the paradigm below.

Gerunds of *legō, legere, lēgī, lēctum*

Nom.	(*legere*)	=	(reading)
Gen.	*legendī*	=	of reading
Dat.	*legendō*	=	to/for reading
Acc.	*legendum*	=	reading
Abl.	*legendō*	=	by/with/from reading

NB: Gerunds are Neuter Singular Verbal Nouns of four cases. Gerunds do not have Plural Forms; Gerunds may or may not have Direct Objects.

1. Reading is fun/pleasant.	*Legere est iucundum.*
2. There are many types of reading.	*Sunt multi modi legendi.*
3. He gives his leisure to reading.	*Otium suum legendo dat.*
4. He threw himself into reading good books.	*In legendum bonos libros se iecit.*
5. By reading good books we help ourselves.	*Legendo bonos libros nos iuvamus nos.*

Gerundives

The **Gerundive** is another name for the **Future Passive Participle**. The nominative singular forms of the Gerundives of *lego, legere, legi, lectum* are: *legendus,-a,-um*. Gerundives are 1st–2nd declension Verbal Adjectives that can be declined completely into Masculine, Feminine, and Neuter singular and plural forms. (See chapter XX for the complete declension.) Since they are Verbal <u>Adjectives</u>, Gerundives must agree in Case, Number, and Gender with the noun they modify.

NB: The Romans preferred Gerundive Constructions, but <u>in English</u> Gerundives are best translated actively. This can easily be demonstrated and remembered by the translation of this simple sentence.

Amo libros legendos.   I love reading books.
(If you told a friend that you loved books to be read, he would think you were crazy.)

So, the best English translations of these sentences would be:

1. *Sunt multi modi **librorum legendorum**.*
    There are many types of reading books.
2. *Otium suum **libris legendis** dat.*
    He gives his leisure to reading books.
3. *In **libros bonos legendos** se iecit.*
    He threw himself into reading good books.
4. ***Libris bonis legendis** nos ipsos iuvamus.*
    By reading good books, we help ourselves.

Two New Ways of Expressing Purpose

So far the only way you have learned to express purpose is by using a Subjunctive Purpose Clause. Like you, the Romans probably avoided the Subjunctive wherever possible, which more than likely accounts for Gerunds and Gerundives of Purpose. By employing the following set constructions, the Romans could indicate purpose without having to use Subjunctive Verbs.

1. ***ad*** + the Accusative Case of the Gerundive (Gerunds in this type construction are best avoided) translated as an Infinitive or as "for the purpose of."
    ***Venit ad pacem <u>faciendam</u>**. (Gerundive)
    He came to make/for the purpose of making peace.
2. ***causā*** preceded by the Genitive Case of a Gerund or Gerundive; translated as an Infinitive or "for the purpose of."
    Pacem <u>faciendi</u> causā venit. (Gerund)
    Pacis <u>faciendae</u> causā venit. (Gerundive)
    He came to make/for the purpose of making peace.

Vocabulary

adversum + acc. against/toward
adversus,-a,-um adverse
cupidus,-a,-um desirous
dolor, dōloris m., pain
opus, operis n., work/task/deed/accomplishment

ignōscō, ignōscere, ignōvī, ignōtum + dat. to grant pardon to/ignore/forgive
parcō, parcere, pepercī + dat. to be lenient to

etsī even if/although
quasi as if

Exercises

A. Using paradigm formats indicating cases, form the Gerunds of the following verbs, giving the English translation of each conjugated form.

    1. facio, facere, feci, factum
    2. moneo, monere, monui, monitum

B. Render each of the following statements into two separate Latin sentences, incorporating:

    (1) a Gerund in the first translation;
    (2) a Gerundive in the second translation.
        1. The teacher gives praise to reading books.
        2. He is coming to destroy the city.
        3. He grants pardon to our love of making war.
        4. By means of forgiving our enemies, we make new friends.

C. Identify the following underlined words as Gerunds or Gerundives then translate the phrase.

    1. huius operis <u>suscipiendi</u>   6. ad ludos <u>videndos</u>
    2. <u>discendi</u> causā   7. <u>vincendo</u> metum
    3. de <u>vivendo</u> bonam vitam   8. armis <u>offerendis</u>
    4. vitae <u>experiendae</u>   9. in exercitu <u>parando</u>
    5. in opere <u>faciendo</u>   10. metibus <u>vincendis</u>

D. Sentence translations. Parse the underlined portions before translating.

    1. Philippus pater meus dedit mihi donum vitae sed Aristoteles magister meus donum <u>vivendi</u>. (Plutarch, "Alexander")
    2. Nullus dolor est <u>quem longinquitas temporis non minuat ac molliat</u>. (Cicero)
        longinquitas, longinquitatis = f., length
        minuo,-uere,-ui,-utum = to diminish
        mollio, mollire = to soften
    3. Nihil est opere et manu factum <u>quod tempus non consumat</u>. (Cicero)
        consumo,-sumere,-sumpsi,-sumptum = to consume
    4. Multi autem propter gloriae cupiditatem sunt cupidi bellorum <u>gerendorum</u>. (Cicero)
    5. Curemus <u>ne poena maior sit quam culpa</u>; maxime autem <u>prohibenda est</u> ira in puniendo (Cicero)
        prohibeo, prohibere = to restrain/hold back
        punio, punire = to punish
    6. Fama vires acquirit in <u>eundo</u>. (Virgil)
        acquiro,-quirere,-quisivi,-quisitum = to acquire
        eundi = Gerund of *eo, ire, ii, itum*
    7. Saepe <u>metuendo</u> sapiens vitat malum. (Publilius Syrus)
        metuo, metuere, metui, metutum = to fear

8. Senectus nos avocat a rebus gerendis et corpus facit <u>infirmius</u>. (Cicero)

   avoco, avocare = to call away

   infirmus,-a,-um = infirm/weak

9. Optima <u>vivendi</u> ratio <u>est eligenda</u>; eam iucundam consuetudo reddet. (Cicero)

   consuetudo,-inis = f., custom/habit

   eligo,-ligere,-legi,-lectum = to choose/select

   reddeo,-dere,-didi,-ditum = to make/render

10. Hae vicissitudines fortunae etsi nobis iucundae in <u>experiendo</u> non fuerunt, in <u>legendo</u> tamen erunt iucundae. Recordatio enim praeteriti doloris delectationem nobis habet. (Cicero)

    delectatio,-onis = f., delight

    recordatio,-onis = f., recollection

    vicissitudo,-inis = f., change

11. Veterem iniuriam <u>ferendo</u> invitamus novam. (Publilius Syrus)

    iniuria,-ae = f., injury/injustice/wrong

    invito (1) = to invite

    vetus, veteris = old

Text Translation

The Romans always boasted that they only fought *bella iusta*. In *De Officiis* as well as in *De Republicā*, Cicero addresses the justifications for war as well as the obligations of the victor to the vanquished.

Parse the underlined portions, then translate the passage.

Quaedam autem officia etiam adversum eos <u>sunt servanda</u>, a quibus iniuriam accepimus. Est enim <u>ulciscendi et puniendi</u> modus; atque haud scio an satis sit eum, <u>qui lacessierit</u>, iniuriae suae paenitere, <u>ne ipse ullum tale posthac faciat</u> et <u>ut ceteri sint ad iniuriam tardiores</u>.

Atque in re publicā maxime <u>conservanda sunt</u> iura belli. Duo autem genera sunt <u>decertandi</u>, unum per disceptationem, alterum per vim: illud proprium est hominis, hoc beluarum; sed bellum vi <u>gerendum est</u> si <u>uti</u> non licet disceptatione.

Quāre quidem bella <u>suscipienda sunt</u> ob eam causam, ut sine iniuriā in pace vivamus, sed post victoriam <u>sunt conservandi</u> qui non crudeles in bello neque immanes fuerunt, ut maiores nostri Tusculanos, Volscos, Sabinos in civitatem etiam <u>acceperunt</u>. At Carthaginem et Numantiam funditus sustulerunt, et etiam Corinthum; sed credo <u>eos hoc fecisse</u> ne loca ipsa <u>ad bellum faciendum</u> hortari possent. Meā sententiā, pax sine insidiis semper est petenda.   (*De Officiis* I, xi, 34–36)

Illa iniusta bella sunt, quae sine causā <u>suscepta sunt</u>. Nam extra <u>ulciscendi aut propulsandorum hostium</u> causam bellum geri iustum nullum potest. Nullum bellum iustum habetur nisi <u>denuntiatum</u>, nisi <u>indictum</u>, nisi <u>repetitis rebus</u>.   (*De Republicā* III, xxiii, 34–35)

an whether
at but
belua,-ae f., wild beast
Carthago,-inis f., Carthage, a Phoenician town in North Africa destroyed by Rome
conservo (1) preserve/maintain/protect
Corinthus,-i m., a city in Greece destroyed by Rome
crudelis,-e cruel
decerto (1) to fight/resolve
denuntio (1) to declare (officially)
disceptatio, disceptationis f., discussion/debate
duo, duae, duo two
extra + acc. beyond
funditus adv., completely
haud adv., not/hardly
immanis,-e inhuman/monstrous

indico,-dicere,-dixi,-dictum to announce/proclaim officially
iniuria,-ae f., injury/wrong/injustice
lacesso,-ere,-ii,itum to provoke
Numantia,-ae f., a town in Spain destroyed by Rome
paeniteo, paenitere + gen. to repent
posthac in the future/afterward
proprius,-a,-um characteristic
propulso (1) to repel
punio, punire to punish
quāre adv, wherefore
repeto,-petere,-petivi,-petitum to claim/demand back
Sabini,-orum m., Sabines, an early people of Italy
tardus,-a,-um slow
talis,-e of such a kind

273

Tusculani,-orum m., Tusculans, an early people of Italy
ulciscor, ulcisci, ultus sum to avenge

victoria,-ae f., victory
Volsci,-orum m., Volscians, an early people of Italy

Text Translation

Omnia tempus habent, et suis spatiis
transeunt universa sub caelo.
Tempus est nascendi, et tempus moriendi;
Tempus plantandi, et tempus evellendi quod plantatum est.
Tempus occidendi, et tempus sanandi;
Tempus destruendi, et tempus aedificandi.
Tempus flendi, et tempus ridendi;
Tempus plangendi, et tempus saltandi.
Tempus spargendi lapides et tempus colligendi,
Tempus amplexandi, et tempus longe fieri ab amplexibus.
Tempus adquirendi, et tempus perdendi;
Tempus custodiendi, et tempus abiciendi.
Tempus scindendi, tempus consuendi;
Tempus tacendi, tempus loquendi.
Tempus dilectionis, et tempus odii;
Tempus belli, et tempus pacis.

(Ecclesiastes III: 1–8)

abicio,-icere,-ieci,-iectum to throw away
adquiro,-quirere,-quisivi,-quisitum to acquire
aedifico (1) to build
amplexor, amplexari to embrace
amplexus,-us m., embrace
colligo,-ligere,-legi,-lectum to bind/bring together
consuo,-suere,-sui,-sutum to sew together
custodio, custodire to keep/watch over
dilectio, dilectionis f., affection/love
evello,-vellere,-velli,-vulsum to tear out
fio, fieri, factus sum to become
fleo, flere, flevi, fletum to weep
lapis, lapidis m., stone

occido, occidere, occidi, occisum to kill
odium,-i n., hatred
perdo,-dere,-didi,-ditum to lose/waste
plango, plangere, planxi, planctum to wail/grieve
planto (1) to plant
salto (1) to dance
sano (1) to heal
scindo, scindere, scidi, scissum to cut/tear apart
spargo, spargere, sparsi, sparsum to scatter
spatium,-ii n., space
taceo,-ere,-ui,-itum to be silent
universus,-a,-um all together

Legal Terminology Work Sheet

Translate the following legal terminology.

1. ab initio
2. actio in personam
3. ad hoc
4. alibi
5. alienus iuris
6. amicus curiae
7. animo et facto
8. bona fide
9. causa mortis
10. compos mentis
11. corpus delicti
12. cui bono
13. de facto
14. habeas corpus
15. in absentiā
16. in communi
17. inter vivos
18. ipso facto
19. ius civile
20. ius civitatis
21. lex scripta

22. malā fide
23. mala in se
24. mala prohibita
25. mens rea
26. modus operandi
27. mos pro lege
28. nolle prosequi
29. nolo contendere
30. nulla bona
31. per curiam
32. per se
33. post mortem
34. primā facie
35. pro formā
36. pro tempore
37. quid pro quo
38. res gestae
39. res ipsa loquitur
40. res iudicata
41. sub iudice
42. sub poenā

absentia,-ae f., absence
actio, actionis f., action
alibi adv., elsewhere
alienus,-a,-um that which belongs to a another
civilis,-e civil
compos, compotis having control/possession of
contendo,-tendere,-tendi,-tentum to contend
curia,-ae f., originally the senate house, the place of judgment

delictum,-i n., crime
facies, faciei f., outward appearance/face
iudex, iudicis m., judge
iudico, iudicare to judge/decide
operor, operari to work/labor
prosequor,-sequi,-secutus sum to pursue/prosecute
reus,-i/rea,-ae originally any party in a lawsuit; later the defendant; later the criminal
vivus,-a,-um living

Cardinal Numerals
Ordinal Numerals
Partitive Genitives
Special Ablative Constructions

Objectives

To enable you to:

1. recognize and translate Cardinal and Ordinal Numbers;
2. understand that all Ordinals Numbers are 1st–2nd Declension Adjectives;
3. recognize and translate Partitive Genitives (Genitive of the Whole);
4. recognize other ways of expressing the idea of the whole using **de** or **ex**.

Cardinal Numerals

Cardinal Numerals are the principal numbers used in counting and indicating "**how many.**" **With the exceptions** of *unus,-a,-um* (one), *duo* (two), *tres* (three), and *mille* (thousand), cardinal numerals through *centum* (100) are indeclinable adjectives. You are already familiar with the declension of *ūnus,-a,-um* (chapter VI). The other **Irregular Cardinal Numbers** are declined this way:

duo two			*trēs* three		*mīlle* (indeclinable adj./noun) thousand *mīlia, milium* (n. pl.,) thousands
m.	f.	n.	m./f.	n.	n.
duo	duae	duo	tres	tria	mīlia
duōrum	duārum	duōrum	trium	trium	mīlium
duōbus	duābus	duōbus	tribus	tribus	mīlibus
duōs	duās	duo	trēs	tria	mīlia
duōbus	duābus	duōbus	tribus	tribus	mīlibus

Ordinal Numerals

Ordinal Numerals indicate the **order of sequence**, i.e., "in which order," and are all **1st–2nd Declension Adjectives**.

	Cardinals		*Ordinals*	
I	1. unus,-a,-um	one	prīmus,-a,-um	first
II	2. duo, duae, duo	(etc.)	secundus,-a,-um	(etc.)
III	3. trēs,tria		tertius,-a,-um	
IV	4. quattuor		quārtus,-a,-um	
V	5. quīnque		quīntus,-a,-um	
VI	6. sex		sextus,-a,-um	
VII	7. septem		septimus,-a,-um	
VIII	8. octō		octāvus,-a,-um	
IX	9. novem		nōnus,-a,-um	
X	10. decem		decimus,-a,-um	
XI	11. ūndecim		ūndecimus,-a,-um	
XII	12. duodecim		duodecimus,-a,-um	
XIII	13. tredecim		tertius decimus	
XIV	14. quattuordecim		quārtus decimus	
XV	15. quīndecim		quīntus decimus	
XVI	16. sēdecim		sextus decimus	
XVII	17. septendecim		septimus decimus	
XVIII	18. duodēvīgintī		duodēvīcēsimus	
XIX	19. ūndēvīgintī		ūndēvīcēsimus	
XX	20. vīgintī		vīcēsimus	
XXI	21. vīgintī ūnus/ūnus et vīgintī		vīcēsimus prīmus	
XXX	30. trīgintā		trīcēsimus	
XXXX/XL	40. quadrāgintā		quadrāgēsimus	
L	50. quīnquāgintā		quīnquāgēsimus	
LX	60. sexāginta		sexāgēsimus	
LXX	70. septuāgintā		septuāgēsimus	
LXXX	80. octūgintā		octōgēsimus	
LXXXX/XC	90. nōnāgintā		nōnagēsimus	
C	100. centum		centēsimus	
CI	101. centum ūnus		centēsimus prīmus	
CC	200. ducentī,-ae,-a		ducentēsimus	
CCC	300. trecentī,-ae,-a		trecentēsimus	
CCCC	400. quadringentī		quadringentēsimus	
D	500. quīngentī		quīngentēsimus	
DC	600. sescentī		sescentēsimus	
DCC	700. septingentī		septingentēsimus	
DCCC	800. octingentī		octingentēsimus	
DCCCC	900. nōngentī		nōngentēsimus	
M	1,000. mīlle		mīllēsimus	
MM	2,000. duo mīlia		bis mīllēsimus	

Partitive Genitives

A **Partitive Genitive** (also called **Genitive of the Whole**) is used to indicate a part of the whole to which it belongs.

1. *pars mei*	part of me
2. *nihil temporis*	no time (nothing of time)
3. *multum boni*	much good (much of good)
4. *aliquis nostrum**	some of us
5. *nemo vestrum**	no one of you

* The Partitive Genitive requires the ***nostrum*** and ***vestrum*** forms of these pronouns.

nōs	*vōs*
****nostrum**/nostrī*	****vestrum**/vestrī*
nōbīs	*vōbīs*
nōs	*vōs*
nōbīs	*vōbīs*

Numbers indicating **more than 1,000** always require a **Partitive Genitive** of the object numbered.

1. *decem milia equorum*	10,000 horses (10,000 of horses)
2. *tria milia virorum*	3,000 men (3,000 of men)

However, for the **number 1,000** the **Nominative Case** of the noun is used with the declinable adjective *mille*:

mille viri	1,000 men
mille feminae	1,000 women
mille tempora	1,000 times

Special Ablative Constructions

With cardinal numbers of **less than 1,000** (i.e., 1 through 999), the idea of the whole is expressed by using *dē* or *ex* with the **Ablative Case**.

1. *tres ex eis*	three of them
2. *centum de viris*	one hundred of the men

Vocabulary

cūnctor, cunctari to delay
cōnor, cōnārī, cōnātus sum to attempt
dēfendō,-fendere,-fendī,-fēnsum to defend
dubitō (1) to hesitate/doubt
occīdō, occidere, occīdī, occīsum to cut down/strike down/kill
patefaciō,-facere,-fēcī,-factum to open/throw open/lay open
reperiō, reperīre, repperī, repertum to discover
respondeō, respondēre, respondī, respōnsum to respond
dēlectātiō, dēlectātiōnis f., pleasure/delight
equus,-ī m., horse
iter, itineris n., march/journey/way
odium,-ī n., hatred
ergā + acc. prep., against
tot indeclinable adjective, so many

Exercises

A. Using paradigm formats, form the Participles (Nom. Sing. forms) of the following verbs. Include the English translation of each.

  1. conor
  2. patefacio
  3. reperio
  4. occido

B. Using paradigm formats, form the Infinitives of:

  1. conor
  2. patefacio
  3. reperio
  4. occido

C. Give the English for the following using a Jussive Subjunctive translation for any Subjunctive forms.

  1. itinera   6. expellent
  2. odiis   7. Reperite!
  3. delectationum   8. occisus erat
  4. equi   9. defendamus
  5. dubitabat   10. cunctatur

D. Give the Latin for the following.

  1. 1,000 horses   6. no good
  2. of the third king 7. 4 of them
  3. 2,000 men   8. 15 of us
  4. the second city 9. 7 friends
  5. to the 5th man   10. no time

E. Parse the underlined portions then translate the sentence.

  1. Vita est donum naturae sed <u>vivere</u> pulchre donum sapientiae. (Gertrude Atherton)
  2. Aetas semper <u>aliquid novi</u> fert. (Terence)
  3. Miror tot <u>milia virorum</u> tam pueriliter identidem cupere currentes equos videre. (Pliny)
       identidem = again and again
       pueriliter = adv., boyishly
  4. Stultus nullam delectationem in <u>intellegendo</u> trahit sed solum in opinione suā <u>declarandā</u>. (Adapted from Proverbs 18:2)
       declaro (1) = to express/declare
       opinio, opinionis = f., opinion

5. Nihil temporis <u>ad litteras scribendas</u> habeo. (Cicero)

6. Omnes qui habent aliquid non solum sapientiae sed etiam sanitatis volunt <u>hanc rem publicam salvam esse</u>. (Cicero)

> *salvus,-a,-um* = safe
>
> *sanitas, sanitatis* = f., sanity

7. Antonius, unus ex inimicis, iussit <u>Ciceronem interfici et caput eius inter duas manus in rostris poni</u>. (Livy)

> *Antonius,-i* = m., Proper Noun
>
> *caput, capitis* = n., head
>
> *inimicus,-i* = m., enemy
>
> *rostra,-orum* = n., speaker's platform

8. De Fabio Maximo Consule poeta Ennius ait: "Unus homo <u>cunctando</u> servavit Romam. Non rumores ponebat ante salutem."

> *consul,-sulis* = m., a consul, chief magistrate of the Roman Republic
>
> *rumor,-oris* = m., rumor
>
> *salus, salutis* = f., safety

9. Noster sensus honoris est sola res quae non <u>senescit</u>; et delectatio ultima, ubi senectute consumimur, non est, ut poeta ait, pecuniam facere sed existimationem amicorum nostrorum habere. (Adapted from Pericles' "Funeral Oration," in Thucydides' *The Peloponnesian War*)

> *consumo,-sumere,-sumpsi,-sumptum* = to consume
>
> *existimatio, existimationis* = f., respect
>
> *senesco, senescere, senui* = to grow old
>
> *sensus,-us* = m., sense
>
> *ultimus,-a,-um* = last

10. Quae spes <u>libertatis</u> manet si illis viris et quod placet licet et quod licet possunt et quod possunt audent et quod faciunt vobis molestum non est? (Cicero)

> *molestus,-a,-um* = troublesome

Text Translation

Cornelius Nepos (born ca. 110 BC) was a biographer from Cisalpine Gaul living at the time of Catullus and Cicero. Of his works, entitled *On Famous Men*, originally at least sixteen volumes, only one volume survives. The surviving book concerns famous foreign generals and, of course, contains a section on Hannibal (247–183 BC), the most famous member of the Barca family of Carthage.

Si verum est, quod nemo dubitat, ut populus Romanus omnes gentes virtute superaverit, non negandum est Hannibalem **tanto** praestitisse ceteros imperatores prudentiā **quanto** populus Romanus antecedat fortitudine omnes nationes. Hic autem odium paternum erga Romanos sic conservavit ut numquam id deponeret. Cum quidem ex patriā expulsus esset, Antiocho potentissimo regi omnium his temporibus fugit. Cum multa de fide suā confirmavisset, de sententiis erga Romanos hoc addidit:

"Me puero novem annos nato," inquit "pater meus Hamilcar, imperator proficiscens in Hispaniam, sacrificium Iovi faciebat. Cum hoc officium fecisset, quaesivit a me vellemne secum in Hispaniam proficisci. Cum id libenter accepissem atque ab eo petere coepissem ne dubitaret me ducere, tum ille 'Faciam,' inquit, 'si fidem mihi quam quaero, dederis.' Simul me ad aram duxit et me iurare iussit numquam in amicitiā cum Romanis me fore. Hoc ius iurandum, patri datum, usque ad hanc aetatem ita conservavi ut nemo sit qui plus odii erga Romanos habeat."

Post mortem in Hispaniā Hamilcaris, Hasdrubale imperatore facto, Hannibal equitatui omni praefuit. Paucis annis, Hasdrubale quoque interfecto, exercitus summum imperii ad Hannibalem detulit. Sic Hannibal, quinque et viginti annos natus, imperator factus est. Proximis tribus annis omnes gentes Hispaniae bello subegit; Saguntum expungnavit; tum tres exercitus maximos paravit. Ex his unum in Africam misit ad patriam defendendam, alterum cum fratre in Hispaniā reliquit, tertium in Italiam secum duxit.

Ad Alpes venit, quae Italiam Galliae iungunt, quasque nemo umquam cum exercitu ante eum transierat. Alpicos conantes prohibere transitum occidit, loca patefecit, itinera munivit, effecitque ut elephantus ire posset, **quā** ante unus homo vix poterat repere. Tandem in Italiam pervenit.

Conflixerat cum Romanis apud Rhodanum cum P Cornelio Scipione consule, tum apud Padum et tum apud Trebiam. In omnibus his proeliis Hannibal erat victor. Inde per Ligures Appenninum transiit, petens Etruriam. In hoc itinere adeo gravi morbo oculorum afflictus est ut postea numquam dextero oculo bene uteretur.

Longum est omnia enumerare proelia inter Hannibalem Romanosque. Quare hoc unum satis erit dictum: post Cannas quamdiu in Italiā fuit nemo ei in acie restitit. Hic invictus ad patriam defendendam revocatus, bellum gessit adversus P. Scipionem, filium eius quem in Italiā superaverat. Hannibal modis suis **Zamae** victus est.

(Liber de Excellentibus Ducibus Exterarum Gentium XXIII, i–vi)

acies, acie, additum f., battle line

addo, addere, addidiī to add

adeo adv., so/to such an extent

affligo,-fligere,-flixi,-flictum to afflict

Africa,-ae f., Africa

Alpes, Alpium f., Alps

Alpici, Alpicorum men of the Alps

alter, altera, alterum another

antecedo,-cedere,-cedi,-cessum to precede/go before

Antiochus,-i m., king of Syria

Appenninus,-i m., Appennines, the mountain range of Italy

ara,-ae f., altar

Cannae,-arum f., small town in Apulia, scene of defeat of the Romans by Hannibal in 216 BC

Carthaginiensis,-e Carthaginian

confirmo (1) to confirm

confligo,-fligere,-flixi,-flictum to clash

defero,-ferre,-tuli,-latum to hand over

depono,-ponere,-posui,-positum to put aside/lay aside

dexter, dextera, dexterum right

enumero (1) to number/enumerate

equitatus,-us m., cavalry

Etruria,-ae f., region across the Tiber from Rome

expello,-pellere,-pulsi,-pulsum to expel

expugno, expugnare to take by storm

fore alternate form of *futurus esse*

fortitudo,-inis f., bravery/fortitude

Gallia,-ae f., Gaul (modern France)

Hamilcar Barca, Hamilcaris Barcae m., (ca. 270–228), commander of the Carthaginian forces in the First Punic War and later in the conquest of Spain

Hannibal Barca, Hannibalis Barcae m., (247–182) son of Hamilcar, leader of the Carthaginian forces in the Second Punic War, one of the greatest military leaders in history

Hasdrubal, Hasdrubalis m., son-in-law of Hamilcar Barca

Hispania,-ae f., Spain

imperator,-oris m., commander in chief

invictus,-a,-um unconquered

Iovis,-is m., Jove/Jupiter

iuro (1) to swear

libenter adv., gladly

Ligures, Ligurum m., Ligurians, a people living along the northwest coast of Italy

morbus,-i m., disease

munio, munire to fortify

Padus,-i m., Po River, in northern Italy

P. Cornelius Scipio, Cornelii Scipionis m., consul of Rome in 218 BC

P. Cornelius Scipio Africanus m., (235–183) a general in the Second Punic War, best known for defeating Hannibal, a feat that earned him the surname "Africanus" and recognition as one of the finest commanders in military history

paternus,-a,-um paternal/belonging to one's father

pervenio,-venire,-veni,-ventum to come through

postea adv., afterward

potens, potentis powerful

praesum,-esse,-fui + dat. to be in charge of

proelium,-ii n., battle

proximus,-a,-um next

prudentia,-ae f., sagacity/foreseeing/skill

quā* adv., where

quamdiu adv., as long as

quārē (quā rē) adv., on which account

quoque adv., also/too

repo, repere, repsi, reptum to crawl

resto,-stare,-stiti + dat. to resist

revoco (1) to call back

Rhodanus,-i m., Rhone River in southern France

sacrificium,-ii n., sacrifice

Saguntum,-i m., a town on the east coast of Spain, south of the Ebro River

simul adv., at the same time

subigo,-igere,-egi,-actum to subject and train

tandem adv., at last

tanto . . . quanto correlative, by so much . . . by how much

transeo,-ire,-ii,-itum to cross over

transitus,-us m., crossing

Trebia,-ae m., Trebbia River, in northern Italy

usque adv., all the way

vix adv., scarcely

Zama,-ae* town in North Africa; *Zamae* locative case, translate "at Zama"

Text Translation

The following excerpt from Livy is based upon a supposed meeting and conversation between Scipio and Hannibal after the Second Punic War. Whether this conversation actually took place or not, it is a good story.

Multis post annis Scipio, cum Hannibale collocutus, qui exsul in Asia vivebat, ab eo quaesivit quem fuisse maximum imperatorem crederet. Respondit Hannibal Alexandrum, Macedonum regem, maximum sibi videri. Cum deinde Scipio quaereret quem secundum poneret, respondit ille Pyrrhum. Scipioni denique roganti quem tertium legeret, Hannibal se ipsum dixit. Tum ridens Scipio, "Quid tu diceres," inquit, "si me vicisses?" "Tum me," respondit Hannibal, "et ante Alexandrum et ante Pyrrhum et ante omnes alios imperatores posuissem."

(*Ab Urbe Condita* Bk. XXXV, xiv)

Alexander,-dri m., Alexander the Great
colloquor,-loqui,-locutus sum to speak together
exsul, exsulis c., an exile
imperator, imperatoris m., commander in chief
Macedones,-um m., Macedonians

Pyrrhus,-i m., Pyrrhus of Epirus, famous mercenary soldier
Scipio, Scipionis m., Roman general who defeated Hannibal at Zama

Review Work Sheet: Chapters XXXII–XXXV

I. List the nine major Subjunctive usages covered in this course.

    1.   6.

    2.   7.

    3.   8.

    4.   9.

    5.

II. Render the following sentence into three possible Latin formats indicating purpose.

"He came to destroy the city."

    1.

    2.

    3.

III. Parse the underlined passages and then render the following sentences into Latin.

    1. There is no one <u>who would believe this</u>.
    2. <u>Had we hesitated, we would all have been killed</u>.
    3. They beg <u>that you be lenient to them</u>.
    4. They asked <u>by what art you were especially benefited</u>.
    5. We thought <u>that you had followed them</u>.
    6. <u>Although we had endured a long war</u>, it was not permitted to us to have peace.
    7. He contains so much hatred <u>that he will never be happy</u>.
    8. <u>May we never hesitate to help our friends</u>!

Locative Case, Special Constructions for
Place to Which, with the names of Towns and Common Places
Place from Which, with the names of Towns and Common Places
Irregular verb *fio, fieri, factus sum*

XXXVI

<table>
<tr><td>

Objectives

To enable you to:

1. recognize and translate the Locative Case;
2. understand that **with common place-names, the Accusative Case without a preposition** is used;
3. understand that **with common place-names, the Ablative Case without a preposition** is used for Place from Which;
4. recognize and conjugate *fio, fieri, factus sum*

</td></tr>
</table>

Locative Case

The Locative Case (denoting location) is almost extinct in Latin. It is used with the names of towns and with nouns denoting commonly frequented places such as *domus* (home). The **Locative Case** answers the question "where?" or "at what place?" **For Singular 1st–2nd Declension Nouns, the Locative Case is the same as the Genitive Singular; for all other Declensions as well as for Plural Place-Names, the Locative is the same as the Ablative**. Be sure to notice that the names of cities differ in declension, gender, and number (i.e., the names of some cities are plural).

Rōma,-ae	f., Rome
Carthāgō, Carthaginis	f., Carthage
Delphī, Delphōrum	m., Delphi
Athēnae, Athēnārum	f., Athens
Syrācūsae, Syrācūsārum	f., Syracuse

286

1. He was seen at Rome.	*Videbatur **Romae**.*
2. He was seen at Carthage.	*Videbatur **Carthagine**.*
3. He was seen at home.	*Videbatur **domi**.* *
4. He was seen at Delphi.	*Videbatur **Delphis**.*
5. He was seen at Athens.	*Videbatur **Athenis**.*
6. He was seen at Syracuse.	*Videbatur **Syracusis**.*

* Irregular locative case of *domus,-us*.

Place to which, with the Names of Towns and Common Places

Normally the prepositions *in* or *ad* + the Accusative are used to denote motion toward or place to which, but **with the names of towns and common locations, the Accusative Case <u>without a preposition</u>** is used.

1. He went to Rome.	*Iit Romam.*
2. He went to Carthage.	*Iit Carthaginem.*
3. He went home.	*Iit domum.*
4. He went to Delphi.	*Iit Delphos.*
5. He went to Athens.	*Iit Athenas.*
6. He went to Syracuse.	*Iit Syracusas.*

Place from which, with the Names of Towns and Common Places

Normally the prepositions *ab, dē, ex* + the Ablative Case are used to indicate Place from Which; **however, with the names of towns and common locations, the Ablative Case <u>without a preposition</u>** is used.

1. He left Rome.	*Abiit Romā.*
2. He left Carthage.	*Abiit Carthagine.*
3. He left home.	*Abiit domo.* *
4. He left Delphi.	*Abiit Delphis.*
5. He left Athens.	*Abiit Athenis.*
6. He left Syracuse.	*Abiit Syracusis.*

* Irregular ablative singular case of *domus,-us*.

Irreglar Verb fio, fieri, factus sum

Fio, fieri, factus sum (to be made/be done/become) is the shortened (contracted) passive form of the verb *faciō, facere*. To conjugate the Present Indicative System as well as the Present Subjunctive of *fio, fieri, factus sum*, simply leave out the *-ac-* in the active forms of the Present Indicative System and the Present Subjunctive of *faciō*.

287

The Imperfect Subjunctive of *fio* is formed the same way as for Deponent Verbs, i.e., by converting the Infinitive to the Active Form then adding the personal endings. **The Perfect System of *fio* has only Passive Forms and is identical to the Perfect Passive System of *facio*.**

Indicative

Pres.	Imp.	Fut.	Perf.	Plup.	FutP.
fīō	fīēbam	fīam	factus sum	factus eram	factus erō
fīs	fīēbās	fīēs	factus es	factus erās	factus eris
fit	fīēbat	fīet	factus est	factus erat	factus erit
fīmus	fīēbāmus	fīēmus	factī sumus	facti erāmus	facti erimus
fītis	fīēbātis	fīētis	factī estis	facti erātis	facti eritis
fiunt	fīēbant	fīent	factī sunt	facti erant	facti erunt

Subjunctive

Pres.	Imp.	Perf.	Plup.
fīam	fierem	factus sim	factus essem
fīās	fierēs	factus sīs	factus essēs
fīat	fieret	factus sit	factus esset
fīāmus	fierēmus	factī sīmus	facti essēmus
fīātis	fierētis	factī sītis	facti essētis
fīant	fierent	factī sint	facti essent

	Participles		**Infinitives**		**Imperatives**	
Pres,	—		Pres.	**fierī**	**fī**	**fīte**
Perf.	**factus,-a,-um**		Perf.	**factus esse**		
Fut.	**faciendus,-a,-um**		Fut.*	—		

* The Future Infinitive is seldom seen and is considered a <u>Supine</u> form, which literally means "dead, on its back face up."

Vocabulary

Athēnae,-ārum f., Athens
Carthāgō,-inis f., Carthage
Delphī,-ōrum m., Delphi
Syrācūsae,-ārum f., Syracuse
necesse indeclinable adj, necessary
sēnsus,-us m., sense/feeling

dēlinquō,-linquere,-līquī,-lictum to fail/be wanting
fīō, fierī, factus sum to be made/be done/become

Exercises

A. Form a Synopsis of *fio, fieri, factus sum* in the Indicative and Subjunctive in 3rd Sing. N. Give the English translations of the Indicative Tenses.

B. Translate the following Indicative and Participle forms; parse the other forms.

1. fiemus	6. factae essemus
2. fite	7. fiunt
3. factus sit	8. fiat
4. fierent	9. factus esse
5. fio	10. fieri

C. Translate the following **Place Constructions**.

1. Delphos	6. Romae
2. Romā	7. domum
3. Carthagine	8. Romam
4. domo	9. Delphis
5. Carthaginem	10. domi

D. Sentence translations.

1. Magnae res non fiunt sine periculo. (Terence)
2. Dixitque Deus: "Fiat lux." Et facta est lux. (Genesis)
3. Hoc durum est; sed levius fit patientiā quidquid corrigere est nefas. (Horace)

    corrigo,-ere,-rexi,-rectum = to correct

    nefas = n., indeclinable, sin/crime/wrong

    patientia,-ae = f., patience/endurance

    quisquis, quaequae, quidquid = whoever/whatever

4. Cedamus! Leve fit onus quod bene fertur. (Ovid)

    onus, oneris = n., burden/load

5. Sunt bona, sunt quaedam mediocria, sunt mala plura quae legis hīc;
   aliter non fit, Avite, liber. (Martial I, xvi)

    aliter = otherwise

    Avitus,-i = m., Proper Noun

6. Si te cum aliis conferes, inanis aut acerbus fies quod homines meliores aut peiores quam tu semper erunt. (Desiderata)

    inanis,-e = vain

    acerbus,-a,-um = bitter

7. Ut recitem tibi nostra rogas epigrammata. Nolo.
   Non audire, Celer, sed recitare cupis. (Martial I, vxiii)

    recito (1) = to read aloud/recite

    epigramma,-atis = n., epigram, a shorty witty poem or saying

    Celer,-eris = m., Proper Noun

8. Vae, puto me fieri deum. (Vespasian)

    vae = alas

9. Docendo, discimus.

10. Historia est philosophia docenda exemplaribus. (Dionysus of Halicarnassus)

11. Beneficium non in eo quod fit aut datur consistit, sed in ipso facientis aut dantis animo; animus est qui beneficiis dat pretium. (Seneca)

    consisto,-sistere,-stiti,-stitum = to consist

    pretium,-i = n., value/worth

Text Translation

In principio creavit Deus caelum et terram.
Terra autem erat inanis et vacua et tenebrae
erant super faciem abyssi, et Spiritus Dei
ferebatur super aquas.

Dixitque Deus: Fiat lux. Et facta est lux.   5
Et vidit Deus lucem quod esset bona: et
divisit lucem a tenebris. Appellavitque
lucem Diem, et tenebras Noctem; factumque
est vespere et mane, dies unus.

Dixitque quoque Deus: Fiat firmamentum in   10
medio aquarum: et dividat aquas ab aquis.
Et fecit Deus firmamentum, divisitque aquas,
quae erant sub firmamento, ab his, quae erant
super firmamentum. Et factum est ita. Vocavitque
Deus firmamentum, Caelum: et factum est vespere   15
et mane, dies secundus.

Dixit vero Deus: Congregentur aquae, quae sub
caelo sunt, in locum unum; et appareat arida.
Et factum est ita. Et vocavit Deus aridam
Terram, congregationesque aquarum appellavit   20
Maria. Et vidit Deus quod esset bonum.
(Genesis I)

abyssum,-i n., abyss/void/bottomless pit
appareo,-ēre,-ui,-itum to appear
aridus,-a,-um dry
congregatio,-onis f., an assembling together
congrego (1) to bring together
divido,-videre,-visi,-visum to divide
facies,-ei f., face
firmamentum,-i n., a means of support/a prop
inanis,-e empty/void/hollow

mane indeclinable noun, morning
medius,-a,-um middle
principium,-i n., beginning
super + acc. adv., above
tenebrae,-arum f., darkness
vacuus,-a,-um empty/void
vero adv., truly/indeed
vesper,-eris m., evening; *vespere* at that time

Text Translation

Between 46 and 44 BC **Cicero's** greatest philosophical works were produced. These dealt not only with the nature of philosophy but with specific ethical thought regarding good and evil, grief and death, duties and law, religion, and old age. The excerpt below which deals with the origin of the term philosophy, is from the *Disputationes Tusculanae*.

Omnes qui in rerum contemplatione studia ponebant, "sapientes" et
habebantur et vocabantur, idque nomen usque ad aetatem
Pythagorae remansit. Sed cum Phliuntem Pythagoras venit, et cum
Leonte, principe Phliasiorum, docte et copiose disceptavit
quaedam, Leon, admiratus ingenium et eloquentiam huius,   5
quaesivit ex eo quā arte maxime uteretur; at Pythagoras dixit se
scire nullam artem sed esse philosophum. Tum Leon admiratus
novitatem nominis, quaesivit qui essent philosophi et quid inter eos
et reliquos interesset. Pythagoras respondit vitam sibi videri
similem ludis Graecis ubi alii corporibus exercitatis gloriam et   10
nobilitatem coronae peterent, alii quaestu et lucro emendi aut
vendendi ducerentur, esset autem genus hominum maxime
ingenuum, qui nec plausum nec lucrum quaererent, sed ad ludos
videndi causā venirent studioseque perspicerent quid ageretur et
quo modo; qui ceteris omnibus habitis pro nihil naturam rerum   15
scire cuperent; hos se appellare sapientiae studiosos, id est
philosophos. Quasi liberrimus ad ludos venit ut spectaret
acquirens sibi nihil plus, sic in vit, sunt qui longe omnibus aliis
studiis contemplationem rerum cognitionemque mallent.

(Disputationes Tusculanae V, iii, 8–9; iv, 10)

acquiro, acquirere, acquisivi, acquisitum to acquire
admiror,-mirari to admire
cognitio,-onis f., study
confido,-fidere,-fisus sum to be assured/trust
contemplatio,-onis f., contemplation
copiose adv., fully/copiously
corona,-ae f., crown
discepto (1) to discuss
docte adv., learnedly
eloquentia,-ae f., eloquence
emo, emere, emi, emptum to buy
exercitatus,-a,-um trained
ingenium,-i n., ability/character/genius
ingenuus,-a,-um noble/honorable
intersum,-esse,-fui to differ
Leon, Leontis m., Proper Noun
lucrum,-i n., reward
ludus,-i m., game

novitas, novitatis f., novelty/newness
perspicio,-spicere,-spexi,-spectum to ascertain
philosophus,-i m., philosopher
Phliasius,-a,-um adj., of Phlius
Phlius, Phliuntis m., Proper Noun, city in Greece near Argos
plausus,-us m., applause
princeps, principis first/foremost
Pythagoras,-ae m., Proper Noun, a famous Greek philosopher
quaestus,-us m., gain
quasi just as
reliquus,-a,-um other
specto (1) to watch
studiose adv., eagerly
studiosus,-a,-um eager for
usque adv., all the way/continuously
vendo,-dere,-didi,-ditum to sell

Text Translation

In this excerpt from *De Senectute*, **Cicero** compares human life spans to the parts assigned to actors. He argues that even a short life can be lived well and honorably.

> Horae quidem cedunt et dies et menses
> et anni, nec praeteritum tempus umquam
> revertitur nec quid sequatur sciri potest.
> Quod cuique temporis ad vivendum datur,
> eo debet esse contentus.   5
>
> Neque enim histrioni, ut placeat,
> peragenda fabula est, modo in quocunque
> fuerit actu probetur; neque sapientibus usque
> ad "plaudite" veniendum est, breve enim tempus
> aetatis satis longum est ad bene honesteque   10
> vivendum.

(*De Senectute* XIX, 69–70)

actus,-us m., act
contentus,-a,-um content
fabula,-ae f., drama/play/fable
histrio, histrionis m., actor
honestus,-a,-um honorable
mensis,-is m., month
modo adv, only
perago,-agere,-egi,-actum to complete
plaudo, plaudere, plausi, plausum to clap;
   "plaudite" was always said at the end of a
   theatrical performance

probo (1) to prove/to be found good
quiscunque, quaecunque, quodcunque
   whoever/whatever
quisque, quaeque, quidque each one/each thing
reverto,-vertere,-verti to return
usque adv., all the way

Text Translation

Virgil's (70–19 BC) *Aeneid,* the epic narrative sequel to Homer's *Iliad* and *Odyssey,* recounts Aeneas's flight from burning Troy, his adventures and mishaps in the Mediterannean, his ultimate arrival in Italy, and the subsequent war that melded the Trojans and the Latins. The first six books of the *Aeneid* are an adventure story; the last six books are concerned with war and character and the reasons why the Romans become the ultimate rulers of the world. Virgil reminds Rome (and Augustus) of the distinctive Roman gift of governing as well as the dangers of irresponsible rule.

Arma virumque cano, Trojae qui primus ab oris
Italiam fato profugus Laviniaque venit
litora, multum ille et terris jactatus et alto
vi superum saevae memorem Junonis ob iram,
multa quoque et bello passus, dum conderet urbem
inferretque deos Latio, genus unde Latinum
Albanique patres atque alta moenia Romae.

(Book I, 1–7)

Excudent alii spirantia mollius aera
(Credo equidem), vivos ducent de marmore voltus,
Orabunt causas melius caelique meatus
Describent radio et surgentia sidera dicent.
Tu regere imperio populos, Romane, memento
(Hae tibi erunt artes) pacisque imponere morem,
Parcere subjectis et debellare superbos.

(Book VI, 847–53)

aes, aeris n., bronze
Albanus,-a,-um Alban; from Alba Longa
altus,-a,-um deep/high
cano, canere, cecini, cantum to sing
condo, condere, condidi, conditum to found
debello (1) to fight to the end
describo,-scribere,-scripsi,-scriptum to describe
dum + subjunctive until
equidem indeed
excudo,-cudere,-cudi,-cusum to strike out
jacto (1) to throw about/fling about
impono,-ponere,-posui,-positum to
    impose/establish
infero,-ferre,-tuli,-latum to carry in
Juno, Junonis f., Juno, queen of the gods
Latinus,-a,-im Latin
Latium,-i n., Latium, a district of Italy
Lavinius,-a,-um Lavinian; from Lavinium
litus, litoris n., shore
marmor, marmoris n., marble

meatus,-us m. motion/path
memento Irregular Imperative, remember!
memor, memoris remembering
moenia, moenium n., walls
mollis,-e soft
profugus,-i m., fugitive
radius,-i m., staff/rod
rego, regere, rexi, rectum to rule
saevus,-a,-um savage
sidus, sideris n., star/constellation
spiro (1) to breathe
subjcio,-jcere,-jeci,-jectum to subject
superbus,-a,-um arrogant
superus,-a,-um above;
superum, super(o)rum of the ones above
surgo, surgere, surrexi, surrectum to arise
Troja,-ae f., Troy
unde whence/from which
vivus,-a,-um lifelike/living
voltus,-us m., face

Review Work Sheet: Chapter XXXVI

I. Provide the Latin forms for the following verbs, being sure to use the verb *fio, fieri, factus sum* for all Passive Forms.

    1. we made
    2. we were made
    3. I do
    4. I become
    5. He had made
    6. He had been made
    7. You (pl.) were making
    8. You (pl.) were becoming
    9. Let them do it.
    10. Let it be done.

II. Translate the following sentences.

    1. Caesar curavit ut imperator fieret.
    2. Fiamus meliores si non maiores quam nostri inimici.
       inimicus,-i = m., enemy
    3. Nisi facti essemus amici, fuissemus difficillimi inimici.
    4. Necesse est ut iura fiant iusta.
    5. Dicunt virum qui fiat rex mox fore sine amicis veris.
       fore = futurum esse

Vocabulary: Chapters XXXIII–XXXVI

adversus + acc. against
adversus, -a, -um adverse
an whether/or
arbitror, arbitrārī, arbitrātus sum to judge/think
Athēnae, -ārum f., Athens

Carthāgō, -inis f., Carthage
cōnor, cōnārī, cōnātus sum to attempt
cūnctor, cūnctārī to delay
cupidus, -a, -um desirous

dēfendo, -fendere, -fendī, -fēnsum to defend
dēlectātiō, dēlectātiōnis f., pleasure/delight
dēlinquo, -linquere, -līquī, -lictum to fail/be wanting
Delphī, -ōrum m., Delphi
dolor, dolōris f., pain
dubitō (1) to hesitate/doubt

equus, -ī m., horse
ergā + acc. prep., against
etsi even if/although
experior, experīrī, expertus sum to experience/try/test

fateor, fatērī, fassus sum to confess
fīō, fierī, factus sum to be made/be done/become

ignōscō, -nōscere, -nōvī, -nōtum + dat. to grant pardon to/forgive/overlook/ignore
īrascor, īrascī, īrātus sum to be angry
iter, itineris n., march/journey/way

licet, licere, licuit impersonal, it is allowed/permitted
loquor, loquī, locūtus sum to say/speak/tell

morior, morī, mortuus sum to die

nāscor, nascī, nātus sum to be born
necesse indeclinable adj., necessary

occidō, occidere, occīdī, occīsum to cut down/strike down/kill
odium, -ī n., hatred
opus, operis n., work/task/deed/accomplishment
orior, orīrī, ortus sum to arise

parcō, parcere, pepercī + dat. to be lenient to
patefaciō, -facere, -fēcī, -factum to open/throw open/lay open
patior, patī, passus sum to endure
placeō, placēre, placuī, placitum + dat. to be pleasing to
proficiscor, proficiscī, profectus sum to set out

quasi as if

reperiō, reperīre, repperī, repertum to discover
respondeō, respondēre, respondī, respōnsum to respond

sēnsus, -us m., sense/feeling
sequor, sequī, secutus sum to follow
Syrācūsae, -ārum f., Syracuse

tot adv., so many

ūtor, ūtī, ūsus sum + abl. of means to benefit oneself by means of/use

Compiled Charts

Regular Verb Conjugations

Indicative Mood—Active Voice

1st	2nd	3rd	3rd-*io*	4th

Present

vocō	videō	mittō	capiō	sciō
vocās	vidēs	mittis	capis	scīs
vocat	videt	mittit	capit	scit
vocāmus	vidēmus	mittimus	capimus	scīmus
vocātis	vidētis	mittitis	capitis	scītis
vocant	vident	mittunt	capiunt	sciunt

Imperfect

vocābam	vidēbam	mittēbam	capiēbam	sciēbam
vocābās	vidēbās	mittēbās	capiēbās	sciēbās
vocābat	vidēbat	mittēbat	capiēbat	sciēbat
vocābāmus	vidēbāmus	mittēbāmus	capiēbāmus	sciēbāmus
vocābātis	vidēbātis	mittēbātis	capiēbātis	sciēbātis
vocābant	vidēbant	mittēbant	capiēbant	sciēbant

Future

vocābō	vidēbō	mittam	capiam	sciam
vocābis	vidēbis	mittēs	capiēs	sciēs
vocābit	vidēbit	mittet	capiet	sciet
vocābimus	vidēbimus	mittēmus	capiēmus	sciēmus
vocābitis	vidēbitis	mittētis	capiētis	sciētis
vocābunt	vidēbunt	mittent	capient	scient

Perfect

vocāvī	vīdī	mīsī	cēpī	scīvī
vocāvistī	vīdistī	mīsistī	cēpistī	scīvistī
vocāvit	vīdit	mīsit	cēpit	scīvit
vocāvimus	vīdimus	mīsimus	cēpimus	scīvimus
vocāvistis	vīdistis	mīsistis	cēpistis	scīvistis
vocāvērunt*	vīdērunt*	mīsērunt*	cepērunt*	scīvērunt*

Pluperfect

vocāveram	vīderam	mīseram	cēperam	scīveram
vocāverās	vīderās	mīserās	cēperās	scīverās
vocāverat	vīderat	mīserat	cēperat	scīverat
vocāverāmus	vīderāmus	mīserāmus	cēperāmus	scīverāmus
vocāverātis	vīderātis	mīserātis	cēperātis	scīverātis
vocāverant	vīderant	mīserant	cēperant	scīverant

Future Perfect

vocāverō	vīderō	mīserō	cēperō	scīverō
vocāveris	vīderis	mīseris	cēperis	scīveris
vocāverit	vīderit	mīserit	cēperit	scīverit
vocāverimus	vīderimus	mīserimus	cēperimus	scīverimus
vocāveritis	vīderitis	mīseritis	cēperitis	scīveritis
vocāverint	vīderint	mīserint	cēperint	scīverint

* Perfect Stem + *ēre* represents an **alternate** 3rd Pl. Perfect form:

vocavēre	vidēre	misēre	cepēre	scivēre

Indicative Mood—Passive Voice

Present

vocor	videor	mittor	capior	scior
vocāris	vidēris	mitteris*	caperis*	scīris
vocātur	vidētur	mittitur	capitur	scītur
vocāmur	vidēmur	mittimur	capimur	scīmur
vocāminī	vidēminī	mittiminī	capiminī	scīminī
vocantur	videntur	mittuntur	capiuntur	sciuntur

Imperfect

vocābar	vidēbar	mittēbar	capiēbar	sciebar
vocābāris	vidēbāris	mittēbāris	capiēbaris	sciēbāris
vocābātur	vidēbātur	mittēbātur	capiēbatur	sciēbātur
vocābāmur	vidēbāmur	mittēbāmur	capiēbamur	sciēbāmur
vocābāminī	vidēbāminī	mittēbāminī	capiēbāminī	sciēbāminī
vocābantur	vidēbantur	mittēbantur	capiēbantur	sciēbantur

Future

vocābor	vidēbor	mittar	capiar	sciar
vocāberis*	vidēberis*	mittēris	capiēris	sciēris
vocābitur	vidēbitur	mittētur	capiētur	sciētur
vocābimur	vidēbimur	mittēmur	capiēmur	sciēmur
vocābiminī	vidēbiminī	mittēminī	capiēminī	sciēminī
vocābuntur	vidēbuntur	mittentur	capientur	scientur

Perfect

vocātus sum	vīsus sum	mīssus sum	captus sum	scītus sum
vocātus es	vīsus es	mīssus es	captus es	scītus es
vocātus est	vīsus est	mīssus est	captus est	scītus est
vocātī sumus	vīsī sumus	mīssī sumus	captī sumus	scītī sumus
vocātī estis	vīsī estis	mīssī estis	captī estis	scītī estis
vocātī sunt	visi sunt	mīssī sunt	captī sunt	scītī sunt

Pluperfect

vocātus eram	visus eram	mīssus eram	captus eram	scītus eram
vocātus erās	visus erās	mīssus erās	captus erās	scītus erās
vocātus erat	vīsus erat	mīssus erat	captus erat	scītus erat
vocātī erāmus	vīsī erāmus	mīssī erāmus	captī erāmus	scītī erāmus
vocātī erātis	vīsī erātis	mīssī erātīs	captī erātis	scītī erātis
vocātī erant	vīsī erant	mīssī erant	captī erant	scītī erant

Future Perfect

vocātus erō	vīsus erō	mīssus erō	captus erō	scītus erō
vocātus eris	vīsus eris	mīssus eris	captus eris	scītus eris
vocātus erit	vīsus erit	mīssus erit	captus erit	scītus erit
vocātī erimus	vīsī erimus	mīssī erimus	captī erimus	scītī erimus
vocātī eritis	vīsī eritis	mīssī eritis	captī eritis	scītī eritis
vocātī erunt	vīsī erunt	mīssī erunt	captī erunt	scītī erunt

* Consistent Irregular Forms.

Subjunctive Mood—Active Voice

Present

vocem	videam	mittam	capiam	sciam
vocēs	videās	mittās	capiās	sciās
vocet	videat	mittat	capiat	sciat
vocēmus	videāmus	mittāmus	capiāmus	sciāmus
vocētis	videātis	mittātis	capiātis	sciātis
vocent	videant	mittant	capiant	sciant

Imperfect

vocārem	viderem	mitterem	caperem	scīrem
vocārēs	vidērēs	mitterēs	caperēs	scīrēs
vocāret	vidēret	mitteret	caperet	scīret
vocārēmus	vidērēmus	mitterēmus	caperēmus	scīrēmus
vocārētis	vidērētis	mitterētis	caperētis	scīrētis
vocārent	vidērent	mitterent	caperent	scīrent

Perfect

vocāverim	vīderim	mīserim	cēperim	scīverim
vocāverīs	vīderīs	mīserīs	cēperīs	scīverīs
vocāverit	vīderit	mīserit	cēperit	scīverit
vocāverīmus	vīderīmus	mīserīmus	cēperīmus	scīverīmus
vocāverītis	vīderītis	mīseritis	cēperītis	scīverītis
vocāverint	vīderint	mīserint	cēperint	scīverint

Pluperfect

vocāvissem	vīdissem	mīsissem	cēpissem	scīvissem
vocāvissēs	vīdissēs	mīsisses	cēpissēs	scīvissēs
vocāvisset	vīdisset	mīsisset	cēpisset	scīvisset
vocāvissēmus	vīdissēmus	mīsissēmus	cēpissēmus	scīvissēmus
vocāvissētis	vīdissētis	mīsissētis	cēpissētis	scīvissētis
vocāvissent	vīdissent	mīsissent	cēpissent	scīvissent

Subjunctive Mood—Passive Voice

Present

vocer	vīdear	mittar	capiar	sciar
vocēris	vīdeāris	mittāris	capiāris	sciāris
vocētur	vīdeātur	mittātur	capiātur	sciātur
vocēmur	vīdeāmur	mittāmur	capiāmur	sciāmur
vocēminī	vīdeāminī	mittāminī	capiāminī	sciāminī
vocentur	vīdeantur	mittantur	capiantur	sciantur

Imperfect

vocārer	vīdērer	mitterer	caperer	scīrer
vocārēris	vīdērēris	mitterēris	caperēris	scīrēris
vocārētur	vīdēretur	mitterētur	caperētur	scīrētur
vocārēmur	vīdēremur	mitterēmur	caperēmur	scīrēmur
vocārēminī	vīdēreminī	mitterēminī	caperēminī	scīrēminī
vocārentur	vīdērentur	mitterentur	caperentur	scīrentur

Perfect

vocātus sim	vīsus sim	mīssus sim	captus sim	scitus sim
vocātus sīs	vīsus sīs	mīssus sīs	captus sīs	scitus sīs
vocātus sit	vīsus sit	mīssus sit	captus sit	scītus sit
vocātī sīmus	vīsī sīmus	mīssī sīmus	captī sīmus	scītī sīmus
vocātī sītis	vīsī sītis	mīssī sītis	captī sītis	scītī sītis
vocātī sint	vīsī sint	mīssī sint	capti sint	sciti sint

Pluperfect

vocātus essem	vīsus essem	mīssus essem	captus essem	scītus essem
vocātus essēs	vīsus essēs	mīssus essēs	captus esses	scitus esses
vocātus esset	vīsus esset	mīssus esset	captus esset	scītus esset
vocātī essēmus	vīsī essēmus	mīssī essēmus	captī essēmus	scītī essēmus
vocātī essētis	vīsī essētis	mīssī essētis	captī essētis	scītī essētis
vocātī essent	vīsī essent	mīssī essent	captī essent	scītī essent

Imperative Mood

Sing.	vocā	vidē	mitte	cape	scī
Pl.	vocāte	vidēte	mittite	capite	scīte

Participles

	Active	Passive	Active	Passive
Pres.	vocāns,-ntis		vidēns,-ntis	
Perf.		vocātus		vīsus
Fut.	vocātūrus	vocandus	vīsūrus	videndus
Pres.	mittēns,-ntis		capiēns,-ntis	
Perf.		mīssus		captus
Fut.	mīssūrus	mittendus	captūrus	capiendus
Pres.	sciēns,-ntis			
Perf.		scītus		
Fut.	scītūrus	sciendus		

Infinitives

	Active	Passive	Active	Passive	Active	Passive
Pres.	vocāre	vocārī	vidēre	viderī	mittere	mittī
Perf.	vocāvisse	vocātus esse	vidisse	vīsus esse	mīsisse	mīssus esse
Fut.	vocātūrus esse		vīsūrus esse		mīssūrus esse	
Pres.	capere	capī	scīre	scīrī		
Perf.	cēpisse	captus esse	scīvisse	scītus esse		
Fut.	captūrus esse		scītūrus esse			

301

Irregular Verb Conjugations

sum, esse, fuī, futurus to be

Indicative Mood

Pres.	Imp.	Fut.	Perf.	Plup.	FutPer.
sum	eram	erō	fuī	fueram	fuerō
es	erās	eris	fuistī	fuerās	fueris
est	erat	erit	fuit	fuerat	fuerit
sumus	erāmus	erimus	fuimus	fuerāmus	fuerimus
estis	erātis	eritis	fuistis	fuerātis	fueritis
sunt	erant	erunt	fuērunt	fuerant	fuerint

Subjunctive Mood

Pres.	Imp.	Perf.	Plup.
sim	essem	fuerim	fuissem
sīs	essēs	fuerīs	fuissēs
sit	esset	fuerit	fuisset
sīmus	essēmus	fuerīmus	fuissēmus
sītis	essētis	fuerītis	fuissētis
sint	essent	fuerint	fuissent

	Infinitives	*Imperatives*	*Participles*
Pres.	esse	es este	**Fut.** futūrus
Per.	fuisse		
Fut.	futūrus esse/fore		

possum, posse, potuī to be able

Indicative Mood

Pres.	Imp.	Fut.	Perf.	Plup.	FutPer.
possum	poteram	poterō	potuī	potueram	potuerō
potes	poterās	poteris	potuistī	potuerās	potueris
potest	poterat	poterit	potuit	potuerat	potuerit
possumus	poterāmus	poterimus	potuimus	potuerāmus	potuerimus
potestis	poterātis	poteritis	potuistis	potuerātis	potueritis
possunt	poterant	poterunt	potuērunt	potuerant	potuerint

Subjunctive Mood

Pres.	Imp.	Perf.	Plup.
possim	possem	potuerim	potuissem
possīs	possēs	potuerīs	potuissēs
possit	posset	potuerit	potuisset
possīmus	possēmus	potuerīmus	potuissēmus
possītis	possētis	potuerītis	potuissētis
possint	possent	potuerint	potuissent

	Infinitives		*Participles*	
Pres.	posse		**Pres.**	potens,-ntis
Perf.	potuisse			

eō, īre, iī, itum to go

Indicative Mood

Pres.	Imp.	Fut.	Perf.	Plup.	FutPer.
eo	ībam	ībō	iī	ieram	ierō
īs	ībās	ībis	īstī	ierās	ieris
it	ībat	ībit	iit	ierat	ierit
īmus	ībāmus	ībimus	iimus	ierāmus	ierimus
ītis	ībātis	ībitis	īstis	ierātis	ieritis
eunt	ībant	ībunt	iērunt	ierant	ierint

Subjunctive Mood

Pres.	Imp.	Perf.	Plup.
eam	īrem	ierim	īssem
eās	īrēs	ierīs	īssēs
eat	īret	ierit	īsset
eāmus	īrēmus	ierīmus	īssēmus
eātis	īrētis	ierītis	īssētis
eant	īrent	ierint	īssent

	Infinitives	**Common**	**Participles**	**Imperatives**
Pres.	īre	**Pres.**	iēns,euntis	ī īte
Perf.	isse	**Perf.**	itūm	
Fut.	itūrus esse	**Fut.**	itūrus	***Gerund***
				eundi

ferō, ferre, tulī, lātum to bring/carry/endure/report

Indicative Mood

Active	Passive	Active	Passive	Active	Passive

Present · Imperfect · Future

ferō	feror	ferēbam	ferēbar	feram	ferar
fers	ferris	ferēbās	ferēbāris	ferēs	ferēris
fert	fertur	ferēbat	ferēbātur	feret	ferētur
ferimus	ferimur	ferēbāmus	ferēbāmur	ferēmus	ferēmur
fertis	ferimini	ferēbātis	ferēbāminī	ferētis	ferēminī
ferunt	feruntur	ferēbant	ferēbantur	ferent	ferentur

Perfect · Pluperfect · Future Perfect

tulī	lātus sum	tuleram	lātus eram	tulerō	lātus erō
tulistī	lātus es	tulerās	lātus erās	tuleris	lātus eris
tulit	lātus est	tulerat	lātus erat	tulerit	lātus erit
tulīmus	lātī sumus	tulerāmus	lātī erāmus	tulerimus	lati erimus
tulīstis	lātī estis	tulerātis	lātī erātis	tuleritis	lati eritis
tulērunt	lātī sunt	tulerant	lātī erant	tulerunt	lati erunt

Subjunctive Mood

Pres. · Imp. · Perf. · Plup.

feram	ferar	ferrem	ferrer	tulerim	lātus sim	tulissem	lātus essem
ferās	ferāris	ferrēs	ferrēris	tulerīs	lātus sīs	tulissēs	lātus essēs
ferat	ferātur	ferret	ferrētur	tulerit	lātus sit	tulisset	lātus esset
ferāmus	ferāmur	ferrēmus	ferrēmur	tulerīmus	lātī sīmus	tulissēmus	lātī essēmus
ferātis	ferāminī	ferrētis	ferrēminī	tulerītis	lātī sītis	tulissētis	lātī essētis
ferant	ferantur	ferrent	ferrentur	tulerint	lātī sint	tulissent	lātī essent

Infinitives · Participles · Imperatives

	Active	Passive	Active	Passive	Imperatives
					fer ferte
Pres.	ferre	ferrī	ferēns,-ntis		
Perf.	tulisse	lātus esse		lātus	
Fut.	lātūrus esse		lātūrus	ferendus	

304

volō, velle, voluī
(to be willing)

nōlō, nōlle, nōluī
(to be unwilling)

mālō, mālle, māluī
(to prefer)

Indicative Mood

Present

volō	nōlō	mālō	
vīs	nōn vīs	māvīs	
vult	nōn vult	māvult	
volumus	nōlumus	mālumus	
vultis	nōn vultis	māvultis	
volunt	nōlunt	mālunt	

Imperfect

volēbam	nōlēbam	mālēbam
volēbās	nōlēbās	mālēbās
volēbat	nōlēbat	mālēbat
volēbāmus	nōlēbāmus	mālēbāmus
volēbātis	nōlēbātis	mālēbātis
volēbant	nōlēbant	mālēbant

Future

volam	nōlam	mālam
volēs	nōlēs	mālēs
volet	nōlet	mālet
volēmus	nōlēmus	mālēmus
volētis	nōlētis	mālētis
volent	nōlent	mālent

Perfect

voluī	nōluī	māluī
voluistī	nōluistī	māluistī
voluit	nōluit	māluit
voluimus	nōluimus	māluimus
voluistis	nōluistis	māluistis
voluērunt	nōluērunt	māluērunt

Pluperfect

volueram	nōlueram	mālueram
voluerās	nōluerās	māluerās
voluerat	nōluerat	māluerat
voluerāmus	nōluerāmus	māluerāmus
voluerātis	nōluerātis	māluerātis
voluerant	nōluerant	māluerant

Future Perfect

voluerō	nōluerō	māluerō
volueris	nōlueris	mālueris
voluerit	nōluerit	māluerit
voluerimus	nōluerimus	māluerimus
volueritis	nōlueritis	mālueritis
voluerint	nōluerint	māluerint

Subjunctive Mood

Present

velim	nōlim	mālim
velīs	nōlīs	mālīs
velit	nōlit	mālit
velīmus	nōlīmus	mālīmus
velītis	nōlītis	mālītis
velint	nōlint	mālint

Imperfect

vellem	nōllem	māllem
vellēs	nōllēs	māllēs
vellet	nōllet	māllet
vellēmus	nōllēmus	māllēmus
vellētis	nōllētis	māllētis
vellent	nōllent	māllent

Perfect

voluerim	nōluerim	māluerim
voluerīs	nōluerīs	māluerīs
voluerit	nōluerit	māluerit
voluerīmus	nōluerīmus	māluerīmus
voluerītis	nōluerītis	māluerītis
voluerint	nōluerint	māluerint

Pluperfect

voluissem	nōluissem	māluissem
voluissēs	nōluissēs	māluissēs
voluisset	nōluisset	māluisset
voluissēmus	nōluissēmus	māluissēmus
voluissētis	nōluissētis	māluissētis
voluissent	nōluissent	māluissent

Infinitives

Pres.	velle	nōlle	mālle
Per.	voluisse	nōluisse	māluisse

Participles

Pres.	volēns,	nōlēns,
	-ntis	-ntis

Imperatives

noli, nolite

fīō, fierī, factus sum to become/be made/be done

Indicative Mood

Pres.	**Imp.**	**Fut.**	**Perf.**	**Plup.**	**FutPer.**
fīō	fīēbam	fīam	factus sum	factus eram	factus erō
fīs	fīēbās	fīēs	factus es	factus erās	factus eris
fit	fīēbat	fīet	factus est	factus erat	factus erit
fīmus	fīēbāmus	fīēmus	factī sumus	factī erāmus	facti erimus
fītis	fīēbātis	fīētis	factī estis	factī erātis	facti eritis
fiunt	fīēbant	fient	factī sunt	factī erant	facti erunt

Subjunctive Mood

Pres.	**Imp.**	**Perf.**	**Plup.**
fīam	fierem	factus sim	factus essem
fīās	fierēs	factus sīs	factus essēs
fīat	fieret	factus sit	factus esset
fīāmus	fierēmus	factī sīmus	factī essēmus
fīātis	fierētis	factī sītis	factī essētis
fīant	fierent	factī sint	factī essent

Participles

Pres.	
Perf.	factus,-a,-um
Fut.	faciendus,-a,-um [factum īrī]

Infinitives

fierī
factus esse

Imperatives

fī, fīte

306

Deponent Verb Conjugations

1st	hortor,	hortārī,	hortātus sum	to urge
2nd	fateor,	faterī,	fassus sum	to confess
3rd	sequor,	sequī,	secutus sum	to follow
3rd -io	morior,	morī,	mortuus sum	to die
4th	orior,	orīrī,	ortus sum	to arise

Indicative Mood

Present

hortor	fateor	sequor	morior	orior
hortāris	fatēris	sequeris	moreris	orīrīs
hortātur	fatētur	sequitur	moritur	orītur
hortāmur	fatēmur	sequimur	morimur	orīmur
hortāminī	fatēminī	sequimini	morimini	orīminī
hortantur	fatentur	sequuntur	moriuntur	oriuntur

Imperfect

hortābar	fatēbar	sequēbar	moriēbar	oriēbar
hortābāris	fatēbāris	sequēbāris	moriēbāris	oriēbāris
hortābātur	fatēbātur	sequēbātur	moriēbātur	oriēbātur
hortābāmur	fatēbāmur	sequēbāmur	moriēbāmur	oriēbāmur
hortābāminī	fatēbāminī	sequēbāminī	moriēbāminī	oriēbāminī
hortābantur	fatēbantur	sequēbantur	moriēbantur	oriēbantur

Future

hortābor	fatēbor	sequar	moriar	oriar
hortāberis	fatēberis	sequēris	moriēris	oriēris
hortābitur	fatēbitur	sequētur	moriētur	oriētur
hortābimur	fatēbimur	sequēmur	moriēmur	oriēmur
hortābiminī	fatēbiminī	sequēminī	moriēminī	oriēminī
hortābuntur	fatēbuntur	sequentur	morientur	orientur

Perfect

hortātus sum	fassus sum	secūtus sum	mortuus sum	ortus sum
hortātus es	fassus es	secūtus es	mortuus es	ortus es
hortātus est	fassus est	secūtus est	mortuus est	ortus est
hortātī sumus	fassī sumus	secūtī sumus	mortuī sumus	ortī sumus
hortātī estis	fassī estis	secūtī estis	mortuī estis	ortī estis
hortātī sunt	fassī sunt	secūtī sunt	mortuī sunt	ortī sunt

Pluperfect

hortātus eram	fassus eram	secūtus eram	mortuus eram	ortus eram
hortātus erās	fassus erās	secūtus erās	mortuus erās	ortus erās
hortātus erat	fassus erat	secūtus erat	mortuus erat	ortus erat
hortātī erāmus	fassī erāmus	secūtī erāmus	mortuī erāmus	ortī eramus
hortātī erātis	fassī erātis	secūtī erātis	mortuī erātis	ortī erātis
hortātī erant	fassī erant	secūtī erant	mortuī erant	ortī erant

Future Perfect

hortātus ero	fassus erō	secūtus erō	mortuus erō	ortus erō
hortātus eris	fassus eris	secūtus eris	mortuus eris	ortus eris
hortātus erit	fassus erit	secūtus erit	mortuus erit	ortus erit
hortātī erimus	fassī erimus	secūtī erimus	mortuī erimus	ortī erimus
hortātī eritis	fassī eritis	secūtī eritis	mortuī eritis	ortī eritis
hortātī erunt	fassī erunt	secūtī erunt	mortuī erunt	ortī erunt

Subjunctive Mood

Present

horter	fatear	sequar	moriar	oriar
hortēris	fateāris	sequāris	moriāris	oriāris
hortētur	fateātur	sequātur	moriātur	oriātur
hortēmur	fateāmur	sequāmur	moriāmur	oriāmur
hortēminī	fateāminī	sequāminī	moriāminī	oriāminī
hortentur	fateantur	sequantur	moriantur	oriantur

Imperfect

hortārer	fatērer	sequerer	morerer	orīrer
hortārēris	fatērēris	sequerēris	morerēris	orīrēris
hortārētur	fatērētur	sequerētur	morerētur	orīrētur
hortārēmur	fatērēmur	sequerēmur	morerēmur	orīrēmur
hortārēminī	fatērēminī	sequerēminī	morerēminī	orīrēminī
hortārentur	fatērentur	sequerentur	morerentur	orīrentur

Perfect

hortātus sim	fassus sim	secūtus sim	mortuus sim	ortus sim
hortātus sīs	fassus sīs	secūtus sīs	mortuus sīs	ortus sīs
hortātus sit	fassus sit	secūtus sit	mortuus sit	ortus sit
hortātī sīmus	fassī sīmus	secūtī sīmus	mortuī sīmus	orti simus
hortātī sītis	fassī sītis	secūtī sītis	mortuī sītis	ortī sītis
hortātī sint	fassī sint	secūtī sint	mortuī sint	ortī sint

Pluperfect

hortātus essem	fassus essem	secūtus essem	mortuus essem	ortus essem
hortātus essēs	fassus essēs	secūtus essēs	mortuus essēs	ortus essēs
hortātus esset	fassus esset	secūtus esset	mortuus esset	ortus esset
hortātī essēmus	fassī essēmus	secūtī essēmus	mortuī essēmus	ortī essēmus
hortātī essētis	fassī essētis	secūtī essētis	mortuī essētis	ortī essētis
hortātī essent	fassī essent	secūtī essent	mortuī essent	ortī essent

Participles

Active

Pres.	hortāns,-ntis	fatēns,-ntis	sequēns,-ntis	moriēns,-ntis	oriēns,-ntis
Per.	hortātus	fassus	secūtus	mortuus	ortus
Fut.	hortātūrus	fassūrus	secūtūrus	moritūrus	ortūrus

Passive

Fut.	hortandus	fatendus	sequendus	moriendus	oriendus

Infinitives

Pres.	hortārī	fatērī	sequī	morī	orīrī
Per.	hortātus esse	fassus esse	secūtus esse	mortuus esse	ortus esse
Fut.	hortātūrus esse	fassūrus esse	secūtūrus esse	moritūrus esse	ortūrus esse

Imperatives

Sing.	hortāre	fatēre	sequere	morere	orīre
Pl.	hortāminī	fatēminī	sequiminī	moriminī	orīminī

Major Subjunctive Usages

Independent Usages

		Translation	Negative
1.	**Jussive**	"Let"	*Nē* "Let not"

Regarded as a soft command; always in the Present Tense; regularly appears in the Present Tense, most frequently in 3rd Person.

Dicat sibi.	Let him speak for himself.
Servi hoc faciant.	Let the slaves do this.

2.	**Optative**	"May"	*Nē* "May . . . not"

Used in expressions of wishing.

Requiescat in pace.	May he rest in peace.
Ne semper sit hoc verum.	May this not always be true.

When used with Past Tenses, regularly accompanied by *utinam* (Would that! O that!)

Utinam studuissem!   Would that I had studied!

3. Other somewhat common Independent Usages:

a. Hortatory	*Eamus!*	Let's go!
b. Deliberative	*Redeam?*	Should I go back?
(Rhetorical Question)		

Dependent Usages

Subjunctive Sequence of Tenses

Independent Main Verb	Dependent Subjunctive Verb	
Present or Future Tense	Present Subjunctive	Same Time or Time After
	Perfect Subjunctive	Time Before
Any Past Tense	Imperfect Subjunctive	Same Time or Time After
	Pluperfect Subjunctive	Time Before

1. **Purpose Clauses**

Pos. Conj.	Neg. Conj.
ut "in order that"	*nē* "lest/in order that not"

Facit hoc ut urbem servet. — He does this to save the city.
Fecit hoc ne urbs deleretur. — He did this lest the city was destroyed.

2. **Result Clauses**

Cue Words	Pos. Conj.	Neg. Conj.
ita, sic, tam "so"	*ut* "that"	*ut nōn* "that . . . not"
tantus,-a,-um		*ut nemo* "that no one"
"such great"		*ut nihil* "that nothing"

Fecit tanta ut urbem servaret.
He did such great things that he saved the city.
Historia erat ita stulta ut nemo ei crederet.
The story was so foolish that no one believed it.

Result by Context

Cue Verbs	Pos Conj	Neg Conj
accido	*(ut)* "that"	*ut non* "that not"
evenio		*ut nemo* "that no one"
efficio		*ut nihil* "that nothing"

Evenit ut nihil factum esset. It turned out that nothing had been done.

3. ***Cum* Clauses**

   Cum followed by a Subjunctive Verb may be translated as "when, since, although." When ***tamen*** occurs in the main clause, *cum* is always translated "**although**."

   > *Cum scirent hoc, discipuli erant feliciores.*
   > When they understood this, the students were happier.
   > *Cum pericula videret, tamen venit.*
   > Although he understood the dangers, nevertheless he came.

4. **Indirect Questions**

   Indirect Questions are introduced by verbs of "asking," "perceiving," "knowing," and "thinking," followed by an Interrogative Pronoun, Adverb, or Adjective cue word.

   Common Interrogative Cue Words:

   > ***quis?quid? qui?quae?quod? cūr? ubi? uter,-tra,-trum? utrum . . .***
   > ***an?quomodo?quam? an? quantus,-a,-um?***

Rogavit ubi fuisses.	He asked where you had been.
Scit quis hoc fecerit.	He knows who did this.

5. **Jussive Noun Clauses**

   Introductory cue verbs: ***rogo, curo, moneo, hortor, oro, peto***

   Pos. Conj.: ***ut***   "to . . . /that"   Neg. Conj.: ***nē***   "not to . . . /that . . . not"

Monui eum ut veniret.	I advised him to come.
Rogo a te ne facias hoc.	I beg you not to do this.
Cura ut venias.	Take care that you come.

6. **Conditional Statements**   Pos. Conj.: ***si***   Neg. Conj.: ***nisi***

   (1) **Less Likely**   "should/would"

   > Verb Form: Present Subjunctive/Present Subjunctive

   Si hoc facias, sis beatior.
   Should you do this you would be happier.
   Nisi facias, sis miserior.
   Should you not do this you would be rather wretched.

   (2) **Contrary to Fact in the Present**   "were/would"

   > Verb Form: Imperfect Subjunctive/Imperfect Subjunctive

   Si ego essem tu, facerem hoc.
   If I were you, I would do this.
   Nisi esset amicus, non faceremus hoc.
   Were he not a friend, we would not do this.

   (3) **Contrary to Fact in the Past**   "had/would have"

   > Verb Form: Pluperfect Subjunctive/Pluperfect Subjunctive

   Si venisset, urbs non amissa esset.
   Had he come, the city would not have been lost.
   Nisi egisset subito, omnes mortuui essent.
   Had he not acted immediately, all would have died.

7. **Relative Clauses of Characteristic**

   Introductory cue phrases: ***quis est qui, nemo est qui, quid est quod, sunt qui, sunt quae, solus est qui***

Quis est qui credat hoc?	Who is there who would believe this?
Sunt qui faciant hoc.	There are (men) who would do this.

8. **Subordinate Clauses in Indirect Statement**

   > *Nescivit viros qui dixissent haec abisse.*
   > He did not know that the men who had said these things had gone away.

9. **Noun Clauses following verbs of "fearing," "preventing," "refusing," "doubting,"** and other Subjective Thoughts Represent the Possibility of Subjunctive Verbs.

311

Noun Declensions

1st Declension Nouns

puella,-ae = f., girl

	sing.	pl.
Nom.	puella	puellae
Gen.	puellae	puellārum
Dat.	puellae	puellīs
Acc.	puellam	puellās
Abl.	puellā	puellīs
Voc.	puella	puellae

2nd Declension Nouns

Nominative Ending in *-ius*

filius,-ī = m., son   *amicus,-ī* = m., friend

	sing.	pl.	sing.	pl
Nom.	filius	filiī	amīcus	amicī
Gen.	filiī	filiōrum	amīcī	amicōrum
Dat.	filiō	filiīs	amīcō	amicīs
Acc.	filium	filiōs	amīcum	amicōs
Abl.	filiō	filiīs	amīcō	amicīs
Voc.	filī	filiī	amice	amicī

2nd Declension Nouns

Nominative Ending in *-ir* or *-er*

vir, virī = m., man   *ager, agrī* = m., field

	sing.	Pl.	sing.	pl.
Nom.	vir	virī	ager	agrī
Gen.	virī	virōrum	agrī	agrōrum
Dat.	virō	virīs	agrō	agrīs
Acc.	virum	virōs	agrum	agrōs
Abl.	virō	virīs	agrō	agrīs
Voc.	vir	virī	ager	agrī

Neuter 2nd Declension Nouns

dōnum,- ī = n., gift

	sing.	pl.
Nom.	dōnum	dōna
Gen.	dōnī	dōnōrum
Dat.	dōnō	dōnīs
Acc.	dōnum	dōna
Abl.	dōnō	dōnīs
Voc.	dōnum	dōna

3rd Declension Nouns

rēx, rēgis = m., king   *pāx, pācis* = f., peace   *tempus, temporis* = n., time

	Sing.	Pl.	Sing.	Pl.	Sing.	Pl.
Nom.	rēx	regēs	pāx	pācēs	tempus	tempora
Gen.	rēgis	regum	pācis	pācum	temporis	temporum
Dat.	rēgī	regibus	pācī	pācibus	temporī	temporibus
Acc.	rēgem	regēs	pācem	pācēs	tempus	tempora
Abl.	rēge	regibus	pāce	pācibus	tempore	temporibus

3rd Declension i-stem Nouns

1. Parisyllabics   2. Consonant Base

cīvis, cīvis = m., citizen   *ars, artis* = f., art/skill

Nom.	cīvis	cīvēs	ars	artēs
Gen.	cīvis	cīvium	artis	artium
Dat.	cīvī	cīvibus	artī	artibus
Acc.	cīvem	cīvēs	artem	artēs
Abl.	cīve	cīvibus	arte	artibus

3. Neuters Ending in *-e,-al,-ar*

mare, maris = n., sea   *animal, animalis* = n., animal

Nom.	mare	maria	animal	animalia
Gen.	maris	marium	animalis	animalium
Dat.	marī	maribus	animalī	animalibus
Acc.	mare	maria	animal	animalia
Abl.	marī	maribus	animali	animalibus

exemplar, exemplaris = n., example/model

Nom.	exemplar	exemplaria
Gem.	exemplaris	exemplarium
Dat.	exemplarī	exemplaribus
Acc.	exemplar	exemplaria
Abl.	exemplarī	exemplaribus

4th Declension Nouns   ### 5th Declension Nouns

exercitus, exercitūs = m., army   *cornū, cornūs* = n., horn   *res, rei* = f., thing

Nom.	exercitus	exercitūs	cornū	cornua	rēs	rēs
Gen.	exercitūs	exercituum	cornūs	cornuum	reī	rērum
Dat.	exercituī	exercitibus	cornū	cornibus	reī	rēbus
Acc.	exercitum	exercitūs	cornū	cornua	rem	rēs
Abl.	exercitū	exercitibus	cornū	cornibus	rē	rēbus
Voc.	exercitus	exercitus				

Irregular Nouns

nemo, neminis = m./f., no one

Nom.	nēmō
Gen.	nēminis
Dat.	nēminī
Acc.	nēminem
Abl.	nūllō/nūllā

vis, vis = f., force; pl. = strength

Nom.	vīs	vīrēs
Gen.	vīs	vīrium
Dat.	vī	vīribus
Acc.	vim	vīrēs
Abl.	vī	vīribus

Pronouns

Demonstrative Pronouns

hic, haec, hoc this, the latter   *ille, illa, illud* that, the former

	m.	f.	n.	m.	f.	n.
Nom.	hic	haec	hoc	ille	illa	illud
Gen.	huius	huius	huius	illius	illius	illius
Dat.	huic	huic	huic	illī	illī	illī
Acc.	hunc	hanc	hoc	illum	illam	illud
Abl.	hōc	hāc	hōc	illō	illā	illō
Nom.	hī	hae	haec	illi	illae	illa
Gen.	hōrum	hārum	hōrum	illōrum	illārum	illōrum
Dat.	hīs	hīs	hīs	illīs	illīs	illīs
Acc.	hōs	hīs	haec	illōs	illās	illa
Abl.	hīs	hīs	hīs	illīs	illīs	illīs

iste, ista, istud such/that of yours

	m.	f.	n.			
Nom.	iste	ista	istud	istī	istae	ista
Gen.	istius	istius	istius	istōrum	istārum	istōrum
Dat.	istī	istī	istī	istīs	istīs	istīs
Acc.	istum	istam	istud	istōs	istās	ista
Abl.	istō	istā	istō	istīs	istīs	istīs

Intensive Pronoun

ipse, ipsa, ipsum himself, herself, itself

Nom.	ipse	ipsa	ipsum	ipsī	ipsae	ipsa
Gen.	ipsius	ipsius	ipsius	ipsōrum	ipsārum	ipsōrum
Dat.	ipsī	ipsī	ipsī	ipsīs	ipsīs	ipsīs
Acc.	ipsum	ipsam	ipsum	ipsōs	ipsās	ipsa
Abl.	ipsō	ipsā	ipsō	ipsīs	ipsīs	ipsīs

Personal Pronouns

1st Person   2nd Person

	sing.	pl.	sing.	pl.
Nom.	*ego* I	*nōs* we	*tū* you	*vōs* you
Gen.	mei	nostrum/nostri	tuī	vestrum/vestri
Dat.	mihi	nōbis	tibi	vōbis
Acc.	mē	nōs	tē	vōs
Abl.	mē	nōbis	tē	vōbis

3rd Person

	sing.				pl.		
Nom.	*is* he	*ea* she	*id* it		**eī**	**eae**	**ea**
Gen.	eius	eius	eius		eōrum	eārum	eōrum
Dat.	eī	eī	eī		eīs	eīs	eīs
Acc.	eum	eam	id		eōs	eās	ea
Abl.	eō	eā	eō		eīs	eīs	eīs

Reflexive Pronouns

1st Person

	sing.	pl.
Nom.	—	—
Gen.	mei *of myself*	nostrum/nostri *of ourselves*
Dat.	mihi	nōbis
Acc.	mē	nōs
Abl.	mē	nōbis

2nd Person

	sing.	pl.
Nom.	—	—
Gen.	tuī *of yourself*	vestrum/vestri *of yourselves*
Dat.	tibi	vōbis
Acc.	tē	vōs
Abl.	tē	vōbis

3rd Person

(same form for singular and plural)

Nom.	—
Gen.	suī *of himself/herself/itself/themselves*
Dat.	sibi
Acc.	sē
Abl.	sē

Interrogative Pronouns

	m./f.	n.	m.	f.	n.
Nom.	*quis* who?	*quid* what?	quī	quae	quae
Gen.	cuius	cuius	quōrum	quārum	quōrum
Dat.	cui	cui	quibus	quibus	quibus
Acc.	quem	quid	quōs	quās	quae
Abl.	quō	quō	quibus	quibus	quibus

Relative Pronouns

	m.	f.	n.
Nom.	*quī* who	*quae* who	*quod* that/which
Gen.	cuius	cuius	cuius
Dat.	cui	cui	cui
Acc.	quem	quam	quod
Abl.	quō	quā	quō
Nom.	quī	quae	quae
Gen.	quōrum	quārum	quōrum
Dat.	quibus	quibus	quibus
Acc.	quōs	quās	quae
Abl.	quibus	quibus	quibus

NB: When *cum* is used with the **Ablative Forms** of the above Pronouns, it is attached to the end: *mēcum, tēcum, sēcum, nōbiscum, vōbiscum, quōcum, quācum, quibuscum*.

Adjectives

1st–2nd Declension *bonus,-a,-um* good

	sing.			pl.		
	m.	f.	n.	m.	f.	n.
Nom.	bonus	bona	bonum	bonī	bonae	bona
Gen.	bonī	bonae	bonī	bonōrum	bonārum	bonōrum
Dat.	bonō	bonae	bonō	bonīs	bonīs	bonīs
Acc.	bonum	bonam	bonum	bonōs	bonās	bona
Abl.	bonō	bonā	bonō	bonīs	bonīs	bonīs
Voc.	bone	bona	bonum	bonī	bonae	bona

Irregular 1st–2nd Declension Adjectives (*alter, nullus, unus, totus, solus, ullus*)

	sing.			pl.		
Nom.	ūllus	ūlla	ūllum	ūllī	ūllae	ūlla
Gen.	ūllius	ūllius	ūllius	ūllōrum	ūllārum	ūllōrum
Dat.	ūllī	ūllī	ūllī	ūllīs	ūllīs	ūllīs
Acc.	ūllum	ūllam	ūllum	ūllōs	ūllās	ūlla
Abl.	ūllō	ūllā	ūllō	ūllīs	ūllīs	ūllīs

3rd Declension Adjective of three endings: *celer, celeris, celere* = swift/fast

	sing.			pl.		
Nom.	celer	celeris	celere	celerēs	celerēs	celeria
Gen.	celeris	celeris	celeris	celerium	celerium	celerium
Dat.	celerī	celerī	celerī	celeribus	celeribus	celeribus
Acc.	celerem	celerem	celere	celerēs	celerēs	celeria
Abl.	celerī	celerī	celerī	celeribus	celeribus	celeribus

3rd Declension Adjective of two endings: *omnis,-e* = every/all

	m./f.		n.	
Nom.	omnis	omnēs	omne	omnia
Gen.	omnis	omnium	omnis	omnium
Dat.	omnī	omnibus	omnī	omnibus
Acc.	omnem	omnēs	omne	omnia
Abl.	omnī	omnibus	omnī	omnibus

3rd Declension Adjective of 1 ending: *fēlix, fēlīcis* = happy

Nom.	fēlix	fēlīcēs	fēlix	fēlīcia
Gen.	fēlīcis	fēlīcium	fēlīcis	fēlīcium
Dat.	fēlīcī	fēlīcibus	fēlīcī	fēlīcibus
Acc.	fēlīcem	fēlīces	fēlix	fēlīcia
Abl.	fēlīcī	fēlīcibus	fēlīcī	fēlīcibus

Possessive Adjectives

	sing.	pl.
1st Person	meus,-a,-um *my*	noster, nostra, nostrum *our*
2nd Person	tuus,-a,-um *your*	vester, vestra, vestrum *your*
3rd Person (Reflexive)	suus,-a,-um *his own, her own, its own*	suus,-a,-um *their own*

Interrogative Adjectives

	sing.			pl.		
	m.	f.	n.	m.	f.	n.
Nom.	*quī* which?	*quae* which?	*quod* which?	quī	quae	quae
Gen.	cuius	cuius	cuius	quōrum	quārum	quōrum
Dat.	cui	cui	cui	quibus	quibus	quibus
Acc.	quem	quam	quod	quōs	quās	quae
Abl.	quō	quā	quō	quibus	quibus	quibus

Common Irregular Adjectives and Adverbs

Positive	*Comparative*	*Superlative*
bonus,-a,-um	melior, melius	optimus,-a,-um
bene	melius	optime
magnus,-a,-um	maior, maius	maximus,-a,-um
magnopere	magis	maxime
malus,-a,-um	peior, peius	pessimus,-a,-um
male	peius	pessime
parvus,-a,-um	minor, minus	minimus,-a,-um
parum	minus	minime
multus,-a,-um	plures, plura	plurimus,-a,-um
multum	plus	plurimum
facilis,-e	facilior, facilius	facillimus,-a,-um
facile	facilius	facillime
diu	diutius	diutissime
saepe	saepius	saepissime

Common Correlatives

alii . . . alii	*some . . . others*
aut . . . aut	*either . . . or*
cum . . . tum	*while . . . at the same time*
et . . . et	*both . . . and*
neque (nec) . . . neque (nec)	*neither . . . nor*
ne . . . quidem	*not even*
non solum . . . sed etiam	*not only . . . but also*
quam . . . tam	*how much . . . so much*
quotiens . . . totiens	*as often as . . . so often as*
sive . . . sive	*if . . . .or if*
tum . . . tum	*not only . . . but also*
utrum . . . an	*whether . . . or*
vel . . . vel	*either . . . or*

Major Ablative Uses

1. Ablative of **Time When** unā horā in one hour
   eō tempore at that time

   The Ablative of Time When is never introduced by a preposition, always contains a noun referring to time, and is translated *in* or *at*.

2. Ablative of **Place Where** in colosseō in the colosseum
   in forō in the forum

   The Ablative of Place Where is always preceded by the preposition *in* and answers the question "where."

3. Ablative of Place **from Which** ē periculō out of danger
   ā bellō away from the war
   dē urbe from the city

   The Ablative of Place from Which is introduced by the prepositions *ab, de,* or *ex* and indicates motion away from a person, place, or thing.

4. Ablative of **Accompaniment** cum amīcō with a friend
   cum puellā with the girl

   The Ablative of Accompaniment is always preceded by the preposition *cum* and answers the question "with whom."

5. Ablative of **Manner** cum laude with praise
   magnā cum laude with great praise
   magnā laude with great praise

   The Ablative of Manner answers the question "how" and must be preceded by *cum* unless used with an adjective; then the use of *cum* is optional. Note that if *cum* is used with an adjective, *cum* falls between the noun and the adjective.

6. Ablative of **Means** pecuniā by means of money
   gladiō by means of a sword

   The Ablative of Means usually occurs as a single-word ablative without a preposition and answers the question "with what" or "by (means of) what."

7. Ablative of **Agent** Factum est ab eō. It was done by him.

   The Ablative of Agent occurs only with Passive Verbs and tells "by whom" an action is done.

8. Ablative of **Separation** Caret pecuniā. He lacks money.
   Liberantur metū. They are free from fear.
   The Ablative of Separation follows verbs of freeing (*līberō*), lacking (*careō*), or depriving (*prīvō*).

9. An **Ablative Absolute** is composed of a noun or a pronoun in the ablative case with a Participle agreeing. An Ablative Absolute may not modify a noun or a pronoun in the Main Clause of a sentence. (For a more complete Explanation and Examples, see chapter XXI.)
   <u>Iure scītō</u>, poena erat clara.
   Since the law was known, the punishment was clear.

322

Glossary: Latin to English

Chapter numbers are in parentheses.

ab (**ā**) **+ abl.** from/away from/by (VIII)

abeō, abīre, abiī, abitum to go away/depart (XXX)

ac/atque and/and also/and even (XVI)

accido, accidere, accidi to happen (XXVIII)

accipiō, accipere, accēpī, acceptum to take/accept (XXII)

ācer, ācris, ācre sharp/fierce/keen (X)

acerbus,-a,-um harsh/bitter (XXIV)

ad + acc. toward/to (with verbs of motion) (VI)

adulēscens, adulēscentis m., youth/adolescent (XXIII)

adversum + acc. against/toward (XXXIV)

adversus,-a,-um adverse (XXXIV)

aequus,-a,-um level/even/equal/just (XXX)

aetās, aetātis f., age/period of life (X)

ager, agrī m., field/farm (III)

agō, agere, ēgī, āctum to do/lead/act/drive (VII)

agricola,-ae m., farmer (III)

ait, aiunt defective verb; he says/they say (XXIII)

aliquis, aliquid someone/something (XXII)

alius, alia, aliud another/other (XI)

alō, alere, aluī, altum to support/nourish/sustain (XIX)

amīca,-ae, f., friend (III)

amīcitia,-ae f., friendship (XV)

amīcus,-ī m., friend (III)

āmittō, āmittere, āmīsī, āmissum to lose (XXVIII)

amō (1) to love (I)

amor, amōris m., love (XII)

an whether/or (XXX)

animal, animalis neut., animal (IX)

animus,-ī m., soul/spirit; pl pride/courage (VI)

annus,-ī m., year (VIII)

ante + acc. before (XII)

antepōnō,-pōnere,-posuī,-positum to prefer/put before (XXXI)

antīquus,-a,-um old/ancient (V)

appellō (1) to call/name (XXV)

apud + acc. among/in the presence of/at the house of (XXX)

arbitror, arbitrārī, arbitratus sum to judge/think (XXXIII)

arma, armōrum neut., weapons/arms (V)

ars, artis f., art/skill (IX)

Asia,-ae f., Asia (XIII)

at but (XVI)

Athēnae,-ārum f., Athens (XXXVI)

atque/ac and/and also/and even (XVI)

auctor, auctōris m., author (XXIV)

audeō, audēre, ausus sum to dare (VIII)

audiō, audīre, audīvī, audītum to hear/listen (IV)

aut or (XV)

aut . . . aut either . . . or (XV)

autem moreover/however (XIV)

auxilium,-ī neut., help/aid (V)

beātus,-a,-um blessed/happy/fortunate (IV)

bellum,-ī neut., war (III)

bellus,-a,-um pretty (III)

bene adv., well (XIV)

beneficium,-ī neut., favor/kindness/benefit (XXVI)

bonus,-a,-um good (III)

brevis,-e brief (XIII)

caelum,-ī neut., sky/heaven (XIII)

Caesar, Caesaris m., Caesar (XIII)

canis,-is c, dog (XXX)

capiō, capere, cēpī, captum to capture/seize (IV)

caput, capitis neut., head

careō, carēre, caruī, caritūrus + abl. of sep. to lack/be deprived of (XVII)

Carthāgō (Karthāgō),-inis f., Carthage (XXXVI)

cārus,-a,-um dear (XIII)

causa,-ae f., cause/reason/case; gen. + causā for the sake of/on account of (XVII)

cēdō, cēdere, cessī, cessum to yield/withdraw/go by/proceed (XXVI)

celer, celeris, celere swift/quick/rapid (X)

cēna,-ae f., dinner (XXXI)

cēnō (1) to dine (XXXI)

certus,-a,-um certain (XVI)

cēterī,-ae,-a the rest/the other (XXIX)

Cicero, Ciceronis m., Cicero (XIII)

circā adv., around (XXI)

cīvis, cīvis m., citizen (IX)

cīvitās, cīvitātis f., state (VIII)

clārus,-a,-um clear/famous (XXIV)

coepī, coepisse, coeptum (defective verb) began (XXIV)

cōgitō (1) to think/understand/consider (I)

cognōscō,-nōscere,-nōvī,-nitum to recognize/know (IX)

committō,-mittere,-mīsī,-missum to commit/entrust (XIII)

commūnis,-e common (XVII)

comprehendō,-hendere,-hendī,-hēnsum to arrest/comprehend/understand (XXIX)

cōnferō,-ferre,-tulī,collātum to bring together/compare; **se conferre** to betake oneself (XXXI)

cōnor, conāri, conātus sum to attempt (XXXV)

cōnsilium,-ī neut., plan (XV)

constituo,-stituere,-stituī,-stitūtum to decide/draw up (XXVIII)

contineō,-tinere,-tinuī,-tentum to contain/hold together (XVII)

cōpia,-ae f., abundance/supply; pl. troops/supplies (XI)

cornū,-ūs neut., horn (XVIII)

corpus, corporis neut., body (VIII)

crēdō, crēdere, crēdidī, crēditum to believe/trust (XXIII)

creō (1) to beget/make (XXVI)

culpa,-ae f., fault (V)

culpō (1) to blame (I)

cum + abl. with (V)

cum + indic. verb when (IX)

cūnctor, cunctāri to delay (XXXV)

cupiditās, cupiditātis f., desire/passion/avarice (XXII)

cupidus,-a,-um desirous (XXXIV)

cupiō, cupere, cupīvī, cupītum to wish/desire (XX)

cūr why? (VII)

cūra,-ae f., care/anxiety (IV)

cūrō (1) to take care (XXXI)

currō, currere, cucurrī, cursum to run (XII)

dē + abl. about/from (II)

dēbeō, dēbēre, dēbuī, debitum to ought/owe (VII)

dēfendō,-fendere,-fendī,-fēnsum to defend (XXXV)

deinde/dein adv., then

dēlectātiō, dēlectātiōnis f., pleasure/delight (XXXV)

dēleō, dēlēre, dēlēvī, dēlētum to destroy/delete/wipe out (VII)

dēlinquo,-linquere,-līquī,-lictum to fail/be wanting (XXXVI)

Delphī,-ōrum m., Delphi (XXXVI)

dēnique adv., at last/finally (V)

deus,-ī m., god (XIX)

dīcō, dicere, dīxī, dictum to say/tell/speak (IV)

diēs, diēī m., day (XIX)

difficilis,-e difficult (XIII)

dīligō, dīligere, dīlēxī, dīlēctum to esteem (XV)

discēdō-cedere,-cessī,-cessum to go away/depart (XXVII)

discipulus,-ī m., student/learner/disciple

discō, discere, didicī to learn (IV)

dissimilis,-e unlike/different/dissimilar (XXV)

diū adv., for a long time (XIII)

dīves, dīvitis adj., wealthy (XXXII)

dīvitiae, dīvitiārum f., wealth/riches (XXI)

doceō, docēre, docuī, doctum to teach (II)

dō, dare, dedī, datum to give (I)

dolor, dolōris m., pain (XXXIV)

domus,-us f, house/home (Loc. *domi*, Abl. *domo*, Acc. *domum/domos*) (XXX)

dōnum,-ī neut., gift (III)

dubitō (1) to hesitate/doubt (XXXV)

dūcō, dūcere, dūxī, ductum to lead/consider (IV)

dulcis,-e sweet/pleasant/agreeable (X)

dum while (XI)

dūrus,-a,-um hard/harsh (VIII)

dux, ducis m., leader (XXI)

efficiō, efficere, effēcī, effectum to effect/bring about (XXVIII)

ego, mei I (XIV)

enim truly/certainly/for/in fact/indeed

eō, īre, iī, itum to go (XXX)

equus,-ī m., horse (XXXV)

ergā + acc. prep., against (XXXV)

ergō adv., therefore (V)

ēripiō, ēripere, ēripuī, ēreptum to rescue/take away (XIX)

errō (1) to err/go astray (I)

et and (I)

etiam adv., even/also (III)

etsī even if/although (XXXIV)

ēveniō, ēvenīre, ēvēnī, eventum to turn out/result (XXVIII)

ex (ē) + abl. away/out of (V)

exemplar, exemplaris neut., example/model (IX)

exercitus,-ūs m., army (XVIII)

expellō, expellere, expulī, expulsum to expel/drive out (XXI)

experior, experīrī, expertus sum to experience/try/test (XXXIII)

exspectō (1) to expect/await (XIII)

facilis,-e easy/agreeable (XXV)

faciō, facere, fēcī, factum to make/do (IV)

factum,-ī neut., deed (XV)

fāma,-ae f., fame/rumor (II)

fateor, fatērī, fassus sum to confess (XXXIII)

fātum,-ī neut., fate (XX)

fēlix, fēlīcis happy/lucky (X)

fēmina,-ae f., woman (XIII)

ferē almost (XV)

ferō, ferre, tulī, lātum to carry/bear/endure/bring (XXXI)

festinō (1) to hasten (I)

fīdēlis,-e faithful/loyal (XXIII)

fīdēs,-eī f., faith/trust (XIX)

filia,-ae f., daughter (III)

filius,-ī m., son (III)

fīnis,-is m., end/limit/boundary; **pl.** territory (XVII)

fīo, fierī, factus sum to be made/be done/become (XXXVI)

fōrma,-ae f., shape/form/beauty (V)

fortis,-e strong/brave (X)

fortūna,-ae f., fortune/luck (II)

frāter, frātris m., brother (XIV)

frūctus,-ūs m., profit/fruit (XVIII)

fugiō, fugere, fūgī, fugitūrus to flee (V)

gēns, gentis f., gens,clan (XVI)

genus, generis neut., class/kind (XIX)

gerō, gerere, gessī, gestum to carry on/conduct/accomplish (IX)

glōria,-ae f., glory (XII)

gracilis,-e slender (XXV)

Graecia,-ae f., Greece (XVI)

Graecus,-a,-um Greek (V)

gravis,-e heavy/serious/severe (XI)

habeō, habere, habuī, habitum to have/hold/possess (IV)

hīc adv., here (XXIII)

hic, haec, hoc this/the latter (VI)

historia,-ae f., story/history (V)

homō, hominis m., human being/man (VIII)

honor, honōris m., honor/office/esteem (VIII)

hōra,-ae f., hour (VIII)

hortor, hortārī, hortātus sum to urge/implore (XXXI)

hostis,-is m., enemy (XXIII)

hūmānus,-a,-um human (XXIII)

humilis,-e humble/lowly (XXV)

iaciō, iacere, iēcī, iactum to throw/hurl (XIII)

iam adv., now/already (XVII)

ibi adv., there (VII)

īdem, eadem, idem the same (XIX)

igitur therefore (XII)

ignis,-is m., fire (XVIII)

ignōscō,-nōscere,-nōvī,-nōtum + dat. to grant pardon to/ignore (XXXIV)

ille, illa, illud that/the former (VI)

immo on the contrary

immortālis,-e immortal (XXIII)

imperium,-ī neut., absolute power/command (XXI)

imperō (1) + dat. to give orders to/command (XXXI)

in + abl. in/on (V)

in + acc. into/against (V)

incertus,-a,-um uncertain (XVI)

incipiō, incipere, incēpī, inceptum to begin (V)

incolō, incolere, incoluī to inhabit (XXIX)

inde thence (XIII)

iniūstus,-a,-um unjust (XXIX)

inquit he says/said (defective verb; occurs after one or more words of a direct quotation) (XXI)

īnsidiae,-ārum f., plots/treachery (VII)

īnsula,-ae f., island (XXV)

intellegō, intellegere, intellēxī, intellēctum to understand (XXIII)

inter + acc. prep, between/among (XIII)

interficiō, interficere, interfēcī, interfectum to kill (XXVI)

inveniō, invenīre, invenī, inventum to discover/ come upon (IV)

ipse, ipsa, ipsum himself/herself/itself (intensive pronoun) (VII)

īra,-ae f., anger (II)

īrascor, īrāscī, īrātus sum to be angry (XXXIII)

is, ea, id, he, she, it, this, that (VI)

iste, ista, istud such (VI)

ita adv., so/thus (XVII)

Italia,-ae f., Italy (V)

itaque and so (XIII)

iter, itineris neut., march/journey (XXXV)

iubeo, iubēre, iussī, iussum to order/command (XVII)

iucundus,-a,-um pleasant (XXII)

iūdicium,-ī neut., judgement/decision/court (XVI)

iungō, iungere, iūnxī, iūnctum to join (XIV)

iūs, iūris neut., right/law (IX)

iūs iūrandum, iuris iurandi neut., oath (XXIII)

iustitia,-ae f., justice (XX)

iūstus,-a,-um just (XXIX)

iuvō, iuvāre, iūvī, iūtum to help/aid (X)

lābor, labōris m., labor/task/effort (VIII)

laudō (1) to praise (I)

laus, laudis f., praise (VIII)

legō, legere, lēgī, lēctum to read/choose (XVI)

lente adv., slowly (I)

levis,-e light/slight (XXVI)

lēx, lēgis f., law (XVIII)

līber, lībera, līberum free (VI)

liber, librī m., book (V)

līberō (1) to free/liberate (XVII)

lībertās, lībertātis f., liberty/freedom (XIII)

licet, licēre, licuit impersonal, to be allowed/permitted (XXXIII)

littera,-ae f., letter of alphabet; **pl.** epistle/literature (XII)

lītus, lītoris neut., shore (XXV)

loca, locōrum neut., region (XI)

locus,-ī m., place/passage in literature (XI)

longus,-a,-um long (VIII)

loquor, loquī, locūtus sum to say/speak/tell (XXXIII)

lūdus,-ī m., school/game (XIX)

lūx, lūcis f., light (XXIV)

magister, magistrī m., teacher/master (IV)

magnus,-a,-um great (III)

maiōrēs, maiōrum m., ancestors (XXV)

mālō, mālle, māluī to prefer (XXXII)

malus,-a,-um bad/evil (III)

manus,-ūs f., hand/handwriting/band of men (XVIII)

mare, maris neut., sea (IX)

māter, mātris f., mother (XIV)

mediocris,-e ordinary/mediocre (XXX)

memoria,-ae f., memory (X)

memoriā teneō to remember (XXIII)

mēns, mentis f., mind/thought (IX)

mereō, merere, meruī, meritum to deserve/earn (XXVI)

metus,-ūs m., fear (XVIII)

meus,-a,-um my (III)

mīles, mīlitis m., soldier (XXVII)

miror, mirārī, mirātus sum to wonder/be astonished (deponent) (XXX)

miser, misera, miserum wretched/miserable (VII)

mittō, mittere, mīsī, missum to send (IV)

modus,-ī m., model/mode/measure/bound (VIII)

moneō, monere, monuī, monitum to advise/warn (II)

mora,-ae f., delay (IV)

morior, morī, mortuus sum to die (XXXIII)

mors, mortis f., death (IX)

mortālis,-e mortal (XXIII)

mortuus,-a,-um dead (XXVI)

mōs, mōris m., custom/habit; **pl.** character/morality (VIII)

moveō, movēre, mōvī, mōtum to move/arouse (XV)

mox adv., soon (X)

multus,-a,-um much/many (III)

mundus,-ī m., world/universe (XVI)

mūtō (1) to change/alter (XIII)

nam for (XII)

narrō (1) to tell/narrate (XXII)

nāscor, nāscī, nātus sum to be born (XXXIII)

natio, nationis f., nation (VIII)

nātūra,-ae f., nature (XI)

nauta,-ae m., sailor (III)

nāvigō (1) to sail (XXVIII)

navis,-is f., ship (XXI)

nē + subjunctive verb neg. conjunction (XXVII)

nē . . . quidem not . . . even (XXVII)

nec adv., not; nec . . . nec neither . . . nor

necesse necessary (indeclinable adj.), (XXXVI)

neglegō,-legere,-lēxī,-lēctum to neglect (XVI)

negō (1) to deny (XXIII)

nēmō, nēminis no one/nobody (XVIII)

neque and not; neque...neque neither/nor

nesciō, nescīre, nescīvī, nescītum to not know (IV)

nihil nothing (I)

nimis (also nimium) nimis indeclinable adj./adv., too much/excessively (VI)

nisi except/unless (XXVII)

nōlō, nōlle, nōluī to wish not/be unwilling/refuse (XXXII)

nōmen, nōminis neut., name (XIV)

nōn adv., not (I)

nōn sōlum . . . sed etiam not only . . . but also (VI)

nōndum adv., not yet (XXVIII)

nōs, nostrum we (XIV)

nosco, noscere, novi, notum to recognize/know (IX)

noster,-tra,-trum our (VI)

novus,-a,-um new (VIII)

nox, noctis f., night (IX)

nūbēs, nūbis f., cloud (IX)

nūllus,-a,-um none/no (VI)

numerus,-ī m., number (VI)

numquam adv., never (XI)

nunc adv., now (IV)

nūntiō (1) to report/announce (XXIII)

ob + acc. on account of (XXVII)

obtineō,-tinēre,-tinuī,-tentum to hold/possess/obtain (VIII)

occāsiō, occāsiōnis f., opportunity/occasion (XVII)

occīdō,-cīdere,-cīdī,-cīsum to cut down/strike down/kill (XXXV)

oculus,-ī m., eye (VII)

odium,-ī neut., hatred (XXXV)

offerō, offerre, obtulī, oblātum to offer (XXXI)

officium,-ī neut., duty/office (VI)

omnis,-e every; pl. all (X)

opus, operis neut., work/task/deed/accomplishment (XXXIV)

ōra,-ae f., shore (XXIX)

ōrātor, ōrātōris m., orator (XX)

orior, orīrī, ortus sum to arise (XXXIII)

ōrō (1) to beg/entreat/beseech (XXXI)

ostendō, ostendere, ostendī, ostentum to show/exhibit (XXI)

ōtium,-ī neut., leisure (IV)

parcō, parcere, pepercī + dat. to be lenient to/sparing (XXXIV)

pār, paris equal (XXXII)

parō (1) to obtain/prepare (XVI)

pars, partis f., part/share (IX)

parvus,-a,-um small (IV)

patefaciō,-facere,-fēcī,-factum to open/throw open/lay open (XXXV)

pater, patris m., father (XIV)

patior, patī, passus sum to endure (XXXIII)

patria,-ae f., fatherland/country (II)

paucī,-ae,-a few (IV)

pauper, pauperis m., pauper/poor man (XXXII)

pāx, pācis f., peace (VIII)

pecūnia,-ae f., money (II)

pellō, pellere, pepulī, pulsum to beat/strike (XXI)

per + acc. through (XIV)

pereō, perīre, periī, peritum to pass away/perish (XXX)

periculum,-ī neut., danger (III)

perpetuus,-a,-um perpetual/continuous (VII)

persuādeō,-suādēre,-suāsī,-suāsum + dat. to persuade (XXXI)

peto, petere, petīvī, petītum to seek/petition (XX)

philosophia,-ae f., philosophy (II)

placeō, placēre, placuī, placitum + dat. to be pleasing to (XXXIII)

poena,-ae f., penalty/punishment (II)

poēta,-ae m., poet (III)

pōnō, pōnere, posuī, positum to put/place (XXIX)

populus,-ī m., people/nation (VI)

porta,-ae f., gate (II)

possum, posse, potuī to be able (VII)

post + acc. after (XII)

praestō,-stāre,-stitī,-stitum to excel/exhibit/supply (XXVII)

praeteritus,-a,-um past (XXII)

premō, premere, pressī, pressum to press/pursue/press hard (XX)

prīvō (1) to deprive (XVII)

prō + abl. for/instead of/in front of (XXIII)

proficiscor, proficiscī, profectus sum to set out (XXXIII)

propter + acc. on account of/because of (VII)

puella,-ae f., girl (II)

puer,-ī m., boy (III)

pugnō (1) to fight (XXIX)

pulcher, pulchra, pulchrum beautiful/handsome (IX)

putō (1) to judge/imagine/suppose/think (XXIII)

quaerō, quaerere, quaesīvī, quaesītum to seek/ask/inquire (XXII)

quam adv., how (X)

quam than; + superlative as . . . as possible (XXIV)

quantus,-a,-um how large/how great/how much (XXX)

quasi as if (XXXIV)

-que enclitic, and (II)

quī? quae? quod? adj., which? what? (XII)

quī, quae, quod who/which/what/that (relative pronoun) (XII)

quia because (XXIII)

quīdam, quaedam, quiddam someone/-thing/a certain one/-thing (XXIV)

quidem indeed/certainly (XXVII)

quis? quid? who? what? (interrogative pronoun) (XVII)

quisque, quidque each one/each thing (XXII)

quod because (VII)

quōmodo adv., how (XXX)

quondam adv., once (V)

quoniam since (XIII)

quoque adv., also/too

rapiō, rapere, rapuī, raptum to seize/carry away/snatch (XVII)

ratiō, ratiōnis f., reason/judgement (XI)

recipiō,-cipere,-cēpī,-ceptum to receive/regain (XXII)

redeō, redīre, rediī, reditum to go back/return (XXX)

relinquo, relinquere, relīquī, relictum to relinquish/abandon/leave (XXII)

(re)maneō,-manēre,-mānsī,-mānsum to remain/stay behind (IX)

remedium, -ī neut., remedy (XXIV)

reperiō, reperīre, repperī, repertum to discover (XXXV)

requiēscō, requiēscere, requiēvī, requiētum to rest/repose (XXVI)

rēs, reī f., thing (XIX)

respondeō, respondēre, respondī, responsum to respond (XXXV)

rēs pūblica, reī publicae f., republic (XIX)

rēx, rēgis m., king (VIII)

rīdeō, rīdēre, rīsī, rīsum to laugh (XXII)

rogō (1) to ask (XXX)

Rōma,-ae f., Rome (V)

Rōmānus,-a,-um Roman (VI)

saepe often (I)

salveō, salvēre to be in good health (II)

sapiēns, sapientis wise man/philosopher; adj. wise (XXV)

sapientia,-ae f., wisdom (III)

satis enough (indecl. noun/adv.) (VI)

scelus, sceleris neut., crime/sin (XVIII)

scientia,-ae f., knowledge (XX)

sciō, scīre, scīvī, scītum to know (IV)

scrībō, scrībere, scrīpsī, scrīptum to write (VI)

sed but (VII)

semper adv., always (V)

senātus,-ūs m., senate (XVIII)

senectūs, senectūtis f., old age (XI)

senex, senis adj./noun old (XVI)

sēnsus,-ūs m., sense/feeling (XXXVI)

sententia,-ae f., feeling/thought/opinion (IX)

sentiō, sentīre, sēnsī, sēnsum to feel/perceive/think (XIV)

sequor, sequī, secūtus sum to follow (XXXIII)

servō (1) to save/protect/preserve (I)

servus,-ī m., slave (XX)

sī if (I)

sīc adv., so/thus (XXVIII)

signum,-ī neut., sign/seal (XX)

similis,-e similar (XXV)

sine + abl. without (V)

sī quis/sī quid indef. pron., if anyone/anything (XXXII)

sōl, sōlis m., sun (XXV)

sōlus,-a,-um alone/ only (VI)

soror, sorōris f., sister (XIV)

spērō (1) to hope (XXIII)

spēs,-eī f., hope (XIX)

stēlla,-ae f., star (XXVII)

stō, stāre, stetī, statum to stand/stand firm (XXVI)

studeō, studēre, studuī + dat. to be eager for/study (XXXII)

studium,-ī neut., study/eagerness (XVI)

stultus,-a,-um foolish (III)

sub + abl. under (sub rege) (VIII)

sub + acc. under (sub terram) (VIII)

subitō adv., immediately (XXIX)

subitus,-a,-um sudden (XV)

————, **suī** himself/herself/itself/themselves (reflexive) (XIV)

sum, esse, fuī, futūrus to be (III)

superō (1) to overcome/surpass (V)

superus,-a,-um above/higher (XXV)

suscipiō, suscipere, suscēpī, susceptum to undertake (XXXII)

suus,-a,-um adj., his own/her own/its own (3rd pers. reflexive possessive) (X)

Syrācūsae,-ārum f., Syracuse (XXXVI)

tamen conj., nevertheless (XXIX)

tam adv., so/to such a degree (XII)

tandem adv., finally/at last (XXI)

tantus,-a,-um so great/so much (XXVIII)

telum,-i neut., spear/weapon (XXI)

tempestās, tempestātis f., storm/wind (VIII)

tempus, temporis neut., time (VIII)

teneō, tenēre, tenuī, tentum to hold/possess (XI)

terra,-ae f., land (VII)

terreō, terrēre, terruī, territum to frighten/terrify (XIX)

timeō, timēre, timuī to fear/to be afraid (XIII)

tolerō (1) to tolerate/endure (VII)

tollō, tollere, sustulī, sublātum to raise/destroy/lift up (XVIII)

tot adv., so many (XXXV)

tōtus,-a,-um whole/entire (VI)

trādō, trādere, trādidī, trāditum to hand down/transmit (XXXII)

trahō, trahere, traxī, tractum to derive/draw/drag/get (XII)

trāns + acc. across (XII)

tū, tuī you (sing.) (XIV)

tum adv., then (VII)

turpis,-e ugly/base/disgraceful (XXIV)

tuus,-a,-um your (sing.) (III)

tyrannus,-ī m., tyrant/absolute ruler (VII)

ubi when/where (V)

ūllus,-a,-um any (VI)

umquam adv., ever (XXII)

unde whence/from which (XIX)

ūnus,-a,-um one (VI)

urbs, urbis f., city (IX)

ut + indic. verb as

uter, utra, utrum which (of two) (XXX)

ūtor, ūtī, ūsus sum + abl. of means to benefit oneself by means of/use/enjoy (XXXIII)

utrum . . . an whether . . . or (XIX)

valeō, valēre, valuī, valitūrus to be strong (II)

-ve or/nor (enclitic) (XXV)

veniō, venīre, vēnī, ventum to come (IV)

verbum,-i n., word (IV)

veritās, veritātis f., truth (XV)

versus,-ūs m., verse/line (XVIII)

vertō, vertere, vertī, versum to turn (XX)

vērus,-a,-um true/real/proper (VI)

vester,-tra,-trum your (pl.) (VI)

via,-ae f., way/road/street (XI)

victor, victōris m., victor (XX)

videō, vidēre, vīdī, vīsum to see/understand (II)

vincō, vincere, vīcī, victum to conquer (VIII)

vīnum,-ī n., wine (XXXI)

vir,-ī m., man (III)

virgō, virginis f., virgin/maiden (XII)

virtūs, virtūtis f., courage/character/virtue (VIII)

vīs, vīs f., force; pl. strength (IX)

vīta,-ae f., life (II)

vitium,-ī n., vice/fault (VII)

vītō (1) to avoid/shun (II)

vīvō, vivere, vīxī, vīctum to live (VIII)

vocō (1) to call (I)

volō, velle, voluī to wish/be willing (XXXII)

vōs,vestrum you (pl.) (XIV)

Glossary: English to Latin

about/from de
above/higher superus,-a,-um
absolute power/command imperium,-i, n.
abundance/supply copia,-ae, f.
across trans
act factum,-i, n.
adverse adversus,-a,-um
advise/warn moneo, monere, monui, monitum
after post
against adversus/erga/in
age/period of life aetas, aetatis, f.
all omnis,-e
almost fere
alone/only solus,-a,-um
already iam
also etiam
always semper
among/in the presence of/at the house of apud
ancestors maiores, maiorum, m
and et
and/and also/and even atque/ac
and so itaque
anger ira,-ae, f.
animal animal, animalis, n.
another/other alius, alia, aliud
any ullus,-a,-um
arise orior, oriri, ortus sum
army exercitus,-us, m.
around circā
art/skill ars, artis, f.
Asia Asia,-ae, f.
as if quasi
ask rogo (1)
Athens Athenae,-arum, f.
at last/finally denique/tandem
attempt conor, conari, conatus sum
author auctor, auctoris, m.
avoid/shun vito (1)
away/out of ex (e)

bad/evil malus,-a,-um
be sum, esse, fui, futurus
be lenient to/sparing parco, parcere, peperci
be able possum, posse, potui
be allowed/permitted to licet, licere, licuit
be angry irascor, irasci, iratus sum
beat/strike pello, pellere, pepuli, pulsum

beautiful/handsome pulcher, pulchra, pulchrum
be born nascor, nasci, natus sum
because quod/quia + indicative verb
be eager for/study studeo, studere, studui
before ante + acc.
beg/entreat/beseech oro (1)
began coepi, coepisse, coeptum
beget/make creo (1)
begin incipio, incipere, incepi, inceptum
be in good health salveo, salvere
believe/trust credo, credere, credidi, creditum
be made/be done/become fio, fieri, factus sum
benefit oneself by means of/use/enjoy utor, uti, usus sum
be pleasing to placeo, placere, placui, placitum
be strong valeo, valere, valui, valiturus
between/among inter
blame culpo (1)
blessed/happy/fortunate beatus,-a,-um
body corpus, corporis, n.
book liber, libri, m.
boy puer,-i, m.
brief brevis,-e
bring together/compare confero, conferre, contuli, collatum
brother frater, fratris, m.
but at/sed
by ab (ā)

Caesar Caesar, Caesaris, m.
call voco (1)
call/name appello (1)
capture/seize capio, capere, cepi, captum
care/anxiety cura,-ae, f.
carry/bear/endure/bring fero, ferre, tuli, latum
carry on/conduct/accomplish gero, gerere, gessi, gestum
Carthage Carthago,-inis, f.
cause/reason/case causa,-ae, f.
certain certus,-a,-um
certain one/certain thing quidam, quaedam, quiddam
change/alter muto (1)
Cicero Cicero,Ciceronis, m.
citizen civis,civis, m.
city urbs,urbis, f.
class/kind genus generis, n.

clear/famous clarus,-a,-um

cloud nubes, nubis, f.

come venio, venire, veni, ventum

commit/entrust committo, committere, commisi, commissum

common communis,-e

comprehend/understand comprehendo, -hendere,-hensi,-hensum

confess fateor, fateri, fassus sum

conquer vinco, vincere, vici, victum

contain/hold together contineo, continere, continui, contentum

courage/character/virtue virtus, virtutis, f.

crime/sin scelus, sceleris, n.

custom/habit/character mos, moris, m.

cut down/stike down/kill occido, occidere, occidi, occisum

danger periculum,-i, n.

dare audeo, audere, ausus sum

daughter filia,-ae, f.

day dies,diei, m.

dead mortuus,-a,-um

dear carus,-a,-um

death mors,mortis, f.

decide/draw up constituo, constituere, constitui, constitutum

deed factum,-i, n.

defend defendo, defendere

delay cunctor, cunctari

delay mora,-ae, f.

Delphi Delphi,-orum, m.

deny nego (1)

deprive privo (1)

derive/draw/drag/get traho, trahere, traxi, tractum

deserve/earn mereo, merere, merui, meritum

desire/passion/avarice cupiditas, cupiditatis, f.

desirous cupidus,-a,-um

destroy/delete/wipe out deleo, delere, delevi, deletum

die morior, mori, mortuus sum

difficult difficilis,-e

dine ceno (1)

dinner cena,-ae, f.

discover reperio, reperire, repperi, repertum

discover (come upon) invenio, invenire, inveni, inventum

do/lead/act/drive ago, agere, egi, actum

dog canis,-is

duty/office officium,-i

each one/each thing quisque, quidque

easy/agreeable facilis,-e

effect/bring about efficio, efficere, effeci, effectum

effort labor, laboris, m.

either . . . or aut . . . aut

end/limit/boundary finis,-is, m.

endure patior, pati, passus sum

enemy hostis,-is, m.

enough satis

equal par, paris

err/go astray erro (1)

esteem diligo, diligere, dilexi, dilectum

even/also etiam, adv.

even if/although etsi

ever umquam, adv.

every omnis,-e

example/model exemplar, exemplaris, n.

excel/exhibit/supply praesto, praestare, praestiti, praestitum

except/unless nisi

expect/await exspecto (1)

expel/drive out expello, expellere, expuli, expulsum

experience/try/test experior, experiri, expertus sum

eye oculus,-i, m.

fail/be wanting delinquo,-quere, -liqui,-lictum

faith/trust fides,-ei, f.

faithful/loyal fidelis,-e

fame/rumor fama,-ae, f.

farmer agricola,-ae, m.

fate fatum,-i, n.

father pater,patris, m.

fatherland/country patria,-ae, f.

fault culpa,-ae, f.

favor/benefit beneficium,-i, n.

fear metus,-us, m.

fear/to be afraid timeo, timere, timui

feel/perceive/think sentio, sentire, sensi, sensum

feeling/thought/opinion sententia, -ae, f.

few pauci,-ae,-a

field ager, agri, m.

fight pugno (1)

fire ignis,-is, m.

flee fugio, fugere, fugi, fugiturus

follow sequor, sequi, secutus sum

foolish stultus,-a,-um

for nam

for a long time diu

for/instead of/in front of pro

force vis, vis, f.

fortune/luck fortuna,-ae, f.

free liber, libera, liberum
free/liberate libero (1)
friend amica,-ae, f.
friend amicus,-i, m.
friendship amicitia,-ae, f.
frighten/terrify terreo, terrere, terrui, territum
from/away from ab (a)

gate porta,-ae, f.
gens, clan gens, gentis, f.
gift donum,-i, n.
girl puella,-ae, f.
give do, dare, dedi, datum
give orders to/command impero (1)
glory gloria,-ae, f.
go eo, ire, ii, itum
go away/depart abeo, abire, abii, abitum
go away/withdraw discedo, discedere, discessi, discessum
go back/return redeo, redire, redii, reditum
go by/proceed cedo, cedere, cessi, cessum
god deus,-i, m.
good bonus,-a,-um
grant pardon to/ignore ignosco, ignoscere, ignovi, ignotum
great magnus,-a,-um
Greece Graecia,-ae, f.
Greek Graecus,-a,-um

hand down/transmit/give over trado, tradere, tradidi, traditum
hand/handwriting/band of men manus,-us, f.
happen accido, accidere, accidi
happy/lucky felix, felicis
hard/harsh durus,-a,-um
harsh/bitter acerbus,-a,-um
hasten festino (1)
hatred odium,-i, n.
have/hold/possess habeo, habere, habui, habitum
he, she, it, this, that is, ea, id
hear/listen to audio, audire, audivi, auditum
heavy/serious/severe gravis,-e
help/aid auxilium,-i, n.
help/aid iuvo, iuvare, iuvi, iutum
here hic
he says/they say ait, aiunt
he says/said inquit
hesitate/doubt dubito (1)
himself/herself/itself ipse, ipsa, ipsum
his own/his own/its own suus,-a,-um, adj.
hold/keep/possess teneo, tenere, tenui, tentum

hold/possess/obtain obtineo, obtinere, obtinui, obtentum
home domus, us, f.
honor/office honor, honoris, m.
hope spero (1)
hope spes,-ei, f.
horn cornu,-us, n.
horse equus,-i, m.
hour hora,-ae, f.
house/home domus,-us, f.
how quam/quomodo
how large/how great/how much quantus,-a,-um
human humanus,-a,-um
human being/man homo, hominis, m.
humble/lowly humilis,-e

I ego, mei
if si
immediately subito
immortal immortalis,-e
in in + abl.
indeed/certainly quidem
inhabit incolo, incolere, incolui
into in + acc.
island insula,-ae, f.
Italy Italia,-ae, f.

join iungo, iungere, iunxi, iunctum
judge/imagine/suppose/think puto (1)
judge/think arbitror, arbitrari, arbitratus sum
judgment/decision iudicium,-i, n.
just iustus,-a,-um
justice iustitia,-ae, f.

kill interficio, interficere, interfeci, interfectum
king rex, regis, m.
know scio, scire, scivi, scitum
knowledge scientia,-ae, f.

labor/work labor, laboris, m.
lack/be deprived of careo, carere, carui, cariturus
land terra,-ae, f.
laugh rideo, ridere, risi, risum
law lex, legis, f.
lead duco, ducere, duxi, ductum
leader dux, ducis, m.
learn disco, discere, didici
leisure otium,-i, n.
letter littera,-ae, f.
level/even/equal/just aequus,-a,-um
liberty/freedom libertas,-tatis, f.

life vita,-ae, f.
light levis,-e
light lux,lucis, f.
live vivo, vivere, vixi, victum
long longus,-a,-um
lose amitto, amittere, amisi, amissum
love amo (1)
love amor, amoris, m.

make/do facio, facere, feci, factum
man vir,-i, m.
march/journey iter, itineris, n.
memory memoria,-ae, f.
mind/thought mens, mentis, f.
model/mode/measure/bound modus,-i, m.
money pecunia,-ae, f.
morality mores,morum, m.
moreove/however autem
mortal mortalis,-e
mother mater,matris, f.
move/arouse moveo, movere, movi, motum
much/many multus,-a,-um
my meus,-a,-um

name nomen, nominis, n.
nature natura,-ae, f.
necessary necesse
neglect/disregard neglego, neglegere, neglexi, neglectum
never numquam
new novus,-a,-um
night nox,noctis, f.
none/no nullus,-a,-um
no one/nobody nemo, neminis
not non
not know nescio, nescire, nescivi, nescitum
not . . . even ne . . . quidem
nothing nihil
not only . . . but also non solum . . . sed etiam
not yet nondum
now nunc
number numerus,-i, m.

oath ius iurandum, iuris iurandi, n.
obtain/prepare paro (1)
offer offero, offerre, obtuli, oblatum
often saepe
old senex, senis
old age senectus, senectutis, f.
old/ancient antiquus,-a,-um
on account of ob
on account of/because of propter

once quondam
one unus,-a,-um
open/throw open/lay open patefacio,-facere,-feci, -factum
opportunity/occasion occasio, occasionis, f.
or aut
or/nor -ve (enclitic)
orator orator, oratoris, m.
order/command iubeo, iubere, iussi, iussum
ordinary/mediocre mediocris,-e
ought/owe debeo, debere, debui, debitum
our noster,-tra,-trum
overcome/surpass supero (1)

pain dolor,doloris, m.
part/share pars,partis, f.
pass away/perish pereo, perire, perii, peritum
past praeteritus,-a,-um
pauper/poor man pauper, pauperis, m.
peace pax,pacis, f.
penalty/punishment poena,-ae, f.
people/nation populus,-i, m.
perpetual/continuous perpetuus,-a,-um
persuade (to make sweet to) persuadeo, -suadere,-suasi,-suasum
philosophy philosophia,-ae, f.
place locus,-i, m.
plan consilium,-i, n.
pleasant iucundus,-a,-um
pleasure/delight delectio, delectionis, f.
plots, treachery insidiae,-arum, f.
poet poeta,-ae, m.
praise laudo (1)
praise laus, laudis, f.
prefer malo, malle, malui
prefer/put before antepono,-ponere,-posui, -positum
press/pursue/press hard premo, premere, pressi, pressum
pretty bellus,-a,-um
profit/fruit fructus,-us, m.
protect servo (1)
put/place pono, ponere, posui, positum

raise/destroy/lift up tollo, tollere, sustuli, sublatum
read/choose lego, legere, legi, lectum
reason/judgement ratio,rationis, f.
receive/regain/take back recipio, recipere, recepi, receptum
recognize/know (cog)nosco, (cog)noscere, (cog)novi, (cog)nitum
refuse nolo, nolle, nolui

region loca, locorum, n.
relinquish/abandon/leave relinquo, relinquere,
  reliqui, relictum
remain/stay behind (re)maneo, (re)manere,
  (re)mansi, (re)mansum
remedy remedium,-i, n.
remember memoriā teneo
report/announce nuntio (1)
republic res publica, rei publicae f.
rescue/take away eripio, eripere, eripui, ereptum
respond respondeo, respondere, respondi,
  responsum
rest/repose requiesco, requiescere, requievi,
  requietum
right/law ius,iuris, n.
Roman Romanus,-a,-um
Rome Roma,-ae, f.
run curro, currere, cucurri, cursum

sail navigo (1)
sailor nauta,-ae, m.
same idem, eadem, idem
save/preserve servo (1)
say/tell dico, dicere, dixi, dictum
school/game ludus,-i, m.
sea mare, maris, n.
see/understand video,-dere, vidi, visum
seek/ask/inquire quaero, quaerere, quaesivi,
  quaesitum
seek/petition peto, petere, petivi, petitum
seize/carry away/snatch rapio, rapere, rapui,
  raptum
senate senatus,-us, m.
send mitto, mittere, misi, missum
sense/feeling sensus,-us, m.
set out proficiscor, proficisci, profectus sum
shape/form/beauty forma,-ae, f.
sharp/fierce/keen acer, acris, acre
shore litus,litoris, n./ ora,-ae, f.
show/exhibit ostendo, ostendere, ostendi, ostentum
sign/seal signum,-i, n.
similar similis,-e
since quoniam
sister soror, sororis, f.
sky/heaven caelum,-i, n.
slave servus,-i, m.
slender gracilis,-e
slowly lente
small parvus,-a,-um
so great/so much tantus,-a,-um
so many tot
so/thus ita/sic

so/to such a degree tam
soldier miles, militis, m.
someone/something aliquis, aliquid
son filius,-i, m.
soon mox
soul/spirit animus,-i, m.
stand/stand firm sto, stare, steti, statum
star stella,-ae, f.
state civitas,civitatis, f.
storm/wind tempestas, tempestatis, f.
story/history historia,-ae, f.
strong/brave fortis,-e
student/learner/disciple discipulus,-i, m.
study/eagerness/zeal studium,-i, n.
such iste, ista, istud
sudden subitus,-a,-um
sun sol, solis, m.
support/nourish/sustain alo, alere, alui, altum
sweet/pleasant/agreeable dulcis,-e
swift/quick/rapid celer, celeris, celere
Syracuse Syracusae,-arum, f.

take/accept accipio, accipere, accepi, acceptum
take care curo (1)
teach doceo, docere, docui, doctum
teacher magister, magistri, m.
tell/narrate narro (1)
than quam
that/the former ille, illa, illud
then tum
thence inde
there ibi
therefore ergo/igitur
the rest/the other ceteri,-ae,-a
thing res, rei, f.
think/understand/consider cogito (1)
this/the latter hic, haec, hoc
through per
throw/hurl iacio, iacere, ieci, iactum
time tempus, temporis, n.
tolerate/endure tolero (1)
too much nimis/nimium
toward/to ad + acc.
true/real/proper verus,-a,-um
truth veritas, veritatis, f.
turn verto, vertere, verti, versum
turn out/result evenio, evenire, eveni, eventum
tyrant/absolute ruler tyrannus,-i, m.

ugly/base/disgraceful turpis,-e
uncertain incertus,-a,-um
under sub

understand intellego, intellegere, intellexi, intellectum
undertake suscipio, suscipere, suscepi, susceptum
unjust iniustus,-a,-um
unlike/different/dissimilar dissimilis,-e
urge/implore hortor, hortari, hortatus sum

verse/line versus,-us, m.
vice/fault vitium,-i, n.
victor victor, victoris, m.
virgin/maiden virgo, virginis, f.

war bellum,-i, n.
way/road/street via,-ae, f.
we nos, nostrum
wealth/riches divitiae, divitiarum, f.
wealthy dives, divitis
weapon telum,-i, n.
weapons/arms arma, armorum, n.
well bene
when cum + indicative verb
whence/thence unde
when/where ubi
whether . . . or utrum . . . an
whether/or an
which (of two) uter, utra, utrum
which? what? qui? quae? quod?
while dum

who? what? quis? quid?
who/which/what/that qui, quae, quod
whole/entire totus,-a,-um
why? cur
wine vinum,-i, n.
wisdom sapientia,-ae, f.
wiseman/philosopher sapiens, sapientis
wish/be willing volo, velle, volui
wish/desire cupio, cupere, cupivi, cupitum
wish not/be unwilling nolo, nolle, nolui
with cum + abl.
without sine + abl.
woman femina,-ae, f.
wonder/be astonished miror, mirari, miratus sum
word verbum,-i, n.
work/labor labor,laboris, m.
work/task/deed/accomplishment opus, operis, n.
world/universe mundus,-i, m.
wretched/miserable miser, misera, miserum
write scribo, scribere, scripsi, scriptum

year annus,-i, m.
yield /withdraw cedo, cedere, cessi, cessum
you (pl.) vos, vestrum
you (sing.) tu, tui
your (pl.) vester,-tra,-trum
your (sing.) tuus,-a,-um
youth/adolescent adulescens, adulescentis, m.

Key To Review Work Sheets

Chapters I–XII

I.

1.
magna	vis	magnae	vires
magnae	vis	magnarum	virium
magnae	vi	magnis	viribus
magnam	vim	magnas	vires
magnā	vi	magnis	viribus

2.
malum	tempus	mala	tempora
mali	temporis	malorum	temporum
malo	tempori	malis	temporibus
malum	tempus	mala	tempora
malo	tempore	malis	temporibus

3.
felix	civis	felices	cives
felicis	civis	felicium	civium
felici	civi	felicibus	civibus
felicem	civem	felices	cives
felici	cive	felicibus	civibus

II.

1.
sum	sumus	eram	eramus	ero	erimus
es	estis	eras	eratis	eris	eritis
est	sunt	erat	erant	erit	erunt

2.
possum	possumus	poteram	poteramus	potero	poterimus
potes	potestis	poteras	poteratis	poteris	poteritis
potest	possunt	poterat	poterant	poterit	poterunt

3.
debeo	debemus	debebam	debebamus	debebo	debebimus
debes	debetis	debebas	debebatis	debebis	debebitis
debet	debent	debebat	debebant	debebit	debebunt

4.
incipio	incipimus	incipiebam	incipiebamus	incipiam	incipiemus
incipis	incipitis	incipiebas	incipiebatis	incipies	incipietis
incipit	incipiunt	incipiebat	incipiebant	incipiet	incipient

III.

1. curre	currite
2. dele	delete
3. fac	facite
4. iuva	iuvate
5. duc	ducite
6. veni	venite
7. dic	dicite

IV.
1. they were coming
2. in that city
3. of which friend?
4. at that time
5. he is leading
6. our history
7. his own labor
8. out of the state
9. the kings whom
10. with a brave citizen
11. will you write?
12. the girl who
13. with honor
14. these plots
15. to your king
16. Begin!
17. by means of force
18. by means of which skills?

Chapters XIII–XIV

A.

1.		2.		**B.** Present System		Perfect System	
libertas	cara	nomen	difficile	traho	trahimus	traxi	traximus
libertatis	carae	nominis	difficilis	trahis	trahitis	traxisti	traxistis
libertati	carae	nomini	difficili	trahit	trahunt	traxit	traxerunt
libertatem	caram	nomen	difficile	trahebam	trahebamus	traxeram	traxeramus
libertate	carā	nomine	difficili	trahebas	trahebatis	traxeras	traxeratis
libertates	carae	nomina	difficilia	trahebat	trahebant	traxerat	traxerant
libertatum	cararum	nominum	difficilium	traham	trahemus	traxero	traxerimus
libertatibus	caris	nominibus	difficilibus	trahes	trahetis	traxeris	traxeritis
libertates	caras	nomina	difficilia	trahet	trahent	traxerit	traxerint
libertatibus	caris	nominibus	difficilibus				

C.
1. me
2. vobiscum
3. nobis
4. is
5. tibi
6. nos
7. se
8. nos
9. mecum
10. se

D.
1. iecerant
2. sensimus/sentiebamus
3. duxisti/duxistisne?
4. id remanebat
5. exspectaveris/-eritis
6. muto
7. discet
8. ea poterat
9. fuisti/fuistis
10. vidi/cogitavi

E.
1. Fraterne meus patrem tuum in urbe iunxit?
2. Cur viri isti se semper laudant?
3. In Asiā diu non fuerat.
4. Eo tempore anni maria difficilia exspectabant.
5. Copias suas expectaverit.

Chapter XVIII

I.
1. disco,discere,didici
2. contineo,-tinere,-tinui,-tentum
3. gero,gerere,gessi,gestum
4. neglego,-legere,-lexi,-lectum
5. muto,mutare,mutavi,mutatum
6. iacio,iacere,ieci,iactum
7. tollo,tollere,sustuli,sublatum
8. iungo,iungere,iunxi,iunctum
9. traho,trahere,traxi,tractum
10. sentio,sentire,sensi,sensum

II.
1. iecerant
2. sensimus/sentiebamus
3. duxistine/duxistisne
4. remanebas
5. exspectati erant
6. terrebamur
7. privabimini
8. potuerat
9. rapietur
10. neglexit

Chapters XVIII–XX

I.

1.

Pres.	vertunt	vertuntur
Imp.	vertebant	vertebantur
Fut.	vertent	vertentur
Perf.	verterunt	versa sunt
Plup.	verterant	versa erant
FutP.	verterint	versa erunt

2.

Pres.	vertens, vertentis	—
Perf.	—	versus,-a,-um
Fut.	versurus,-a,-um	vertendus,-a,-um

3. verte, vertite

II.

1.

		3.	
premens	exercitus	alta	spes
prementis	exercitus	altae	spei
prementi	exercitui	altae	spei
prementem	exercitum	altam	spem
premente	exercitu	altā	spe
prementes	exercitus	altae	spes
prementium	exercituum	altarum	sperum
prementibus	exercitibus	altis	spebus
prementes	exercitus	altas	spes
prementibus	exercitibus	altis	spebus

2.

		4.	
dies	cupiendus	manus	scriptura
diei	cupiendi	manus	scripturae
diei	cupiendo	manui	scripturae
diem	cupiendum	manum	scripturam
die	cupiendo	manu	scripturā
dies	cupiendi	manus	scripturae
dierum	cupiendorum	manuum	scripturarum
diebus	cupiendis	manibus	scripturis
dies	cupiendos	manus	scripturas
diebus	cupiendis	manibus	scripturis

III. 1. femina dictura
2. populo petenti pacem
3. in re publicā carente metibus gravibus
4. scelerum scitorum
5. petendum

IV. 1. Viros terrentes civitatem cepimus.
2. Terrens civitatem, exercitus tyranni denique continebatur.
3. Petita pax a senatu timente bellum alta est.
4. Spes in eis fugituris non deleta erat.
5. Eademne scelera vitiaque nostram novam rem publicam delebunt?
6. Orator dicturus a nullo cognitus est.
7. Poterimusne nunc vivere in pace et sine metibus gravibus?

Grammar Review Chapters I-XX

Review Sheet I: Nouns

I.

Nominative	Subject of Verb
Genitive	Shows possession
Dative	Indirect Object of the Verb
Accusative	Direct Object of the Verb
Ablative	Prepositional Phrases
Vocative	Direct Address

II.   1st:-ae   2nd:-i   3rd:-is   4th:-us   5th:-ei

III.

1. gloria, glory
   gloriae
   gloriae
   gloriam
   gloriā
   gloriae
   gloriarum
   gloriis
   glorias
   gloriis

3. senatus, senate
   senatus
   senatui
   senatum
   senatu
   senatus
   senatuum
   senatibus
   senatus
   senatibus

2. officium, duty
   officii
   officio
   officium
   officio
   officia
   officiorum
   officiis
   officia
   officiis

4. oculus, eye
   oculi
   oculo
   oculum
   oculo
   oculi
   oculorum
   oculis
   oculos
   oculis

340

5. nomen, name
nominis
nomini
nomen
nomine
nomina
nominum
nominibus
nomina
nominibus

7. lex, law
legis
legi
legem
lege
leges
legum
legibus
leges
legibus

6. mare, sea
maris
mari
mare
mari
maria
marium
maribus
maria
maribus

8. res publica, republic
rei publicae
rei publicae
rem publicam
re publicā
res publicae
rerum publicarum
rebus publicis
res publicas
rebus publicis

IV.

1. causa
2. amicitiae
3. virtutem/animos
4. regi, a servo

5. inter populos
6. dona, ducibus
7. Amor, vis

Review Sheet II: Verbs

I. 1. tense 2. voice 3. mood 4. number 5. person

II. 2nd Principal Part, Infinitive

III. 1. 4th 2. 3rd–io 3. 2nd 4. 1st 5. 3rd

IV.

1. veni	venite	4. fac	facite
2. aude	audete	5. vive	vivite
3. lauda	laudate	6. fuge	fugite

V.

-o/-m	-mus	-r	-mur
-s	-tis	-ris	-mini
-t	-nt	-tur	-ntur

VI. 1. Pres.   est   she is

	Pres.	est	she is
	Imp.	erat	she was
	Fut.	erit	she will be
	Perf.	fuit	she has been
	Plup.	fuerat	she had been
	FutP.	fuerit	she will have been

2.
	Pres.	possunt	they are able
	Imp.	poterant	they were able
	Fut.	poterunt	they will be able
	Perf.	potuerunt	they have been able
	Plup.	potuerant	they had been able
	FutP.	potuerint	they will have been able

VII.   -bi; -e; -ba

VIII. 1.
	Pres.	tenemus we hold	tenemur we are held
	Imp.	tenebamus	tenebamur
	Fut.	tenebimus	tenebimur
	Perf.	tenuimus	tenti sumus
	Plup.	tenueramus	tenti eramus
	FutP.	tenuerimus	tenti erimus

2.
	Pres.	dant they give	dantur they are given
	Imp.	dabant	dabantur
	Fut.	dabunt	dabuntur
	Perf.	dederunt	data sunt
	Plup.	dederant	data erant
	FutP.	dederint	data erunt

3.
	Pres.	sciunt they know	sciuntur they are known
	Imp.	sciebant	sciebantur
	Fut.	scient	scientur
	Perf.	sciverunt	scitae sunt
	Plup.	sciverant	scitae erant
	FutP.	sciverint	scitae erunt

4.
	Pres.	legitis you choose	legimini you are chosen
	Imp.	legebatis	legebamini
	Fut.	legetis	legemini
	Perf	legistis	lecti estis
	Plup.	legeratis	lecti eratis
	FutP.	legeritis	lecti eritis

5.
	Pres.	cupitis you desire	cupimini you are desired
	Imp.	cupiebatis	cupiebamini
	Fut.	cupietis	cupiemini
	Perf.	cupivistis	cupitae estis
	Plup.	cupiveratis	cupitae eratis
	FutP.	cupiveritis	cupitae eritis

Review Sheet III: Adjectives

I.   1. case   2. number   3. gender

II.   1.

Nom.	multus	multa	multum
Gen.	multi	multae	multi
Dat.	multo	multae	multo
Acc.	multum	multam	multum
Abl.	multo	multā	multo
Nom.	multi	multae	multa
Gen.	multorum	multarum	multorum
Dat.	multis	multis	multis
Acc.	multos	multas	multa
Abl.	multis	multis	multis

2.

Nom.	felix	felix	felices	felicia
Gen.	felicis	felicis	felicium	felicium
Dat.	felici	felici	felicibus	felicibus
Acc.	felicem	felix	felices	felicia
Abl.	felici	felici	felicibus	felicibus

3.

Nom.	fortis	forte	fortes	fortia
Gen.	fortis	fortis	fortium	fortium
Dat.	forti	forti	fortibus	fortibus
Acc.	fortem	forte	fortes	fortia
Abl.	forti	forti	fortibus	fortibus

4.

Nom.	celer	celeris	celere
Gen.	celeris	celeris	celeris
Dat.	celeri	celeri	celeri
Acc.	celerem	celerem	celere
Abl.	celeri	celeri	celeri
Nom.	celeres	celeres	celeria
Gen.	celerium	celerium	celerium
Dat.	celeribus	celeribus	celeribus
Acc.	celeres	celeres	celeria
bl.	celeribus	celeribus	celeribus

III.   meus,-a,-um   noster, nostra, nostrum
tuus,-a,-um   vester, vestra, vestrum
suus,-a,-um   suus,-a,-um

IV.

Nom.	qui	quae	quod
Gen.	cuius	cuius	cuius
Dat.	cui	cui	cui
Acc.	quem	quam	quod
Abl.	quo	quā	quo
Nom.	qui	quae	quae
Gen.	quorum	quarum	quorum
Dat.	quibus	quibus	quibus
Acc.	quos	quas	quae
Abl.	quibus	quibus	quibus

343

V. Verbal Adjectives

1.	Pres.	delens, delentis	—
	Perf.	—	deletus,-a,-um
	Fut.	deleturus,-a,-um	delendus,-a,-um
2.	Pres.	vocans, vocantis	—
	Perf.	—	vocatus,-a,-um
	Fut.	vocaturus,-a,-um	vocandus,-a,-um
3.	Pres.	faciens, facientis	—
	Perf.	—	factus,-a,-um
	Fut.	facturus,-a,-um	faciendus,-a,-um
4.	Pres.	inveniens, invenientis	—
	Perf.	—	inventus,-a,-um
	Fut.	inventurus,-a,-um	inveniendus,-a,-um
5.	Pres.	petens, petentis	—
	Perf.	—	petitus,-a,-um
	Fut.	petiturus,-a,-um	petendus,-a,-um

VI.

1. amantes
2. magnum
3. tuae
4. quibus?
5. vestrae
6. dicturum
7. vocata
8. faciendae
9. mei
10. qui?

Review Sheet IV: Pronouns

I.

1.

	hic	haec	hoc
Nom.	hic	haec	hoc
Gen.	huius	huius	huius
Dat.	huic	huic	huic
Acc.	hunc	hanc	hoc
Abl.	hoc	hāc	hoc
Nom.	hi	hae	haec
Gen.	horum	harum	horum
Dat.	his	his	his
Acc.	hos	has	haec
Abl.	his	his	his

2.

	ille	illa	illud
Nom.	ille	illa	illud
Gen.	illius	illius	illius
Dat.	illi	illi	illi
Acc.	illum	illam	illud
Abl.	illo	illā	illo
Nom.	illi	illae	illa
Gen.	illorum	illarum	illorum
Dat.	illis	illis	illis
Acc.	illos	illas	illa
Abl.	illis	illis	illis

II.

Nom.	ego		nos			
Gen.	mei		nostrum/nostri			
Dat.	mihi		nobis			
Acc.	me		nos			
Abl.	me		nobis			
Nom.	tu		vos			
Gen.	tui		vestrum/vestri			
Dat.	tibi		vobis			
Acc.	te		vos			
Abl.	te		vobis			
Nom.	is	ea	id	ei	eae	ea
Gen.	eius	eius	eius	eorum	earum	eorum
Dat.	ei	ei	ei	eis	eis	eis
Acc.	eum	eam	id	eos	eas	ea
Abl.	eo	eā	eo	eis	eis	eis

III. emphasis; ipse, ipsa, ipsum; himself, herself, itself
subject; nominative

IV. Nom. -, Gen sui, Dat sibi, Acc se, Abl se

V.
1. ipsi, eum
2. ego, eisdem
3. Tu, te; is, se
4. ipsa, se
5. se
6. eius

VI.

Nom.	quis	quid	qui	quae	quae
Gen.	cuius	cuius	quorum	quarum	quorum
Dat.	cui	cui	quibus	quibus	quibus
Acc.	quem	quid	quos	quas	quae
Abl.	quo	quo	quibus	quibus	quibus

VII.
1. quae
2. Qui
3. Quem/Quos
4. quorum
5. Quid
6. Cui/Quibus
7. Quā
8. quas
9. cui
10. Quis

Chapter XXI

I.   Subject—Modifiers—Indirect Object—Direct Object—Adverb—Verb

II.   1. 1st superari,   2. 2nd moveri,   3. 3rd *-io* iaci,
       4. 3rd mitti.   5. 4th sciri

III.   case, number, gender; tense, voice

IV.   noun, pronoun, participle

V.   with, since, because, if, although, when, after

VI.   1. SP   2. AA   3. SP   4. AA   5. SP   6. AA

VII.
1. accompaniment   cum amico
2. manner   cum laude
3. place where   in urbe
4. place from which   ex urbe
5. agent   ab eo
6. separation   Caruit metu.
7. means   vi
8. time when   eo tempore
9. absolute   rebus his factis

VIII. **legens, legentis** choosing/reading   **lectus,-a,-um** having been chosen
    lecturus,-a,-um   **legendus,-a,-um**
    about to choose   fit to be chosen

1. I know the man reading the book.
Cognosco virum legentem librum.

2. After the books had been read, the students were happy.
Libris lectis, discipuli erant felices.

3. We helped the citizens about to petition the senate.
Iuvabamus cives petituros senatum.

4. The women were called by the tasks to be done.
Feminae vocabantur laboribus faciendis.

Chapters XXII–XXV

I.   1. esse   2. pellere   pelli   3. recipere   recipi
       fuisse   pepulisse   pulsus esse   recepisse   receptum esse
       futurus esse/fore   pulsurus esse   recepturus esse

II.   1. "Hostis," inquit, "pellendus erit."
     2. Ducibus optimis lectis, cives putabant/putaverunt mox pacem venturam esse.
     3. Maiores nostri sciverunt/sciebant patres suos fecisse eas res.
     4. Auctores recepturi dona scribunt dissimiliores libros sed sunt amici optimi.
     5. Insulā iucundiore, viri erant quam felicissimi.

6. Memoriā tenebunt hoc dicendum esse.
7. Loco nescito, naves nostras ad litus/oram egimus.
8. Senserunt/sentiebant nos scribere breviores litteras.

Chapters XXVI–XXIX

I.
amittunt	they lose	amittuntur	they are lost
amittebant	they lost	amittebantur	they were lost
amittent	they will lose	amittentur	they will be lost
amiserunt	they have lost	amissa sunt	they have been lost
amiserant	they had lost	amissa erant	they had been lost
amiserint	they will have lost	amissa erunt	they will have been lost
amittant	amittantur		
amitterent	amitterentur		
amiserint	amissa sint		
amissent	amissa essent		

II.
Imperatives	amitte!	amittite!	
Pres.	amittens, amittentis		
Perf.		amissus,-a,-um	
Fut.	amissurus,-a,-um	amittendus,-a,-um	
Infinitives			
Pres.	amittere	amitti	
Perf.	amisisse	amissus,-a,-um esse	
Fut.	amissurus,-a,-um esse		

III.
1. longe
2. peius
3. graviter
4. liberius
5. melius
6. parum
7. magis
8. maxime
9. longius
10. acerrime

IV.
1. Semper simus amici optimi.
2. Cum eum cognoscerem, tamen venimus.
3. Ne hoc faciamus ne bellum sit.
4. Sciebant nos non intellecturos esse.
5. Tanta vitia eius erant ut non posset iuvari.
6. Diligimus eos qui mala non faciunt/agunt.
7. Discedentes a bello milites nullum metum ostenderunt.
8. Remediis scitis, remedium (erat) facillimum.
9. Duce expulso milites abierunt.

Chapter XXX

I.
Indicative	Subjunctive
is	eas
ibas	ires
ibis	
īsti	ieris
ieras	isses
ieris	

II.
1. (the man) going
2. Perf. Inf.
3. they go
4. they will have gone/Perf. Subj. 3rd
5. Return!

6. he has departed
7. Imp. Subj. 1st Pl.
8. you will perish
9. Pres. Inf.
10. Plup Pass. Subj. 3rd Sing. N.

III.
1. ibimus
2. redibimus
3. iit
4. perierat
5. ibas

6. Eamus!
7. Redeat!
8. Itisne?
9. perire
10. Uter redit?

IV.
1. I know that he is doing this, did this, will do this, it is being done by him, was done by him.
2. I knew that he was doing/did this, had done this, would do this.
   it was being done by him, had been done by him.
3. I know who is doing this, who did this.
   why it is being done by him, it was done by him.
4. I knew who was doing this, who had done this.
   why it was done by him, it had been done by him.

Chapter XXXII

I.
1. abierant
2. maluerunt/malebant
3. noluerunt/nolebant
4. ferent
5. volumus
6. redii
7. redis/reditis
8. traditum est
9. Peribitne?
10. ponitum erit

II.
1. Suscipiamus consilium pacis ut bellum vitemus.
2. Hortor vos ut memoriā teneatis qui sitis.
3. Obtulit tantum auxilium ut possemus ferre multos dies sine amicis nostris.
4. Si rogetis eum, redeat.
5. Si intellexissent iniustitiam, negavissent facere hoc.
6. Sciebant nos non esse divites.
7. Volumus scire quis auxilium mittat.
8. Cum petivissemus eorum auxilium multos annos, tamen numquam venerunt.
9. Di persuadeant tibi ne eas.
10. Si vir quem petitis hīc viveret, vobis possem dicere quod vultis scire.

Pre-Chapter XXXIII

I.

Nom.	qui	quae	quod
Gen.	cuius	cuius	cuius
Dat.	cui	cui	cui
Acc.	quem	quam	quod
Abl.	quo	quā	quo

	Nom.	qui	quae	quae
	Gen.	quorum	quarum	quorum
	Dat.	quibus	quibus	quibus
	Acc.	quos	quas	quae
	Abl.	quibus	quibus	quibus

II.	Nom.	quis	quid
	Gen.	cuius	cuius
	Dat.	cui	cui
	Acc.	quem	quod
	Abl.	quo	quo

Plural same as plural for **I.**

III.
1. He left with the man whom/*quem* you saw.
2. Which/*Qui* tasks were undertaken?
3. To whom/*Cui/Quibus* had help been offered?
4. Other things which/*quae* have been handed down are not true.
5. The men about whom/*quibus* you were speaking had endured many evils.
6. The life of which/*cuius* mortal lacks anxiety?
7. Who/*Quis* is astonished that such things happen?
8. With whom/*quocum/quibuscum* did they dine on that night?
9. They wish to know which/*qui* men did this.
10. They asked me who/*quis* had undertaken this duty?

Chapter XXXIII

1. they will use
2. Fut. Inf.
3. arising
4. he thought
5. they had followed
6. Pres. Inf.
7. Pres. Inf.
8. Speak!
9. Perf. Subj. 3rd Sing. M.
10. they will please
11. it had been permitted
12. Endure!/they are enduring
13. he sprang forth/was born
14. (those) permitting/enduring
15. PlPer Subj. 3rd Pl.
16. it arises
17. Pres. Subj. 1st Pl.
18. Perf. Inf.
19. having died
20. Set out!

Chapter XXXII–XXXV

I.
1. Purpose
2. Result
3. Cum Clauses
4. Indirect Question
5. Jussive
6. Optative
7. Jussive Noun
8. Relative Clause of Characteristic
9. Conditional Subjunctives

II.
1. Venit ut urbem deleret.
2. Urbis delendae causā venit.
3. Venit ad delendam urbem.

III.
1. Rel. Cl. Char.   Nemo est qui huic credat.
2. Cond. Subj.   Si dubitavissemus, omnes occisi essemus.
3. Juss. Noun   Petunt te ut ignoscas eis.
4. Indirect Question   Rogaverunt quā arte maxime utereris.
5. Indirect Statement   Credidimus vos secutos esse eos.
6. Cum. Clause   Cum bellum longum tulissemus, tamen non licuit nobis habere pacem.
7. Result   Tantum odium continet ut numquam sit felix.
8. Optative   Ne dubitemus iuvare amicos nostros!

Chapter XXXVI

A.
1. faciebamus/fecimus
2. fiebamus/facti sumus
3. facio
4. fio
5. fecerat
6. factus erat
7. faciebatis
8. fiebatis
9. Faciant id.
10. Fiat id.

B.
1. Caesar took care that he became/was made commander.
2. Let us become better if not greater than our enemies.
3. Had we not become friends, we would have been very difficult enemies.
4. It is necessary that laws be made just.
5. They say that a man who becomes a king soon will be without true friends.